FLORENCE

How to use this book

The main text provides a survey of the city's cultural history from its origins under the Romans to the present time. It is illustrated with paintings, sculpture, architecture and general views.

The map (pp. 238-39) shows the principal monuments, museums and historic buildings, using symbols and colours for quick reference.

To find a museum or gallery turn to Appendix I, which lists them alphabetically, with their address, opening times and a note on their scope and contents. The larger collections are sub-divided into departments. Page numbers indicate where these are mentioned or illustrated in the text.

To find a historic building or a church turn to Appendix II, which gives a similar alphabetical list of important buildings, landmarks, monuments, fountains, squares, etc. Grid-references enable the most important places to be easily located on the map (e.g., S. Maria del Fiore, HC, means horizontal reference H, vertical reference C).

For information on artists—painters, sculptors, architects, goldsmiths, engravers, etc.—turn to Appendix III. Here are listed those who contributed to the cultural greatness of Florence and whose works are now to be seen there. Each entry consists of a biographical note, details of where the artist's works are located and references to the main text where they are mentioned or illustrated.

World Cultural Guides

FLORENCE

Bruno Molajoli

150 illustrations
in colour and black and white

special photography
by Mario Carrieri

Holt, Rinehart and Winston
New York • Chicago • San Francisco

Fiore d'Italia e sua parte più bella
(Flower of Italy and its fairest part)

Coluccio Salutati (14th century)

Translated from the Italian
Main text by Muriel Grindrod
Appendices by Geoffrey Webb
Captions by Jocelyn Selson

The World Cultural Guides
have been devised and produced by
Park and Roche Establishment, Schaan.

French edition published by Editions Albin Michel, Paris.

Library of Congress Catalog Card Number: 72-155539
First Edition

ISBN: 0 03 091932 0

Printed and bound in Italy by Amilcare Pizzi S.p.A.

Contents

Jacket illustration: the dome of
S. Maria del Fiore

End-paper illustration: coloured
engraving of old city of Florence

Significant dates
in the history of Florence

BC 59	Julius Caesar establishes colony of 'Florentia'.
AD 535-54	Italy reconquered by Justinian. Florence under Byzantine influence.
568-72	Lombard conquest of Italy.
854	The County District of Florence absorbs Fiesole.
1055	Florence a city of the Holy Roman Empire.
1059	Consecration of the Baptistry as Cathedral of Florence
1138	Foundation of Florentine Commune.
1154-87	Frederick Barbarossa's campaigns in Italy.
1172-74	Construction of 'Second Circle' of walls.
12th-14th centuries	Guelf and Ghibelline strife.
1252	Florentine gold florin standard in Europe.
1255	Foundation of Palazzo Pubblico, seat of the Mayor, later called 'Bargello'.
1265-1321	Dante's poetry establishes Tuscan as literary vernacular.
1266-1337	Giotto's humanistic painting a major innovation.
1284-1333	The 'Third Circle' built round Florence enclosing 1,556 acres with 118 churches.
1296	Duomo begun by Arnolfo di Cambio.
1298	Foundation of Palazzo Vecchio.
1304-74	Petrarch, Italy's greatest lyrist.
1313-75	Boccaccio, founder of Italian prose.
1333	Great flood destroys bridges and many art works.
1345	Ponte Vecchio (10th century) rebuilt.
1347-48	Famine and black death reduce population.
1360-1429	Giovanni de' Medici restores fortunes of banking family.
1378	'Tumult of the Ciompi', a struggle between wealthy merchant class and ordinary people.

1401	Competition to design Baptistry doors won by Ghiberti.
1418	Competition to design dome of Duomo won by Brunelleschi
1452-1519	Leonardo da Vinci.
1455-1510	Botticelli.
1469-92	Lorenzo de' Medici.
1469-1527	Niccolò Macchiavelli.
1475-1564	Michelangelo.
1491	Savonarola, prior of San Marco, denounces new paganism of Renaissance.
1494-95	French invade Italy. Charles VIII takes Florence.
1527-30	Florentine Republic.
1536-1608	Buontalenti, impresario at Ducal Court.
1537-74	Cosimo de' Medici, Duke of Florence.
1558-70	Palazzo Pitti completed by Ammannati.
1560	Vasari plans Uffizi as administrative offices.
1569	Florence becomes Grand Duchy of Tuscany.
1737	Dukes of Lorraine succeed to throne of Tuscany.
1799-1815	French rule in Italy.
1801	Treaty of Florence with Naples.
1848-49	Italian war of independence. Grand Duke Leopold grants constitution to Florence.
1849-70	Unification of Italy.
1850-60	Tuscan Macchiaioli art movement emerges.
1865	Florence becomes provisional capital of new unified Italy. New urban development.
1944	Centre of Florence devastated by retreating army and occupation.
1966	Arno floods inundate town.

The Medieval City

'Florentia' was the auspicious name of the colony established by Caesar in 59 BC and repopulated by Octavian's veterans after the war of Perugia. Nothing else then existed on the right bank of the Arno except for a few small inhabited settlements of not much earlier date and the buried remains of an Italic village which had become extinct at least seven hundred years before. It was certainly not the *'municipium splendidissimum'* which, according to the ancient historians, Sulla had devastated during the social war. There may have been some confusion between it and the nearby Fiesole, whose traditional sway over the little Etruscan centres of the mid-Arno valley went further back; and there are certain historical records of an invasion by the Gauls in 225 BC and the existence of a military colony with the new function of centre of the region and a newly-planned Roman city endowed with a forum, a capitol, a theatre and various temples.

But like Tuscany this colony lay outside all the main lines of traffic in ancient times, because the chief lines of communication between north and south correspondend to the axis of the Via Flaminia and the Via Salaria, while the great cultural currents followed a similar course, flowing towards the Po region in the north and towards Apulia and Sicily in the south. This isolation was broken only with the Roman conquest.

Thus 'Florentia' developed as a Roman city according to military and geographical needs; and it was connected with a *centuria* (century, or tribal division), numerous and definite traces of which remain in the plain north of the Arno.

The lines of the medieval and modern city clearly follow the Roman road-pattern, and fragmentary archaeological remains have been found in the subsoil: these, in the absence of any visible indications above ground, are the only definite existing clues to the site and form of the ancient city, enclosed within rectangular walls (about 480 by 420 metres) and with the traditional plan along right-angled axes, supposedly based on analogy with the augural division of the heavens.

The recognizable town plan of the *castrum* or defended garrison town is divided into four parts by the junction of the two main roads, the *cardo maximus* and the *decumanus maximus;* the first, from north to south, followed the line of the present-day Via Roma and Via Calimala, while the second, from east to west, corresponded to the Corso,

◁
The Palazzo Vecchio, in the Piazza della Signoria, 1298-1314,
with Arnolfo's elegant tower rising in the centre of medieval Florence.

Via degli Speziali and Via Strozzi. At the crossing-point, where today the nineteenth-century Piazza della Repubblica makes a violent gash in the harmonious texture of the historic centre, stood the Forum, which in the Middle Ages became the market-place. It thus remained the centre throughout the city's successive building transformations, even when, as political aspects took on greater significance, the two poles of Piazza della Signoria and Piazza del Duomo, representing respectively political power and religious activity, became more definitely distinguishable as rising centres of importance.

Facing the Forum were the capitoline temple and various public buildings. In subsequent years, especially during the first century AD, as public and private building developed other public buildings arose, the Thermae (the memory of which survives in the present Via delle Terme), the theatre (in the area now corresponding to Palazzo Vecchio and Palazzo Gondi) and, not far off, the temple of Isis and the amphitheatre (near Piazza di Santa Croce, where the houses are built following the curve of the ancient Roman construction, along the present Via Torta, Via de' Bentaccordi, and Piazza de' Peruzzi).

Recent excavations have brought to light remains of the southern gateway of the surrounding wall, connecting with the branch of the Via Cassia on the left of the Arno. However, no visible ruins remain above ground in the city that subsequently grew up on the same site: systematic excavations or chance discoveries have merely provided traces and documentation for historical reconstruction. Anyone hoping for such evidence in the modern archaeological museum will find very little, by comparison with its vast collection of Etruscan antiquities and art objects, deriving from the huge territory of ancient Etruria which extended to the south of Florence.

But traces can be recognized of one particular urbanistic phenomenon which was to continue until very much later: the progressive pressure of the countryside upon the town, the influx into the town of ever-increasing numbers of people from the countryside, who became town-dwellers, and the attraction exercised by the town on distant routes of communication crossing the plain. Hence the natural formation of the *borghi*, or suburbs, came about in a spontaneous and unregulated expansion outside the city walls, with the largest settlements occurring around the gates and along the main roads.

An element of continuity in the history of Florence is provided by this growing and continuous characteristic of the life of the town as a focus of attraction and expansion, and as a point of confluence of old and new routes of communication which, converging from many distant directions, found a meeting-point in the renovated urban centre.

Florentia became the connecting link between the principal centres of the region, with the attraction of the *via pubblica*, the old Cassian Way, which, coming directly from Rome, passed below the hills of Fiesole and by way of Rifredi, Quinto and Sesto arrived at Pistoia and Lucca, then continuing to Luni along the new stretch of the Cassia opened from Arezzo during the Imperial period, with the roads from Siena, Volterra and Bologna. In a wider sense, Florence came to be the focal point between the two coasts of the Adriatic and the Tyrrhenian Sea by the roads to Faenza and Pisa. Road communications, as we know, played a most important part in the development and the economic and political prosperity of towns in antiquity.

The spread of Christianity in the second half of the third century gave the town a martyr, San Miniato, and caused it to be chosen as the seat

The Chimaera, *detail an Etruscan bronze of* c. 350 BC, *discovered in Arezzo in 1555.*

of a bishopric at the beginning of the fourth century. The first Christian church, dedicated to San Lorenzo and originally designed to be the cathedral, was consecrated in 397 by Sant'Ambrogio, bishop of Milan. It was outside the walls, as indeed were almost all the churches built soon after.

But the era of the so-called 'Dark Ages', and their barbarian invasions, marked a long interruption in the development of the life of Florence. The Byzantines who occupied Florentia after 539 did little to further its fortunes. They even reduced its boundaries to facilitate defence, confining it to the interior of the Roman city which was then largely in a ruined condition. Round this they built new walls, the line of which, described in the fourteenth century by Malispini, has been verified topographically by recent researches and still includes two surviving ruins, identifiable as towers forming part of the fortifications and recognizable from their cylindrical form as Byzantine. One of them has been transformed into the campanile of the church of San Michele in Palchetto, while the other has been absorbed into the complex of buildings known as Capaccio. The first constructions of the churches of Sant'Apollinare and San Roffilo also belong to this period.

No less obscurity surrounds the next lengthy period, the Lombard era. Churches were built then also—Or San Michele and S. Michele Bertelde (now San Gaetano), in honour of the archangel venerated by the

Lombards, San Frediano and San Piero in Ciel d'oro, as in Pavia—all of which were destined to undergo successive transformations or reconstructions.

Under the Franks, whose rule lasted from the beginning of the ninth century to 1027, assisted by the dukes and later the counts and margraves of Tuscany, the town emerged laboriously from its state of collapse and isolation. The surrounding walls of the Roman city which had been disregarded during the Byzantine era were restored more or less accurately. An extension was made towards the Arno to link up with the only bridge then crossing the river, which later became known as the Ponte Vecchio.

There is no precise historical documentation about this restoration of the fortifications, but it is thought probable that it goes back to the beginning of the ninth century, to the time of Charlemagne, according to tradition handed down by early chroniclers. It is the *cerchia antica* mentioned to Dante by his great-grandfather Cacciaguida in Canto XV of the *Paradiso*.

The wall started out from the Castello di Altafronte, near the Arno, which was the city's stronghold, and continued along a line corresponding to the present Vie dei Castellani, dei Leoni, Piazza San Firenze, Via del Proconsolo, Piazze del Duomo and di S. Giovanni, Via dei Cerretani, Via dei Rondinelli, Via Tornabuoni, and Piazza S. Trinità, then went parallel to the course of the river, excluding Borgo SS. Apostoli, and finally rejoined the Castello di Altafronte. It had four main gateways, three of which were on the site of the Roman gateways, at the two extremities of the ancient decuman—Porta San Pancrazio and Porta San Piero—and at the northern extremity of the Roman enclosure—Porta del Vescovo e del Duomo, while to the south Porta Santa Maria was placed further off to allow for the town's development towards the river. But several other smaller openings were created, known as *postierle* or posterns (the only surviving record of them is in the name of Via Portarossa), to facilitate communications with the *borghi* which were growing up outside the walls and near the gateways, from which, moreover, they took their names, which have survived in modern nomenclature: Borgo di San Piero, beyond the gateway of that name, later known as Borgo degli Albizi; Borgo Santi Apostoli, between the Arno and the walls; the Borgo known later as dei Greci, outside the Peruzza postern (also mentioned by Dante, *Paradiso* XVI, 125-126: *nel picciol cerchio si entrava per porta che si nomava da quei della Pera*—'the little circuit was entered by a gate named after those of Pera').

In 854, as a mark of its newly-achieved supremacy reversing the old relationship, the *contado* of Florence absorbed Fiesole. The Church assumed both temporal jurisdiction and economic and political primacy, soon to be supported by the lay noblemen of the Margraviate of Tuscany. At the end of the tenth century the hermit Romualda founded the Florentine Badia, or Abbey, with the help of the mother of Ugo, Margrave of Tuscany, 'the great baron' (Dante), who was buried there in 1001.

Florence then began to emerge from the shadows, through the vitality and consciousness of her own strength shown by her people during the religious struggles, and an increasingly vigorous spirit of renewal,

▷

The Certosa dei Galluzzo, a Carthusian monastery, begun 1341 and later extended, with three cloisters and a church which dominates the Montaguto hill.

especially after the city was released from obedience to the Margraviate to become, in 1055, a city of the Holy Roman Empire.

Another influence was the great economic and agrarian transformation then beginning in the Arno valley, which hitherto had been mainly marshland. At the same time industrial and mercantile developments were going on in several towns, foremost among them Pisa and Lucca. In Florence in 1018 renovations began in the church of San Miniato, on the hill dominating the town on the left bank of the Arno. The popes frequently made long stays in the town. Pope Stephen IX died there in 1058 and was buried in the church of S. Reparata.

Bishop Gerardo, who succeeded him under the name of Nicolas II while continuing to exercise the office of Bishop of Florence,

S. Miniato al Monte. Florentine Romanesque, altered in the 12th-13th centuries. The coloured marble revetment of the façade is a Tuscan speciality.

consecrated the restoration of the Baptistry and the basilica of San Miniato and also of the churches of S. Lorenzo (1059) and S. Felicità, both of which were later destroyed and rebuilt in their present form. With the exception of the Baptistry, which for some time was used as the cathedral, these churches were all in the peripheral area outside the ancient quadrangular walled enclosure.

A new and unusual influence was already making itself apparent with the spread of Romanesque architecture. In Florence this is often spoken of as classical in character, to convey the adherence to the geometrical criteria of Early Christian architecture, which here had been spared from barbarian pressure when it moved eastwards after the defeat of the Goths outside the walls of Florence at the beginning of the

fifth century. There is thus some uncertainty as to whether the Baptistry, that cardinal monument of Florentine life, retains an original Early Christian plan of the fifth century or is a completely new structure of the tenth-eleventh century (it was reconsecrated in 1059). The original character of the other great Florentine Romanesque building, the church of San Miniato al Monte, with the rhythmic splendour of its marble façade, its five blind arches (in which the ancient form of the narthex seems to be sublimated), and its basilical plan and vaulted roof, seems to be detached from the widespread Lombard influence and more directly related to late Latin roots. Among the small but noble group of Romanesque churches in Florence, San Pietro Scheraggio, incorporated by Vasari in the fabric of the Uffizi and now still preserved in its surviving parts, had a similar structure not unlike that of the church of the SS. Apostoli, with colonnades whose proportions attracted the interest of Brunelleschi, while the unfinished façade of the Badia at Fiesole re-echoes, in its distribution of white and green marble, motifs both of the Baptistry and of San Miniato.

As religious conflicts intensified and the investiture dispute between the Papacy and the Empire became more fierce, intolerance of feudal subordination began to emerge more clearly together with the birth and growth of a spirit of autonomy among the population.

Among the signs of a progress towards independence were the interventions by the Florentines in the wars fought against the great feudal nobles of the region, such as these against Prato (1107), Val di Pesa (1110), and Castello di Montecascioli.

The Florentines used their own militia to come to the aid of the Pisans, who were threatened by Lucca while they themselves were involved against the Saracens in the Balearic isles; and there is an old tradition that as a mark of gratitude they were given the two porphyry columns which were placed on either side of the main doorway of the Baptistry.

Following the example of Pisa and Lucca, which towns had already embarked on a communal regime, the people of Florence demanded not only the charge of their common interests in the ecclesiastical organization but also the exercise and defence of certain collective rights. They were placed under the charge of the *boni homines,* citizens chosen for their probity and competence. Thus a form of popular representation was initiated, soon to be followed by the creation of consuls and the division of the city into smaller administrative units. The death of Countess Matilde of Tuscany in 1115 marked the relaxation of feudal servitudes and the dawn of a new era.

The Florentine commune came to birth in the last years of the eleventh century and the early years of the twelfth. It was still bound by dependence on the middle and lower aristocracy and constricted by the surviving feudal links with the Church and the Margraviate. Consequently the evolution of the communal constitution went on throughout the whole of the twelfth century. Meanwhile the first steps were taken towards securing dominion over the surrounding countryside and differentiating between the various economic activities. Thanks to the energy

▷

Fiesole. The green hills from whence emerged the primitive town of the Etruscan settlement, centre of the region until the barbarian invasions of the 'Dark Ages'.

P. 18/19

Fiesole. The Roman theatre which was built in the 1st century AD.

Palazzo dei Vescovi at S. Miniato. The episcopal palace, begun 1295, was incorporated in the monastery of S. Miniato in 1594.

of its citizens, Florence forged ahead of all the other Tuscan towns in transforming its economy. Once merely a consumer of the agricultural resources of the surrounding countryside, the town now became a producer of industrial goods, and particularly of textiles, and the idea made headway that the investment of capital, trade in money, might find an outlet in foreign and even in distant markets. The population grew concurrently with a greater degree of urbanization and concentration of manpower.

Complex and often confused political vicissitudes accompanied these slow but sure advances in the civil, social and economic life of Florence. Among these were the war with Fiesole and its destruction following its association with the great feudal lords of the countryside (1123-25) and constant disputes with them; the campaigns of Frederick Barbarossa (1154-87); and a rapid sequence of victories and defeats in struggles with the Tuscan towns and in Florence's relations with the Emperor, until the final recognition in 1187 of the Commune and its rights of jurisdiction. All this formed the background to the continual and recognizable evolution of the outward aspect of the city, which in its flourishing trade and growing economic prosperity found ever-increasing stimulus and resources for its own development. But there was no room for that development within the narrow urban structure, conditioned as it was by the predominant interests of defence, by the influx of the 'new aristocracy' from the countryside, and by the rise of contending factions.

So the old nucleus of the town with its modest buildings in course of renovation, while still maintaining the rectangular Roman plan, began to take on two highly characteristic new aspects. First, a change was introduced in the planning of streets, alley-ways and squares, which were nearly always kept narrow so as to correspond to the interests of defence in the disputes arising from house to house and at street-corners; and secondly, vertical development was introduced in the construction of tower-dwellings, narrow and very tall, built to fit into a small space and crowded together close to each other, isolated but, if need arose, possible to connect for purposes of defence by means of wooden bridges, or accessible from outside by temporary ladders.

By 1170 there were quite a number of these towers, the strongholds of the 'tower society' consisting of the nobles, the *optimates,* and the *boni homines* who chiefly discharged the offices of the consulate. In that year it was decreed that a second circle of walls should be built to embrace the outer *borghi* and preserve new land for the city's expansion. The new walls, roughly quadrangular in form, did not follow the line of the original enclosure but were situated at right angles to it. Construction of this new defensive belt began in 1172 and was swiftly completed within two years. It still took the Castello di Altafronte as its starting-point, but then it turned, eastwards and followed a line via, in modern terms, Piazza Mentana, Via dei Benci, the northwestern side of the Piazza Santa Croce, Via Verdi (formerly Via del

A view of the medieval precinct in the Oltrarno quarter.

Porta alla Croce, 1284, now isolated in the centre of the Piazza Beccaria.

Fosso, recalling the moat along the walls), Borgo degli Albizi, Via S. Egidio, Via Bufalini, Via dei Pucci, Via dei Gori, the northern side of the Piazza S. Lorenzo, Canto dei Nelli, then veering towards the Arno by way of the Piazza Madonna, Via del Giglio, and Via dei Pozzi, then back along the river to the Castello di Altafronte.

The numerous main gateways took on new names except for the eastern gate, which was still known as Porta S. Pietro but was moved to the end of the present Borgo degli Albizi; to the north was Porta San Lorenzo, to the north-west Porta San Paolo, and nearby Porta alla Carraia, near the Arno; and finally, on the south-east, the last of the main gateways, Porta dei Buoci, later known as Porta a Quona. The suburb which had developed on the other side of the Arno was included to form a *sestiere* within the city (Florence was then divided into *sestieri,* or 'sixths'), with the backs of the outermost houses looking towards the countryside serving in place of a surrounding wall. But gateways were built here too: the Porta a Roma, in the present Via de' Bardi; the Porta a San Pier Gattolini, at the boundary of the Borgo di Piazza (now Piazza San Felice); and Porta S. Jacopo, to protect the Borgo of that name (which extended beyond it into the Borgo di San Frediano).

Towards the end of the twelfth century building activity was greatly intensified. The city underwent a startling transformation, and there was an ever-increasing tendency to seek space outside the new walls. Small workshops belonging to wool-dyers and tanners developed along-

Porta San Frediano. Built in 1332, it closed the town in the southwest.

side the river, which gave them the water needed for their trade, and this provided the stimulus for fresh building. New and populous suburbs arose, and are still recalled in Florentine nomenclature (on the near side of the Arno, Borgognissanti, Borgo la Noce, Borgo Pinti, Borgo Allegri, Borgo la Croce, Borgo Santa Croce; on the far side, Borgo Stella, Borgo Tegolaio, and Borgo San Frediano).

Building became even more concentrated in the centre of the city, in its oldest part; for lack of space houses were crowded together and became higher and higher, adding to the dense forest of tall slender towers that gave a marked character to the city's appearance. This was noted by contemporary chroniclers, who gave the number of towers as over a hundred and fifty and their height as up to 130 *braccia* (nearly 250 feet) and spoke of the astonishing general effect, whereby Florence 'showed herself from afar and from without the most beautiful and luxuriant city that could be found on its small site' (Villani). But within, it was a nest of vipers. Ever since the fatal Easter day of 1215, when during a marriage dispute the young Buondelmonte dei Buondelmonti was stabbed to death on the Ponte Vecchio, groups of Florentines had become increasingly hostile to each other. Family hatreds had become party hatreds. The parties were known as Guelphs and Ghibellines, the Guelphs friends of the Church, the Ghibellines friends of the Empire. Factions dominated the whole inner life of the city.

They also had a visible influence on its outward appearance. For the overwhelming vision of the towered city lasted only a few years. In

1250, when the *Primo Popolo* was established for the government of the Commune, a decree was issued, inspired by the desire to curb the rivalries, ambitions and fratricidal hatred of the Florentines, imposing a limit on the height of the towers and ordering all those of over one hundred feet high to be decapitated.

It was a tremendous downfall, on a par with that produced two years before by the destruction of the Guelphs' houses and towers after the victory of the Ghibellines. Eight years later it was repeated when, with the parties' changing fortunes, it was the turn of the Ghibelline towers, palaces and emblems to be razed to the ground. And this time the destruction involved works of value for their architecture and rich ornamentation.

Thus the face of the city was changed yet again, though not entirely through outrage and destruction. For the Florentines with their innate practical sense extracted from those heaps of ruined masonry the stones needed to complete the enclosing defensive wall on the far side of the Arno. Picturesque stretches of the wall still exist on the hill of San Giorgio, which had at its summit the Porta San Giorgio (1260-84), the most ancient of the surviving gateways, for that of San Miniato, also in the same stretch of wall, is of later date. The new stretch included the church of San Niccolò, the ancient church of San Felice, Borgo Stella and Borgo Tegolaio, and the church of San Frediano with a large part of that Borgo.

But this was only the prelude to the construction of a new and much more extensive surrounding wall, the 'third circle', begun in 1284 and finished in 1333. Conceived on such a large scale, it could contain all the city's building development up to the last century, when it was demolished to make way for the present ring of roads from which the modern residential and suburban quarters radiate.

The new walls, enclosing an area of 630 hectares (1,556 acres) as compared with 23 hectares (57 acres) within the first walls and 80 hectares (198 acres) in the second, provided even more room than was necessary for the building requirements of the flourishing city. Old buildings could be enlarged and new ones, whether public or private, civil or religious, could be planned on an ample scale. In the first decades of the fourteenth century the chronicler Giovanni Villani counted 110 churches and monasteries and thirty hospitals in the city, and he described them as 'well situated in it and surrounded by many fine houses'.

Outside the walls, too, the Florentines' wealth and taste for good living were beginning to make themselves felt in the building of villas and country residences on the gentle slopes around the city. There, so says Villani, 'most of the wealthy and well-to-do citizens and nobles with their families spent four months of the year', and it was 'so splendid a thing to see, that outsiders, coming in from the countryside, generally imagined that the rich buildings and fine palaces they found some three miles outside were part of the city, as in Rome.'

While the walls were necessary for security, political freedom was a necessary condition of freedom to work and trade and of the prosperity resulting therefrom. The Florentines sustained a crushing defeat by the Sienese at Montaperti in 1260; but after that certain events of vital importance—their revenge victory over Siena at Colle seven years later, the defeat of Pisa by the Genoese at Meloria in 1284, the

The verdure clad hill of S. Miniato dominating the left bank of the Arno.

Florentine victory over Arezzo at Campaldino in 1289—marked the stages of Florence's advance on the road towards political pre-eminence both externally, as the main centre of Tuscany, and internally, where public administration became stabilized on democratic lines, population rose, and considerable social and economic developments took place. Florence had already begun to coin her own money—hitherto the sole privilege of the empire—in the twelfth century. From 1252 onwards the gold florin circulated in the world at large as the symbol and instrument of the city's prosperity and power: it bore the imprint of Florence's emblem, the lily, and of her patron saint, St John.

Florentine merchants, who for the past century had combined in Guilds, spread their trading networks abroad and sent their exports to distant countries to an extent unparalleled in Italy or even in Europe itself. They also strengthened their influence in the city's popular government, participating in it, urging reforms, and supporting new initiatives.

Though factional strife and civil discord continued, growing prosperity united people in their old and constant ambition to increase the grandeur and beauty of the city, endowing it with new buildings and works of art and so providing the prelude to the splendours of the Renaissance.

The *palazzo pubblico,* or town hall, then came into being in Tuscany as an expression of the achievement of the Communes' autonomy. This and the cathedral were henceforth to be the respective central points in the new structure of the Italian towns.

In Florence, under the *Capitano del popolo,* the new magistrature established side by side with the offices of *Podestà* (mayor) and councillors, the constructions of the Palazzo began in 1255; five years later it became the seat of the Podestà, by which name it was known until two hundred years later it took the name of Bargello.

Massive as a fortress but harmoniously proportioned even after its successive alterations, the Bargello achieved an added gracefulness with its battlemented tower, known as the Volognana, which soared above the surrounding buildings, dominating them unrivalled until the campanile of the Badia rose up beside it, for the towers of the nobles' palaces had all been truncated or destroyed.

The real seat of popular power, however, was initiated only in 1298, when the building of an even more grandiose structure began, the Palazzo del Popolo, which in the following century became known as the Palazzo dei Signori, or 'della Signoria', and later still as the Palazzo Vecchio. Its tall tower, asymmetrically placed so as to use the older tower of the Foraboschi palace as sub-structure, its projecting battlements and the rugged thickness of its walls recall the fortified medieval castles of the feudal nobles; but nevertheless it remained for centuries the model for Florentine civic architecture, admired for the organic composition of the building as a whole, for the design and rhythms of its two-arched windows, and for its use of the rustic ashlar, the rugged hewn stone quarried from the Boboli hillside, whose variegated tones gave an effect of light and shade to the exterior of the austere edifice. It was still unfinished when, in the summer of 1300, it became the seat of the *Gonfaloniere della Giustizia* (Chief Magistrate) and the Priors of the Guilds, among them Dante Alighieri.

▷

The Baptistry seen from the campanile of S. Maria del Fiore (Duomo).

Thus the Palazzo della Signoria became not only the symbol but the immediate expression of the revolutionary force of the new bourgeois class which had achieved power, and of its consolidation with the proclamation of *Ordinamenti della Giustizia* (Ordinance of Justice).

The new civic pride was evident in the fervour of building activity, to which all citizens were called upon to contribute financially. Contemporary documents repeat the splendid formula of the dedication to God and 'in honour of the Commune and people of Florence and for the embellishment of the City'.

The religious orders became promoters and agents for some of the major undertakings. In 1246 the Dominicans initiated the first of the great Florentine Gothic churches, Santa Maria Novella, adapting to a new sense of space the style of Gothic architecture which, originating

S. Miniato al Monte, interior.
The design is still in the tradition of the Early Christian basilica.

in France, had been taken over and spread throughout Europe by the most powerful of the religious orders.

In 1258 the rebuilding of the church of Santa Trinità began. It differs considerably both structurally and aesthetically from the

standards of northern Gothic in the width of its arcades and aisles, which determine the breadth of the cross-vaulting, and in the relationship of space values.

Building activity became even more intense in the last years of the thirteenth century. The ancient Badia was renovated (1284), and the first loggia of Or San Michele was built (a few decades later it was destroyed by fire and had to be rebuilt). Some extensive undertakings were initiated which were to give a new appearance to the medieval city. Among these were the new and extended circle of walls and the city's four main gateways; the prisons, know as the *Stinche;* the foundation of the Hospital of S. Maria Nuova; demolition of the Hospital of S. Giovanni Evangelista; and the extension of the Piazza del Battistero to make room for the replacement of the old Cathedral of Santa Reparata by the new and much larger Santa Maria del Fiore. While the Dominicans continued to build Santa Maria Novella, the Franciscans started on the church of Santa Croce and the Silvestrine monks founded their monastery and church of San Marco.

Arnolfo di Cambio, one of the greatest followers of Nicola Pisano, came to Florence in 1294 and his name became linked with the chief monuments of his time, the Palazzo Vecchio, Santa Croce, and Santa Maria del Fiore. In Santa Croce, in particular, he accentuated the sense of space already inherent in Florentine Romanesque architecture and used it to give new relationships of proportion and effects of atmosphere and light which were the very negation of Gothic, even while they seemed to draw their inspiration from it. The vertical trend of Gothic is broken up by the width and unusual gracefulness of the

*Fiesole. Interior of the Duomo, begun 1028,
enlarged 1256 and in the 14th century.*

The Baptistry, consecrated 1059. The black and white marble revetment is 12th century. The door is Ghiberti's masterpiece.

ogival arches, by the continuous horizontal band of the entablature, and by the dark mass of the trussed roofs of the very wide naves. There is a more open view, a clearer, more rational impression by comparison with the Gothic churches of France and Germany, and this applies also to the plan of the church, which can be taken in at a glance in its harmonious relationships of space, almost like a single hall, so all-embracing is the rhythm of the arches. This also served a practical end, no less significant of the times and the complex motives to which art had to conform—namely, the need for the mass of the faithful to be able easily to see and hear the celebrant at the altar, and the preacher in the pulpit, in a community, at once religious and civil, which was becoming increasingly democratic.

A stronger Gothic emphasis is to be found in the structural consistency of Santa Maria del Fiore, in the coordination of the plan of the vaulting with the spacing and complexity of the pilasters, and above all in the grafting onto the longitudinal body of the nave of the gigantic apse, framed on a grandiose scale, according to a strict central plan around the octagon destined to crown the cupola, already envisaged a hundred years before Brunelleschi gave to it the final form of unimaginable grandeur within that vast enclosed space.

Arnolfo brought to 'modern' architecture that revival of classical foundations and of proportions of space and volume on a human scale which had characterized his sculptures (see, for instance, those designed for the façade of Santa Maria del Fiore, now in the Museo dell'Opera).

Palazzo Spini-Ferroni, an imposing medieval building with feudal battlements.
Built in 1289, it was restored in 1874.

*Palazzo del Podestà (Bargello).
The rooms of the Podestà
(Mayoralty) and the priors who
assisted them in the administration
of the city give on to this
central courtyard.*

And this confirms the view that with Arnolfo, as with Giotto, the cultural position of Florentine art was already advancing in what could be termed a humanistic direction.

This was equally true of painting. The slow pruning of the great Western branch of Byzantine painting and the new graftings introduced in Lucca, Siena and Arezzo developed the first timid offshoots of a new painting in the thirteenth century, and in Florence itself, in the mosaics of the Baptistry, where the new 'expressionism' insinuated itself into the 'automatic formalism' of Byzantine art. These pathetic, tragically contorted figures are the forerunners of that 'popularization' in art, with its parallel in literature, which caused Cennini to say of Giotto that he 'translated the art of painting from Greek into Latin'. Here too the fundamental change is in the human quality, breaking through the hardened shell of traditional and conventional Byzantine typological representation.

Various Florentine master-craftsmen worked on the mosaics in the Baptistry, among them probably the young Cimabue and Coppo di Marcovaldo, possibly the originator of the great *Last Judgment,* where the change is less in the traditional iconography than in the striking methods of expression.

But Cimabue was the artist who advanced most rapidly along the new road. He marks one of the main turning-points in the history of Florentine painting between the end of one stage and the opening of the next, as does Arnolfo in architecture and sculpture.

This period, which began in Florence at the end of the thirteenth century and ended at the beginning of the fifteenth, is traditionally, if incorrectly, described as 'Gothic'. This refers, however, less to typical outward stylistic preferences than to a new inclination towards human nature and individuality and to the free search for thoughts and feelings in the inner consciousness, as compared with the transcendental world of medieval religious practice.

In this sense it is possible to speak of 'classicism' in Cimabue's painting, derived not from Rome (which the artist visited in 1272) but from that Byzantine 'neo-Hellenism' which in Tuscany was to be found not only in the mosaics of the Baptistry but also in the painted crucifixes of Giunta Pisano and the paintings of Coppo di Marcovaldo.

Masterpieces such as the *Crucifixion* in Santa Croce and the *Madonna* in Santa Trinità, a youthful work (*c.* 1275), already express in an archaic solemnity those values of passionate common humanity which were to attain stupendous dramatic tones in the fresco, unhappily now much altered by time, of the *Crucifixion* in the upper church at Assisi: a naked, powerful eloquence which has its parallel in the lyric poetry of Jacopone da Todi and in much of Dante's verse.

Cimabue's feeling for plasticity, expressed in an elaboration of language which had no such models as sculpture found in the ancient sarcophagi, advanced in a different direction from the still abstract treatment of his contemporary Duccio di Boninsegna, who dissolved the traditional Byzantine stylism in the fluid aristocratic elegance of the *Madonna Rucellai* (Uffizi).

But—according to Dante—Cimabue's reputation was now to be obscured by a new man, Giotto, creator of a *stil nuovo* in painting as Guido Cavalcanti was to do in poetry.

Giotto personifies the Florentine genius for incorporating in art its

▷

A typical Florentine street with shuttered windows, and overhanging eaves.

own conceptions of life, which are given concrete expression in ever
new and relevant forms and are never exhausted by him in any single
form of expression, so that, as Berenson says, 'we feel that the artist
is greater than the work, and the man towers over the artist'.

Almost contemporary with Dante, Giotto shares with him the honour
of the conquest of rational clarity over medieval obscurity, and the
privilege of bequeathing to Florence the foundations of a new language both of words and of imagery. Like Dante, Giotto possesses the
gift of pictorial clarity and, as Goethe saw, the power to isolate the
image with serene sureness of touch.

◁

*S. Croce. This magnificent Gothic basilica was completed in the second
half of the 14th century. The façade and campanile are 19th century.
It contains a many great works of art, including
Michelangelo's tomb by Vasari. Below, ground plan of S. Croce.*

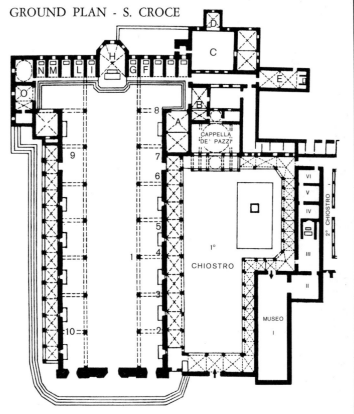

GROUND PLAN - S. CROCE

1 Pulpit (Maiano). 2 Michelangelo Monument (Vasari). 3 Dante Ceno-
taph (S. Ricci). 4 Vittorio Alfieri Monument (Canova). 5 Machiavelli
Monument (Spinazzi). 6 Annunciation (Donatello and Michelozzo).
7 Leonardo Bruni Tomb (Rossellino). 8 Ugo Foscolo Sepulchre (Berti).
A Castellani Chapel (A. Gaddi). B Baroncelli Chapel (T. Gaddi).
C Sacristy (T. Gaddi). D Rinuccini Chapel (G. da Milano). E Novi-
ziato Chapel (Michelozzo). F Peruzzi Chapel (Giotto). G Bardi Chapel
(Giotto). H Greater Chapel (A. Gaddi). I. Tosinghi and Spinelli Chapel
(G. del Biondi). L Capponi Chapel (Pietà by L. Andreotti). M Pulci
& Berardi Chapel (B. Daddi). N Bardi & Vernio Chapel (Maso di
Banco). O Bardi Chapel (Crucifix by Donatello). 9 Marsuppini Monu-
ment (Settignano). 10 Galileo Monument (Foggini & Ticciati).

Thanks to them, the literary and the pictorial languages of the fourteenth century were to form the inseparable basis and foundation for the humanistic renaissance. This is not to say, however, that in both of them no continuing infiltrations come from the rich and fruitful soil of the Middle Ages, with its strong spiritual and religious qualities, to which Romanesque and Gothic architectonic civilization bears witness throughout Europe. Giotto in his genius does not reject this heritage but absorbs it and by his own treatment heightens its vital impulses. As André Malraux has well said, '*Lorsque Giotto rompt avec la tradition bizantine, il l'abolit; dans la mesure ou il rompt avec la tradition gothique, il l'accomplit*'. (When Giotto breaks with the Byzantine tradition he abolishes it; whenever he breaks with the Gothic tradition he completes it.)

Giotto spent his youth in Florence but then left it for much of his life to work in Assisi, Rome and Padua, though he still frequently returned to Florence to paint there. In the city of St Francis, with his innate spirit of rationalism he greatly enhanced that revelation of human qualities represented by the facts of the Saint's life. In portraying those facts he had no iconographical tradition behind him to call upon, no already existing plan or models to follow, as in the vast series of religious subjects that had been handed down and still formed the obligatory themes of evocative and didactic figurative art—a sort of 'poor man's Bible'—such as the churches and monasteries commissioned. Instead, he was dealing with recent events, real people who had lived in the still existing town, facts to be recounted with constant reference to the memories of yesterday and to an almost contemporary situation, which had to be brought alive and translated into Florentine terms, in other words popular and 'civil' rather than courtly and feudal terms, just as Dante was to do in the *Divine Comedy* and Boccaccio in the stories of the *Decameron*.

Light and shadow, colour, and empirical perspective of essential buildings fitting into a space framework related to man's natural size—all these expressed a new conception of life introduced into art with a sense of reality and concreteness hitherto unknown.

The *Madonna di Ognissanti,* today in the Uffizi, side by side with Cimabue's painting of the same subject, reveals the extent of the change effected by Giotto, in the monumental treatment of the figure of the Virgin, constructed as a unified whole with strong and simple modelling, among angels wrapped in absorption but breathing humanity.

The *Crucifixion* in Santa Maria attributed in part to Giotto, the mutilated *Madonna* in San Giorgio alla Costa, the polyptych in the Badia, and the surviving fragments of the fresco with *Scenes from the Life of the Madonna*, also in the Badia, recorded by Ghiberti and Vasari and restored to light some years ago by Procacci, all belong to Giotto's pre-Padua period (i.e. pre-1302-06).

From Assisi to Padua Giotto's work strengthened in its formal structure and in the deep spiritual expressiveness which goes far beyond its obvious narrative capability, great and new though that was.

Giotto returned to Florence in 1320, almost as if to resume and conclude his own experiences there, with the frescoes in Santa Croce, before dedicating himself in the last years of his life to the undertaking of the Campanile of Santa Maria del Fiore (the Duomo), which was

▷

The Donati tower house in San Piero Maggiore, dating from the late Middle Ages.

*The ramparts from the Porta
S. Giorgio to the Porta
S. Niccolò, both built in 1324.*

Remains of the ancient walls of the town on the Costa S. Giorgio, seen from the Belvedere.

The Bargello, 1254-1346. The austerity of this fortress-like building is accented by these sharp angles.

designed by him and which bears his name. There, pursuing Arnolfo's method of a polychrome outer casing, derived from Florentine Romanesque, he effectively modified the solidity of the structure and the stern outline of the octagonal angled buttresses in the part corresponding most closely to the architect's idea (e.g. in the first two storeys, built between 1334 and 1337).

Of the four chapels frescoed by Giotto in Santa Croce, only two have preserved the master's paintings, and even those are seriously impaired. The frescoes of the Bardi chapel take up again the themes of Assisi in a vision of supreme tranquillity. Recently freed from the repainting of the last century, despite mutilation they reveal paintings of a strength and limpid quality comparable with those of Assisi. The mural paintings in the nearby Peruzzi Chapel, which have come down to us in poor condition, are of a later period.

Giotto exercised a dominating influence on the Florentine art of his day and on subsequent developments. His new pictorial structure satisfied in many ways the expectations of an artistic world in ferment which also offered great opportunities in the flourishing political and economic conditions of the city.

During the Middle Ages, in mural painting the aesthetic aim appears subordinated to the evocative and edifying function. Figurative representation, when not purely symbolical and abstract, seems to be following a text, like the illustrations of a book, aiming to arouse the imagination by the simplest means relating to ordinary visual experience.

The Volognana tower, left, with the straight lines typical of medieval Florence and, right, the hexagonal campanile 1310-30 of the Badia Fiorentina.

With Giotto the relationship is reversed in favour of aesthetic experience; the surface of the wall is penetrated by a new, multi-dimensional sense of space in structure and colour, and while still subdivided into compartments it shows in each one of them an autonomous figurative representation, finished in itself and coordinated in relation to the space defined by the architecture. This achievement was at once understood by contemporary artists and absorbed by pupils and followers.
The Florentine churches of the fourteenth century afford an outstanding example of the striking diffusion of the new mural painting, which covered whole walls of chapels reaching even to the roof, retaining only in the frames, which were also minutely decorated, the essential features of the architectonic structure. This narrative ardour finds a parallel only in the rising literature of the *novella*, or short story.

Among the followers of Giotto some relics of archaism, still steeped in thirteenth-century influences, remained, as in the Maestro della Santa Cecilia (so called from the painting of this subject, now in the Uffizi). But complete and direct adherence to Giotto's teachings is to be seen in Taddeo Gaddi, who lived side by side with the Master for twenty-four years, deriving from him his elegance of technique in the arrangement of long narrative sequences, his freshness of analytical observation in enlivening them with episodes, and, to a slightly lesser degree, his plastic sense and constructive power, as can be clearly seen in his *Life of Mary* painted in fresco in the Baroncelli chapel in Santa Croce

(1322-38), which is the most important of the many works, mainly panels, which emerged from his prolific studio.

Another pupil of Giotto's, and according to Ghiberti the greatest, is Maso di Banco, who, in his *Life of San Silvestro* (c. 1340), in the Bardi Chapel of Santa Croce, rhythmically combines the spaces of the composition and the groups of austere figures, showing great clarity in his definition of form and colour and in the architectonic layout, in a way which recalls the work of Ambrogio Lorenzetti.

The relationship between Florentine and Sienese painting, in other words between a plastic, naturalistic treatment and an accentuation of the factors of colour and poetry, became increasingly close. An interpreter of this trend, sensitive to the most subtle rhythmic and chromatic values, is Bernardo Daddi, in the *Lives of St Stephen and St Lawrence* in the Pulci Berardi Chapel of Santa Croce, and with greater lyricism in the predella of the polyptych in the Uffizi, and in his smaller paintings such as, for example, the Altaroli del Bigallo, now in the Galleria dell'Accademia.

Giotto's influence can also be clearly seen in architecture and sculpture. The chief witness to it is the Campanile of Santa Maria del Fiore, designed by him with a clear determination of geometrical harmonies which was later echoed by Jacopo Talenti in the chapter house (now the Cappellone degli Spagnoli) of Santa Maria Novella, by Francesco Talenti in the enlargement of Santa Maria del Fiore, and by Simone Talenti and Benci di Cione in the Loggia della Signoria.

Among the sculptors, Andrea da Pontedera, known as Andrea Pisano, between 1330 and 1333 modelled the first bronze door of the Baptistry, uniting echoes of French Gothic with the vigour and harmony of a medieval classicism learnt from Giotto. Andrea Pisano succeeded Giotto as master builder of the Duomo and carried on the construction of the Campanile, modelling in accordance with the Master's intentions the panels of the first storey which are among the masterpieces of sculpture of that period. Pupils from his workshop and Alberto Arnoldi collaborated in the work and continued it beyond the middle of the century in the panels of the north side of the second storey, with the series of the Sacraments, showing great plastic vigour in the extreme simplification of the subjects represented.

In essential form, Arnoldi and some other artists of the second half of the fourteenth century re-echo, rather than return to, Romanesque styles. This is particularly true of Andrea di Cione, known as Orcagna. As architect and sculptor, his masterpiece is the tabernacle of Or San Michele (1359), Gothic in form and ornamented with marbles sculptured with forceful modelling and a realistic ruggedness that is highly expressive . As a painter, he portrayed in Santa Croce the *Triumph of Death*, now in a fragmentary condition, and in the refectory of Santo Spirito a great Crucifixion, frescoed in collaboration with his brother Nardo di Cione; and he also painted for the Strozzi the superb altarpiece (1357) for the family chapel in Santa Maria Novella, a typical product, both refined and sumptuous, of a tendency to substitute for the more universal conceptions of the Giottoesque world the resources of a great and proudly displayed technical mastery.

◁
The Palazzo Vecchio, begun 1298-1314, a superb building with crenellated parapets surmounted by a rectangular tower with overhanging chamber and belfry above.

S. Croce, main cloister, 13th century.

In the Strozzi chapel Nardo di Cione painted frescoes of lyrical imaginative quality, inspired by Dante's *Inferno*, *Paradiso*, and *Purgatorio*.

Throughout the second half of the fourteenth century, once the brief period of crisis and uncertainty, described in a story of Sacchetti's, had been overcome, artists were unceasingly active in producing altar-paintings and frescoes to adorn the main churches of Florence. Giovanni da Milano, in collaboration with a talented unknown pupil of Orcagna, between 1355 and 1365 painted the *Scenes from the Life of the Virgin* in the Rinuccini Chapel of the Sacristy of Santa Croce, showing that he had derived from his northern training a taste for topical realism, from the school of Taddeo Gaddi, and especially from Maso and Nardo di Cione, consistency of modelling, and from the Sienese delicacy of colour.

Agnolo Gaddi illustrated with episodic richness and decorative fluency the *Legend of the Cross* in the choir of Santa Croce. After 1387 Spinello Aretino portrayed with dry touch and an almost abstract and polemical sense of chromatic clarity the *Life of St Benedict*, translated into popular terms as if in contrast to a tendency of the times towards the celebration and diffusion of great doctrinal themes. The most

Seated figure, 1310, by Arnolfo, probably Boniface VIII.
It was originally on the façade of the Duomo. Museo dell'Opera del Duomo.

obvious example of this had been given by the Dominicans, who around 1366 commissioned Andrea di Bonaiuto (also known as Andrea da Firenze) to decorate their chapter-house—the scene of memorable disputes—in the monastery of Santa Maria Novella (later known as the Capellone degli Spagnuoli, or Spanish Chapel, when after 1540 it was used by Eleonora of Toledo, wife of Cosimo I, for the religious services of her suite). There the artist translated into fluent imagery the complex and thought-provoking sequence of theological symbols, probably selected by Jacopo Passavanti, then Prior of the monastery and author of the celebrated *Specchio della vera penitenza* (Mirror of true penitence), to extol the work of the Dominican Order and its saints and martyrs, culminating in the *Triumph of St Thomas Aquinas.*

Among the very large number of artists working in Florence at this time the capacity for refinements of technique compensates, to judge by the results, for the comparative lack of that inventiveness and inspiration which had distinguished the painting of Giotto and his immediate followers.

Amid the plethora of works of pictorial art it is not always easy to distinguish the most independent personalities and authentic voices. Some of them remain positively enigmatic, like Giottino, author of one

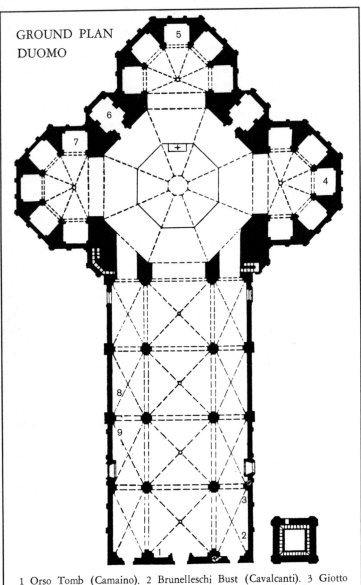

GROUND PLAN
DUOMO

1 Orso Tomb (Camaino). 2 Brunelleschi Bust (Cavalcanti). 3 Giotto Bust (Maiano). 4 Old Sacristy. 5 S. Zanobius, Urn (Ghiberti). 6 New Sacristy (Luca della Robbia). 7 Pietà (Michelangelo). 8 Giovanni Acuto Monument (Uccello). 9 Nicolò da Tolentino Monument (Castagno).

of the greatest masterpieces of painting of the second half of the four-teenth century, the *Pietà*, formerly in San Remigio and now in the Uffizi. Giottino is mentioned by Vasari but confused by him with Maso di Banco and his father Stefano, then rehabilitated by Longhi, who explains his strongly northern character not only by the influence of Giovanni da Milano, a Lombard migrated to Florence, and his contacts with Giusto de' Menabusi, a Florentine migrated to Padua, but also by his own probable stay in Milan, together with his father, around 1350. But there is in him a dramatic power and poetic pene-tration rare in the environment and times in which he was working.

S. Maria del Fiore (Duomo) The octagonal dome with frescoes in the cupola of The Last Judgment *by Vasari, Zuccari and assistants (16th century).*

Outstanding among the most prolific of the Florentine workshops were those of Niccolò Gerini and Lorenzo di Bicci, who with almost dialectical accents developed an eclectic, fluent and open language of painting which was to continue to resound even beyond the end of the century and the beginning of the next.

In the great hive of artistic industry of fourteenth-century Florence, the architects are no less important than the painters and sculptors. They were involved in great enterprises, foremost among them the continuation of the fabric of the Cathedral which, already of ambitious proportions in the original plan adopted by Arnolfo, was further enlarged in Francesco Talenti's plans initiated in 1357, and was finally redesigned ten years later following a competition. The last three decades of the fourteenth century and the first two of the fifteenth saw the great edifice take shape, with the roof of the nave and aisles and the building of the platforms and drum upon which a few years later the cupola was to arise—a half century of superhuman effort, a dream proudly brought to realization, a creation of giants in the midst of a city proportioned to the measure of man.

But there were also energies for other things, nourished by the growing economic prosperity brought to the city by its flourishing textile industry and trading activities. This remarkable good fortune enabled it to withstand various adversities and calamities: the siege by Emperor Henry VII in 1312, disputes with the other Tuscan towns, the defeats of Montecatini in 1315 and Altopascio in 1325, the devastating flood of 1333 which destroyed the bridges and many of the city's works of art, the serious plague of 1348, and the episode of Walter of Brienne, known as the Duke of Athens, who was acclaimed as Governor of Florence in 1343 but swiftly expelled by the populace. Despite all this, the city's prestige and wealth increased. In 1336 Florence, to counter the encroachments of Mastino della Scala, Lord of Verona, became an important factor in the Italian political scene by entering into an association with Venice, Milan and Ferrara; and the old term of Commune was then gradually replaced by that of Florentine Republic. Even the violent upheaval which arose some decades later (1378) through the contrasting interests of the wealthy merchant class and the ordinary people, a revolt known as the 'Tumult of the Ciompi'

Loggia dei Lanzi, Piazza della Signoria; works by Giambologna and Cellini.

and led by Michele di Lando, was unable to shake the solid foundations of order in the city and its outward sign, pursuit of artistic undertakings. In 1337 Francesco Talenti, Neri di Fioravante and Benci di Cione had begun the reconstruction of Or San Michele, the ancient loggia originally intended for a grain market, on more extensive lines than those of Arnolfo's edifice of 1290 which had been burnt down in 1304. Later, after the broad arcades of the ground floor had been enclosed, in 1380, by Simone Talenti's ornate triple windows, the two upper storeys were completed with two great halls whose wide windows pierced the walls on every side, framing with an extraordinary effect of nearness the main landmarks of the town's ancient centre, from the tower of the Palazzo Vecchio to the cupola of the Cathedral, against the background of the hills.

Before the middle of the century the Palazzo del Podestà was enlarged with the Sala del Consiglio Generale (Hall of the General Council) with its majestic cross-vaulting, the great window and the staircase by Neri di Fioravante and Benci di Cione. These same architects in 1349 began the church of San Carlo dei Lombardi, in simple and austere ogival style, facing Or San Michele.

Between 1352 and 1358 there arose near the Cathedral the marble

Loggia del Bigallo, with its oratory, attributed to Alberto Arnoldi, a rare example of both religious and secular architecture, the product of one of the most noble and ancient Florentine traditions, public assistance for the sick and for homeless children.

After the death of Giotto's successor Andrea Pisano, Francesco Talenti carried on the construction of the Campanile and completed it in 1359, boldly resolving the accentuated verticalism with a jutting horizontal cornice.

Between 1376 and 1382 Francesco Talenti's son Simone with Benci di Cione built the Loggia for the public ceremonies of the Signoria; it was traditionally attributed to Orcagna and consequently is sometimes known by that name as well as by that of Loggia dei Lanzi, so called because the Grand Duke Cosimo I de' Medici stationed a guard of German lancers there. The Loggia, with its grandiose and simple definition of space and its three lofty semi-circular arches, re-echoes and advances the new conception of architecture established by the Duomo, linked to Gothic only by the reference in the profiles of the supporting columns and at the same time to the new and the old rhythms of space. Thus here too we find an anticipation of the spirit of the Renaissance.

The City of the Renaissance

When we think of Florence, we think of the Renaissance—in other words, of the beginning of a new civilization, the formative moment of the modern world. Certain typical features—the competition for the Baptistry doors, the first buildings of Brunelleschi, the Brancacci Chapel—and the general tendency to simplify the intricacies of history and fix its focal points in conventional chronological terms, have led to the identification of the rise of this great phenomenon with the beginning of the fifteenth century and a return to the past, to the ancient sources of thought and beauty.

Modern studies have brought about a profound change in the standards of evaluation and historical perspective of the Renaissance as compared with the traditional view, confirmed in the last century by no less an authority than Burckhardt. We no longer think now in terms of the 'discovery' and 'rebirth' of classical antiquity after what Petrarch defined as the 'dark ages', the 'shades' of the Middle Ages. We think, rather, of a new interpretation of that ancient world, carried on through the centuries uninterrupted and preserved in the secret veins of a mainly figurative culture, and of a new desire to penetrate and critically compare its essential values by re-exploring the historical relationship between modern man and the man of antiquity. Hence comes the chronological extension of the concept of the Renaissance and its reabsorption in that of Humanism, as an integral, comprehensive phenomenon of art, as of every other form of thought and of human life itself, in all its historical and political aspects. But this extension is also geographical on the European plane, embracing different and distant manifestations, from the famous tapestries of the Apocalypse in Angers (1380) to the illuminated manuscripts of the international school of the Loire, from the sculptures of Champmol to the paintings of the flourishing Flemish school: all of them examples

▷

Giotto, Madonna in Majesty, *1285, Uffizi.*

which show how trans-Alpine Gothic art in the course of its evolution ventured along new paths and participated in the ceaseless elaboration of artistic and cultural values which absorbed and progressively replaced those of the Middle Ages.

But these facts of history in no way diminish the importance of the privilege that fell to Florence as the crucible of the supreme synthesis of all these experiments, both her own and those of others, finding thereby the answers most closely in tune with contemporary aspirations. These answers had, in fact, been maturing there over a long time in the tradition of that virtual classicism expressed in Arnolfo's architecture and sculpture, in the perfect proportions of Santa Croce and the Loggia of the Signoria, in the formal purity of Andrea Pisano, in the massive imagery of Orcagna.

Man had come once again to give the measure of all things. The great fourteenth-century masters had already more or less consciously anticipated the *humanitas* of the Renaissance in their passionate adherence to the realities of the world.

Dante, Petrarch and Boccaccio had celebrated the individual above and beyond the objective data classified by scholastic philosophy. Their message had been fully understood by a great many Florentines of secular culture; and with their open mentality of men experienced in affairs and familiar with the ways of the world they offered the favourable social terrain for the birth of the new civilization.

For Humanism, the sign of man's greatness lies in the activity he carries out in the world; his power is celebrated in terrestrial toil,

Giotto, Death of St Francis, *detail, c. 1318. Fresco in S. Croce.*

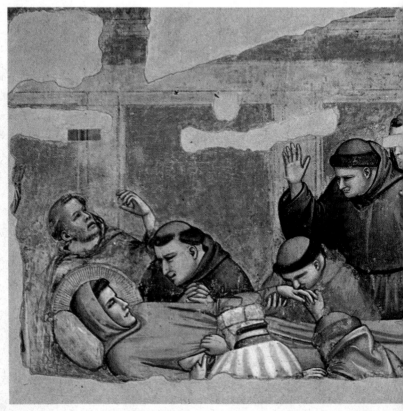

employed towards making the 'city of all men'. For the philosopher Giannozzo Manetti, the ideal is the dignity of the active life. In one of his finest pages he exalts the splendour of Florence as a document of the nobility of man: Brunelleschi's buildings, its pictures, palaces, mercantile activities, great wealth: 'all the things we see are ours, and therefore human because made by man... ours are the paintings, ours the sculptures, the craftsmanship, the sciences; ours the knowledge...; ours all the infinite inventions, ours the language and letters.'

Marsilio Ficino, who opened men's minds to the thought of Plato and Plotinus, discerned in reality life, order, truth and beauty, and in man the eye of the world, the mirror of the universe.

The humanists of the fifteenth century had the feeling that they were confronted by a new age, by something that was being 'reborn' over and above the literary and artistic forms of the classical era to which they turned as a symbol of revolt against medieval life and thought. What counted was the creation of the modern world, even amid the illusion of resuscitating the world of antiquity. The early humanists drew the image of man as *poet* in the full sense of the word, meaning *creator*: creator in his every human manifestation, and above all in his measure of himself against the things of nature; creator of literary and figurative expression no less than of the laws and regulations that order the free and civilized life of human society.

It is not without significance that early humanism in Florence derived its impulse, especially in the sphere of the moral and political sciences, from the culture of an intellectual aristocracy, from the chancellors of

Taddeo Gaddi, Crucifixion, *c. 1340-55, and detail. S. Croce.*

the Republic, the representatives of the great families, the leading class
which was coming into power in the Commune side by side with
learned churchmen and university professors. It was a wealthy wool-
merchant and banker, Giovanni Villani, who, visiting Rome for the
Jubilee of 1300, was so much impressed by the sight of the ancient
ruins that on his return to Florence he decided to become his city's
historian and thus wrote his *Chronicle.*

Guided by a lively consciousness of man and his destiny, the Florentines
discerned in the florin, rather than the sword, the weapon of power,
and they became the foremost citizens in the world. Among the
complex of propulsive forces that went to produce Florence's pre-
eminence, her extraordinary economic vitality played a decisive role.
From the thirteenth century onwards the Florentines dominated the
economic life of the West with their industry, trade and banking.
They formed business companies with representatives, correspondents
and trade links in every part of Europe, especially in France, Flanders
and England. They produced and sold; and they created and diffused

the laws of credit and the essential instruments of banking and account-
ancy. They spread the capitalist mentality throughout the world. They
lent money to popes and to the kings of France and England. Despite
crises and losses—the failure of the Spini, Cerchi and Frescobaldi
houses at the beginning of the fourteenth century, and later on the
recession at the time of the Black Death and the social struggles—the
advance seemed irresistible for at least three generations of the Peruzzi,
Bardi and Acciaiuoli families, and then of the Alberti, the Strozzi, and
above all the Medici. Some fortunes were unstable but all immense.

The Middle Ages was the time of the people, of groups and corporations. The Renaissance saw the increasing emergence of the individual,
and of his pride in the consciousness of his own merits. Whereas
Petrarch, the great innovator of the *studia humanitatis*, had declared
that man is not born noble but becomes it, Cristoforo Landini, the
friend of Lorenzo the Magnificent, attributed the merit of this nobility
to *virtù*—in other words, to the will to forge one's own destiny and the
capacity to realise it with daring, intelligence, and greatness of soul.

For this reason, too, the harking-back to the ancients and their exaltation of the heroic provided a stimulus for the moderns to emulate on the same level, on the plane of the absolute.

Art conformed to this new situation and reinforced it. The artist acquired a high opinion of himself, his creative powers and the dignity accruing to him therefrom. Alberti, in the letter to Brunelleschi at the opening of his treatise on painting, claims that the Florentines of his day are the equal of the greatest artists of antiquity. But already in the fourteenth century glorification of artists had developed in the stories and anecdotes of Boccaccio and Sacchetti; and in his *Lives* the chronicler Filippo Villani linked the work of the artists and poets with the memory of the city's Roman origins and the glories of its history, thus giving the first impetus to the art-historical literature that was to develop during the Renaissance.

The Florentine Renaissance is a theatre of great protagonists. Their role and presence seems constantly to occupy the entire stage in an almost overwhelming display of creative power. But from the Middle Ages to the early Renaissance this unprecedented artistic development would not in fact have been possible without an active link with the intermediary social strata, which meant that the artist never remained isolated in the society in which he worked. Side by side with him in his workshop apprentices and pupils helped and collaborated in his creations, and spread the news of them abroad.

These works of art destined for an elevated and restricted cultural class ranging from the prince to the wealthy merchant constituted at the same time models for other lower classes, the bourgeoisie and the ordinary people, who were also themselves consumers of art at a different level of price and quality. Consequently through the medium of the workshops skilled and careful craftsmen drew constant inspiration from these unique works of art, elaborating variations of them, copying them, and thus making generally accessible a body of artistic production which from a combination of different elements acquired a surprising homogeneity of taste and quality.

In this way art permeated every sphere of society and every occasion of life. And the artists themselves, whether great or humble, felt themselves the centre of attention, always on trial and therefore in a unique position, masters of all the skills and artifices of their trade, ready to find a felicitous solution for every undertaking.

'Let us forget for a moment our standardized and faceless civilization, the mechanical fatality which bit by bit lays its stamp on us and makes us all alike until we cease to be aware of it. Let us try to revert to the spirit of the little Renaissance *polis*, the almost portable city, where everything that exists and is useful is under our hands; where everyone knows each other if they are not actually related; and where all experience is exemplary and within the compass of lively sensation. The Socratic city, punctilious as a beehive, pellucid as a Pythagorean table, precise as a card-index; and where culture is carried on entirely in the form of dialogue if not of disputation.' And when a

◁
A closer view of the campanile with its double and triple arched windows so proportioned as to look the same height when seen from the ground up.

P. 62/63
Over the red-tiled roofs of Florence can be seen S. Maria del Fiore (Duomo) with Giotto's campanile on the left and Brunelleschi's dome on the right.

Hexagonal panels, 1337-43, by Andrea Pisano, which decorate the base of the campanile: animal husbandry, agriculture and architecture.

piece of work is to be undertaken 'the whole beehive is in a ferment; a competition is a national test no less serious than a war, and the chosen craftsman must be answerable in detail to the community which has placed its own preference in his hands.' (Emilio Cecchi).

It is easy to understand how, as such a situation developed, at the beginning of the fifteenth century a clash occurred between conservatives and innovators. The former, the flagging disciples of late Gothic painting, followers of Orcagna, and the craftsmen of the workshops of Gerini's followers, viewed with suspicion the sallies of the Camaldulensian Lorenzo Monaco, active champion of the Florentine-Sienese tradition refurbished with modern asceticism, but not unheedful of the voices from the north, especially through the medium of illuminated manuscripts.

At this time that 'International' or 'Cosmopolitan' Gothic which had been first cultivated in the European courts, in Burgundy, Flanders and Bohemia, became more widely diffused, bringing with it calligraphic elegance and naturalistic accents employed in secular tales. It was an art no longer linked with religious ends as of old but adapted to satisfy in spiritualized guise the worldly aspirations of an aristocracy that found its new myths in power and wealth and discovered new sources of pleasure in nature and in an art that copied it with patient analysis and joyous contemplation. The greatest interpreter of this international trend in Italy at the beginning of the fifteenth century was Gentile da Fabriano, who came from the Marches.

One can imagine the consternation caused by the arrival in Florence from Lombardy of this already famous painter, who was at once commissioned by Palla Strozzi, richest and most powerful of all the Florentine magnates, to paint for the chapel in Santa Trinità the

Adoration of the Magi (now in the Uffizi) which, completed in 1423, revealed itself as a masterpiece. It was the most splendid and astonishing work to be seen in Florence at that time: a sumptuous and fabulous display of worldly elegance, aristocratic ambitions, comfortable truths, and dreamlike appearance, touched by serenity as if by the gentle light of an ideal dawn. Two years later, in the polyptych for the chapel of the Quaratesi family in San Niccolò Oltrarno (later dismembered: four saints in the Uffizi) he produced another masterpiece, showing some signs of contact with Florentine culture and also of affinity and contact with Masolino da Panicale, a sensitive and still timid champion of new things.

When Felice Brancacci, on his return from the embassy to the Sultan of Egypt in 1422, fulfilled his vow to decorate his own chapel, dedicated to St Peter, in the church of the Carmine, he asked Masolino to undertake the work and Masolino began on it. But in those same years he had accepted, for the *Madonna and St Anne* in the Church of St Ambrogio (now in the Uffizi), the overwhelming collaboration of the young Masaccio; and soon afterwards Masaccio took a hand in the frescoes of the Brancacci chapel. This was to be the new gospel of Renaissance painting.

Thus the innovators' advance-patrols had arrived on the scene: Masaccio the painter, Filippo Brunelleschi the architect, Donatello the sculptor, and side by side with them Leon Battista Alberti, also an architect but above all a theoretician and writer of lucid genius.

There was also Lorenzo Ghiberti, who at the beginning of the century had taken part with Brunelleschi, Niccolò Lamberti, and the Sienese sculptors Jacopo della Quercia and Francesco di Valdambrino in the famous competition for the second door of the Baptistry which had excited all Florence. He had emerged victorious with the model of

S. Maria del Fiore,
east end and
south transept.

Right, above, Brunelleschi, The Sacrifice of Isaac, 1402 entered for the competition to design the door which Ghiberti won. Bargello.

Right, below, detail showing Moses receiving the Tables of the Law.

Ghiberti. The Baptistry door, known as the 'Porta del Paradiso', 1425-52, whose bronze panels depict scenes from the Old Testament, below.

the panel in bas-relief representing the *Sacrifice of Isaac* (Bargello Museum). He had introduced new methods of composition and rhythm as compared with the fourteenth-century door modelled by Andrea Pisano. The general system was still Gothic, but within it he introduced modulations of chiselling vaguely verging on the classical, executed with the finesse of a goldsmith. These elements were further enriched in the third door, executed later, between 1425 and 1452, with freer mastery in the rhythm of the composition and the graduation of the plastic effects, according to the principles of perspective worked out by Brunelleschi and Donatello. 'The gate of Paradise', it was called by Michelangelo. But modern critics have entertained some reserves about his assertion of classicism, especially since a recent restoration removing the incrustations of centuries has revealed in the incomparable chiselling persistent reminders of late Gothic taste.

Brunelleschi, Ghiberti's rival in the competition for the Baptistry door (panels in the Museum of the Bargello), appears more constructive and substantial, ready to grasp the realistic fact in all its implications, including those of space. But not even he seemed sufficiently advanced to Donatello, who, twenty years later, in competition for the wooden *Crucifix* in the Gondi Chapel of Santa Maria Novella, said to him, so Vasari reports: 'You can make Christs, I peasants.'

Such are the stages along a road that is historical, political and social rather than artistic, the landmarks of a civil morality of which the new artists are the pioneers and the apostles rather than the interpreters. And foremost among them is Masaccio.

The Brancacci Chapel is almost the paradigm of the transformation and contradictions that distinguish these first decades of the fifteenth century, in the transition from a 'courtly' society—bound by feudal customs and still sunk in the gentle nostalgia of Masolino— to the moral consciousness of the popular soul as Masaccio understood it. His hand is recognizable in the architectonic background—a contemporary view of Florence—in the fresco by Masolino representing the *Raising of Tabitha* and the *Healing of the Lame Man,* where the frail, elegant figures in the foreground stand in an illusionary setting in a perspective space: it is already the vision of Masaccio. And when Masaccio stands alone, master of his own work, his overpowering genius brings to life on these walls (in the personages of the *Tribute Money, Peter enthroned, Peter baptizing, Peter healing the sick and distributing alms,* and, in part, in the *Raising of the son of Theophilus*) a new race of men, a stern and open humanity imbued with purpose, identified in the aspects and essence of natural realities and in their setting, which is itself a historical reality, living and present. 'How quickly a race like this would possess itself of the earth and brook no rivals but the forces of nature.' (Berenson).

This massive achievement, expressive of an almost mysteriously sudden maturity, is the more impressive when we recall the artist's premature death, only a few months later, at the age of twenty-seven.

The span of less than four years, from 1425 to 1428, which covers the painting of the frescoes in the Brancacci Chapel is the crucial period of the assertion of the Renaissance in Florence. During part of it, between September 1425 and August 1427, Masolino was absent in Hungary. Then work was resumed with Masaccio's participation; but in the following year it was again interrupted when both artists, one

▷

General view showing the River Arno with the Ponte Vecchio in the distance.

Andrea di Bonaiuto, The Mission and Triumph of the Dominicans, *1366, and right, detail. S. Maria Novella, Spanish Chapel.*

after the other, left for Rome, from which neither was to return to Florence. And the work, destined to be the school for artists throughout the Renaissance down to Leonardo, Raphael and Michelangelo, was resumed and completed fifty years later, by the hand of Filippino Lippi.

But it was also during the short period of feverish activity on the scaffolding of the Brancacci chapel that Masaccio completed another masterpiece: the *Trinity*, painted in fresco on a wall of Santa Maria Novella, which takes its scale from the human figures, solemn in their stern sadness: monumental frescoes within the imaginary setting of a chapel of classical style which seems, as Vasari said, 'like a hole in the wall': an illusive construction of perspective space, of profound and solemn symmetry, in accordance with a science so intellectually rigorous as to recall the theoretical intuitions of Leon Battista Alberti and to confirm the direct collaboration of that great master of perspective, Filippo Brunelleschi.

All classes of the population participated closely in the development of the city's artistic activities, which were looked upon as a vital part of everyday life. This can be clearly seen from the widespread custom of placing works of sculpture in the open, either on the outside of main buildings or isolated, as in front of the Palazzo della Signoria as a symbol of civil liberty, or inserted in niches, tabernacles or recesses in buildings, as in Arnolfo's façade of Santa Maria del Fiore. Here the tradition of northern Gothic architecture was influential. Most of the extensive statuary decoration of the lower part of the façade, built in Arnolfo's time and preserved until 1587, can be seen today in the Museo dell'Opera, and it bears witness to the importance of the sculptors' role, right from the outset and

Masaccio, Payment of the Tribute Money, *1426-27, detail. S. Maria del Carmine.*

into the fifteenth century. Indeed it determined a plastic tradition developed for centuries in the workshops of the Florentine cathedral, from Arnolfo himself to Jacopo di Piero Guidi and Giovanni d'Ambrogio, from Piero di Giovanni Tedesco to Niccolò Lamberti, down to Nanni di Banco, who in the first years of the fifteenth century affirmed his position among the new sculptors with the tympanum of the Porta della Mandorla and the great solemn statues of *Isaiah* and *St Luke the Evangelist* (1410-13), not unworthy of comparison with the *St John the Evangelist* which Donatello sculptured (1415) in those same workshops where as a young artisan he had learnt the first rudiments of his trade. Donatello also continued to work on Giotto's Campanile until 1436, executing the group of the *Sacrifice of Isaac, St John the Baptist,*

and the prophets *Jeremiah and Habakkuk,* popularly known as the 'Zuccone', or bald-head.

But meanwhile the young sculptors were offered another important opportunity to display their work in public, in the church of Or San Michele. The Guilds, the ancient and powerful corporations of Florentine merchants and craftsmen, wanted to adorn the outside of the church with statues of their patron saints which became an anthology of the most splendid development of Florentine fifteenth-century sculpture. They were all there: Niccolò Lamberti, with *St Luke the Evangelist* (*c.* 1405, now in the Bargello, since 1601 replaced by Giambologna's statue of him) and *St James* (also attributed to Ciuffagni); Nanni di Banco, with *St Eligius* (1413), *St Philip* (*c.* 1415) and the *Four*

Masaccio, St Peter baptizing,
*1426-27, detail. S. Maria
del Carmine, Brancacci Chapel.*

Crowned Saints (1413); Lorenzo Ghiberti, with *St John the Baptist* (1414-16), *St Matthew* (1419-23) and *St Stephen* (1428); Donatello, with *St Mark the Evangelist* (1411), *St Peter* (1413), *St George* (1416, now in the Bargello), and *St Louis of Toulouse* (1423-25), subsequently transferred to Santa Croce and replaced by Andrea Verrocchio's *Incredulity of St Thomas* (1466-83).

These works are listed here with their dates to give evidence of the swiftly succeeding stages along a stupendous road going from the residual Gothicism of Lamberti and still to a slight extent of Ghiberti to the new vigour of body and spirit and the first original application of perspective seen respectively in the statue and the bas-relief of *St George* by Donatello. They also demonstrate how great a stimulus it must have been for the young Masaccio to have there before his eyes in the street these solemn examples of an idealized humanity, and certain of their cadences and harmonies which find an echo in the *Tribute* in the Carmine (as for instance in the group of the *Four Crowned Saints*); or the skilful depth of perspective in the bas-relief of Donatello's *St George*, later recalled in the spacial inventiveness of the *Trinity* in Santa Maria Novella.

Donatello, who lived longer than the others, was able to sum up in himself and develop with an extraordinary vigour and intensive activity all the creative heritage of Florentine Humanism. Originally a workman and craftsman before becoming a great artist, he drew upon and exalted the popular aspects of that heritage, finding in the ancient tenacious virtues, still alive in speech and customs, the components of a classical culture that welcomed them without subjection or archaeological nostalgia. Thus at the outset of his dazzling career, the boy *David*, the sturdy young *St George* (Bargello Museum) and the saints and prophets that he portrayed in marble and bronze for the Duomo, the Campanile and Or San Michele are not spiritualized ascetics but living men each with their own individual bodily traits and mental attributes: middle-class citizens and workmen such as could be met with every day in the streets of Florence, active in the life of the town, men of thought and action, sharing in and defending by their civic virtues the freedom and prestige of their 'city-state'.

Events in municipal life were closely connected with events in the sphere of art, and especially of architecture, through the common civic involvement that determined them; for from the first decades of the fifteenth century onwards artists, men of letters, scholars, merchants and craftsmen shared in the administration of public affairs. The Republic, in entrusting the office of Chancellor to such learned humanists as Coluccio Salutati, Leonardo Bruni, Carlo Marsuppini and Poggio Bracciolini, was not motivated solely by the desire to give classical dignity to public documents and diplomatic letters. The great ideas of liberty, justice and civic pride which the humanists drew from their study of the classics became common currency in the political and economic conduct of a state that was changing from a democratic regime to an oligarchical government, from Signoria to Principality.

Thus the knowledge and study of the great models of classical architecture aroused cultural ambitions which found expression in building activity and in the disposition of the civic organism, even though

◁

Masaccio, The Expulsion from Paradise, *1426-27.*
S. Maria del Carmine, Brancacci Chapel.

these were conditioned by reduced economic and financial resources, which only began to improve after the middle of the century. During the repression which followed the Tumult of the Ciompi in 1382, such popular energies as might have promoted substantial changes in the city's structure had become exhausted, and public finances had been eroded by the struggles with Pisa and Lucca. Thus the ruling oligarchy concentrated on completing works already begun and supplementing them by private initiatives on the part of the wealthiest families, among them the gradually rising star of the Medici.

The city was still in the forefront of everyone's thoughts. Though it meant tightening their belts, it was decided to embark on the great undertaking of completing the cathedral with the construction of the dome, planned by the early architects to rise immense upon the walls of the octagonal drum. In 1418 the Guild of the Wool Merchants, which provided for the fabric of the cathedral, announced a public competition for the dome. It was won by Filippo Brunelleschi, who soon afterwards also began the building of the Spedale degli Innocenti, or Foundling Hospital. These were two outstanding works of Renaissance architecture.

Amid doubts and violent arguments, Brunelleschi overrode what had hitherto been regarded as the insurmountable difficulties of constructing keystones and supporting armatures for so great a height. The building procedure he chose had been used by the Romans, but in its application to those colossal dimensions and in its subsequent influence on Tuscan architecture it was the true invention of his own 'mechanical' genius. His method was to turn the immense mass into a double ogival cap or vault in eight segments, without keystones, and develop it above the great void with no other support than the structure itself as it gradually grew, articulated in ribs and sections, by means of an ingenious placing of the materials—bricks and stone— herring-bone-wise, in contracting rings, with perfect gradual distribution of the stresses and loads, until after sixteen years of work the summit was sealed 91 metres (280 feet) above the drum and 114 metres (370 feet) from the ground.

A construction of such great height, grandeur and perfection had never been seen. The most daring undertaking of the century not only completed the building, the centre and symbol of the traditions and religious ideals of the Florentine people, but also gave it a new significance. From Arnolfo's original structure a singular plan had emerged like a great flowering cross, in which the development of the nave and aisles was related to the spacial, visual expansion of the octagonal choir and the fifteen chapels radiating from it.

With the dome, Brunelleschi welded together these spaces, giving them unity and as it were drawing them upwards to an apex in the dynamic tension of the airy roof; and thus he raised the spaces and volumes, both within and without, from the simple value of dimension to the more complex and coordinated relationship of proportion.

Only then was it possible fully to appreciate how the colossal mass of the cathedral, at first seemingly unassimilable into the architectonic texture of Florence, emerged as a fitting part of it, dominating and supreme amid the network of streets and districts and in the panorama of the city as a whole. The dome, resolving the many-sided form

▷

Donatello, Habakkuk, 1423-24, one of sixteen figures notable for its realistic treatment which formerly adorned the campanile. Museo dell'Opera del Duomo.

Nanno di Banco, St Luke, 1413,
formerly in one of the niches
of the original façade of the
cathedral which was destroyed
in 1587. Museo dell'Opera
del Duomo.

◁
Spedale degli Innocenti,
the 15th-century courtyard.

P. 84/85
Brunelleschi's dome which,
according to specification,
had 'to reach such a height and
magnificence that one could
not expect anything more
noble, more beautiful from
human handiwork'.

of the great drum with the ogival curve—eight white ribs gleaming out amid the red of the terracotta brickwork—and with the wonderful lantern at the summit (1436, wooden model in the Museo dell'Opera del Duomo), constitutes the visual pivot for the surrounding city framework and the geometrical symbol of the new perspective space, the intersecting point of the diametrical planes which stretch out from the building as far as the horizon (Benevolo). Thus Brunelleschi's creation assumes a significance far beyond the municipal circle, as that returned exile, Leon Battista Alberti, recognised with pride when he termed it 'a structure so great, towering above the skies, and so ample as to cover with its shadow all the Tuscan people'. The other landmark of fifteenth-century architecture is the Spedale degli Innocenti with its outer portico and two inner cloisters, which Brunelleschi began to build in 1419. This was not an isolated building but part of a coordinated whole: it was in fact one side of a symmetrical piazza, the prolongation of a street (the Via dei Servi), which ran south-west through the old Borgo di Balla to the Piazza del Duomo. Brunelleschi's project coincided with Alberti's theoretical concept of the regularity and symmetry of the 'new city's' plan, where streets, squares and market-places were to be flanked by porticoes or symmetrical or less similar buildings. Thus the piazza, which was to be completed about a century later, was visualized as forming with the cupola of the church of the Annunziata one of the outlets of the long, straight Via dei Servi, which at its other end terminated and was dominated in perspective by the cupola of the Duomo: a gigantic apparition, in the distance and by contrast, not to be seen from any other viewpoint. Another characteristic of the piazza was its seeming enclosure on every side, because the side streets entering it were not obvious and only the Via dei Servi was clearly a continuation of it and related to the whole. Yet the piazza was not a reserved shut-in enclosure; on the contrary, it was a hospitable place, designed for civic uses and meant to be much frequented. And the portico is the ingenious link between this open space and the buildings surrounding it, like an extension of a domestic courtyard.

From the platform at the top of the wide flight of steps, like the stage of a theatre, the nine arches of the colonnade, resting broad and supple on their slender pillars of Tuscan stone (*pietra serena*), fill the space with their limpid proportions. Elements taken from classical architecture, like words from an ancient vocabulary, are used with a new significance, given fresh life by an inventive power that coordinates them into an original form in a truly creative process, in the fusion of so many imponderable elements—rhythm, proportion, light, colour—with a figurative coherence owing nothing to the near and remote tradition of classicism since it is itself the new classicism.

In the same way Brunelleschi confronted at this time the task of giving a new form to the Romanesque church of San Lorenzo. He drew up the plan for the Medici in 1419 and started work on it two years later (like some others of his works, it was to be completed, after a long pause, by other hands). In it he did not depart from the traditional plans of Santa Croce and Santa Maria Novella, with the frontal alignment of the chapels in the transept; and he seems to re-echo their spaciousness in the rhythm and extraordinary élan of the columns that unite, rather than separate, the nave and aisles with highly original perspective links. But he dominates, moulds and articulates space—the supreme value of his architectonic vision—in accordance with strict geometrical rules, creating in it planes of projection, interpenetration of volumes, escalations of size in both directions, axial and transversal. He replaces the straight surface of the perimeter walls by a wall modulated by a series of recessed chapels. In this series of arches, in the architectonic order that governs them, and in the contrasting depth of their shadow we find repeated and as it were scaled down to a minor key the grandiose and harmonious rhythm of the central nave. The essential character of the forms and their logical connections are accentuated by the chromatic detachment of their frameworks of *pietra serena* against the white of the plaster walls: a feature to become typical of Tuscan Renaissance architecture.

The geometrical principle which governed the architect in the composition of the whole building is especially exemplified in the Sacristy of San Lorenzo (built on the left flank of the transept, it later came to be known as the Old Sacristy, in contrast to the New Sacristy on the opposite side, built a century later by Michelangelo): a square chamber covered by a polygonal dome, supported and connected by spherical pendentives with the arches of the walls: interpenetration of pure geometrical forms within the disposition of the architectonic parts, all of the highest ingenuity: and of supreme quality, too, are the stuccoes, bas-reliefs, bronzes and glazed terracotta lunettes, all the work of Donatello, for which the word 'decoration' seems a misnomer, so closely do they form part of, and are governed by, the supreme rigour of the architecture.

The same principle is at work in the Pazzi Chapel, in the cloister of Santa Croce, but there with a more intense plasticism, in the measured division of the walls, in the rarified harmony it conveys, in the

The façade of S. Lorenzo. In front stands the memorial to Giovanni delle Bande Nere, 1540, by Baccio Bandinelli.

S. Croce, the Pazzi Chapel. Begun in 1430 by Brunelleschi, it is one of the earliest and best-known examples of Renaissance architecture.

limpid, tranquil accord between the interior and the exterior, which is highly original, even though the façade, as always with Brunelleschi's works, remains incomplete; and also in the contemporary unfinished 'Rotonda', which was to have been the oratory of the Camaldulensian monastery of Santa Maria degli Angioli, unique in its day (1433) for its unusual octagonal central plan with radiating apses, in a plastic articulation which has been attributed to Brunelleschi's resumed contact with classical architecture during his second visit to Rome in that year. It was a trial of the type of solution adopted three years later in the walls of the basilica of Santo Spirito. Of this last masterpiece of Brunelleschi's, only a part of the perimeter walls and eight of the 31 columns of the nave and transepts had been completed at the time of his death; but the model he left was used for its completion during the next forty years by Antonio Manetti, Giovanni da Gaiole and Salvi d'Andrea. There we find again Brunelleschi's rational, unitary vision of spaces articulated in perspective, in the multiplication of relations and contrasts of light and shadow, in the rigorous sequence of the apsidal chapels, in the structural connections of the arches of the vaults and the cupolas over the aisles, and especially in the original expansion of the central crossing (before it was encumbered by the screen and the Baroque baldacchino) with the addition of the surrounding aisles which extend the effect of projection and interpenetration in depth of the columns and arches.

The name of the Medici has already cropped up here in connection with some of the fundamental works in the history of Renaissance

P. 90/91
S. Lorenzo. This basilica, consecrated by S. Ambrogio, was renovated in the 11th century and rebuilt by the Medici. Designed by Brunelleschi, 1442, it was completed after his death by A. Manetti, 1447-60.

One of two pulpits by Donatello in S. Lorenzo. Set on a marble substructure the reliefs are in bronze. The work was completed by the school of Giambologna.

architecture of the fifteenth century. They were a family of nobles of bourgeois origin who, like other great Florentine families, had prospered in trade and financial affairs. After suffering a set-back for their espousal of the popular cause at the time of the Tumult of the Ciompi, their fortunes were restored by Giovanni de' Medici (1360-1429), a shrewd and careful administrator of his fortune who succeeded in creating a vast network of banking affairs with branches in sixteen European capitals: an eminent position among the eighty banks of Florence. Indifferent to political ambitions, he sought no rewards of government though, as Machiavelli records, enjoying them all; and it was not until 1421, when he was already advanced in years and at the height of his wealth and popularity in spite of disputes with the Albizzi faction, that he accepted election to the office of *Gonfaloniere della Giustizia*. He had always been interested in and supported the progress of the arts. In 1401 he had been one of the judges in the famous competition for the Baptistry door. He had given hospitality in his own house to the anti-Pope John XXIII after the latter's deposition from the papal throne; and when John XXIII died in 1419 he caused a splendid tomb, on which Donatello and Michelozzo worked, to be erected to him in the Baptistry. But his greatest merit in Florentine art is his support for the genius of Brunelleschi, to whom he gave the opportunity and the large financial means to create two masterpieces of the new architecture: the Spedale degli Innocenti and the church of San Lorenzo, eventually church of the Medici family.

His son Cosimo (1389-1464) followed in his father's footsteps and went further. Educated in the famous school of the Camaldulensian monastery of Santa Maria degli Angioli, he possessed a humanistic culture which in no wise detracted from his keen business sense. He quickly demonstrated his ability to add to the family fortune; and he also had political ambitions. This sharpened the old rivalry of the nobility, and especially of the Albizzi family, and even caused him,

in 1433, to be regarded as suspect to the state and sent into exile. On his return in the following year he reversed the situation, compelling the Albizzi and two hundred of their followers to leave Florence, and established his own political power, skilfully evading all public offices, which instead he got his friends to fill, but in effect always retaining the dominant position as banker of the Republic and trusted adviser of the government. He was clever in reconciling his own interests with those of the state, himself assuming much of the public expenditure on things that could add to its splendour and dignity. Following the example of his father, he did a great deal to further the arts and culture, for which there was a widespread interest in Florence amounting to emulation. We recall, for example, how Palla Strozzi, Niccolò da Uzzano and Cosimo de' Medici competed to support the Florentine Studio where classical languages were taught; and how the most powerful families vied with each other to secure the work of artists to enrich churches and houses with paintings and sculpture, and, even more, to enlist architects in the building of prestigious new dwellings. Before his exile, Cosimo had decided to build a new palace, worthy of their rank, for himself and his family; and he had asked Brunelleschi, who was already the family architect and controlled the building situation in the city, to provide the plans for it. Brunelleschi had long desired this opportunity, and the model he prepared reflected his most daring and original ideas. The site proposed was, not unintentionally, right opposite San Lorenzo, the church of the Medici. But Cosimo was not satisfied; he considered the model too imposing and sumptuous, an ostentation of wealth that would not please his fellow-citizens; and he rejected it, says Vasari 'to avoid envy rather than expense'. So the commission went to Michelozzo, Donatello's companion in the work on Or San Michele. The site was transferred to a short distance from the church of San Lorenzo, on the Via Larga (now Via Cavour), at that time the widest street in the city.

Brunelleschi's plan, rejected by Cosimo, was eventually utilized by Luca Pitti, friend and later rival of the Medici, for the construction of the Pitti Palace. That palace was not begun until 1458, several years after Brunelleschi's death, under the direction of Luca Fancelli.

The story runs that Luca Pitti, who became *Gonfaloniere della Giustizia* in 1458, owed his acquisition of that important title to the gratitude of Cosimo de' Medici, thereby thwarting the intrigues of a group of citizens, led by Gerolamo Macchiavelli, who were determined to remove from the Medici faction the privilege of granting state appointments. And there is a theory that among the very considerable rewards he received, to say nothing of the vast sums of money he derived therefrom, may have been the gift of the model prepared by Brunelleschi for the Medici palace. (Procacci).

Pitti had begun to build at once, on the far side of the Arno, beside the old and modest house of his family, on the slope of the hill where the Boboli Gardens now lie; and the work went on so rapidly that in 1461 he obtained possession from the Signoria of the street opposite the house to avoid disturbance to the family, who were already living

▷

A general view of Florence.

P. 94/95

S. Croce, the Pazzi Chapel. This small masterpiece by Brunelleschi has a portico in classical style.

Palazzo Pitti, façade. The original core was erected by Luca Fancelli, to Brunelleschi's design, between 1451 and 1466.

there while building was going on. It soon slowed down, however, as a result of Pitti's changing fortunes, and came to a standstill after his death in 1472. The back of the palace remained unfinished, while the outer façade corresponded to the plan, being originally confined to only seven central windows on the two upper floors and three great portals of similar design on the ground floor. The most unusual features of the building—its massive severity, its exceptional proportions, the original distribution of the windows, which is identical on the two upper storeys, and with windows open to the ground on the bottom floor, linked by a single outside balcony—confirm the traditional attribution of the architectonic invention to Brunelleschi

and the priority of the themes which were to exercise the greatest influence on subsequent developments in Florentine architecture.

Among these, the most immediate are to be found in Michelozzo's work, and in the Palazzo Medici, built between 1444 and around 1460 following the interruption caused by Cosimo's exile and political vicissitudes. This too, in more eclectic form, is a splendid example of the Renaissance nobleman's palace, typical for the planimetric development round the great porticoed courtyard, for the unsymmetrical façade, the design of the two-arched windows, and the surmounting classical cornice, here seen for the first time instead of an overhanging roof; and, lastly, for the varied rustication in the different storeys, from rough-hewn

Palazzo Rucellai. Designed by Alberti, it was built by B. Rossellino, 1451-55. A fine example of the classical revival, it was very influential in Florence.

on the ground floor to smooth on the top storey, which seems to echo the succession of the orders of classical architecture and is aimed to augment the perspective effect from below to above.

Another powerful Florentine banker, Giovanni Rucellai, in those same years wanted to build a new palace and a loggia in Via della Vigna Nuova; and he had recourse to a literary man, theoretician and expert who for the occasion turned architect—Leon Battista Alberti, the first and most complete example of what is meant by the 'universal man'. Alberti was born in Genoa in 1404, of a wealthy Florentine family exiled by the Albizzi. He was educated in Venice in music and mathematics, and at Bologna and Padua in law. He wrote in Latin well enough to deceive the scholars, who took for an ancient work a comedy he composed when twenty years old. He was recalled to Florence in 1428, and in 1434, after a period in Rome, he returned there again. There he lived among artists and humanists, published a treatise on painting, and prepared another on architecture, *De re aedificatoria* (1452, but published only posthumously in 1485), to demonstrate, in the wake of Vitruvius and with recourse to Plato's ideas and to mathematical terms, the intellectual range of architecture and its mediatory influence between man and the universe: ideas that were to gain ground in his time and secure a following, like his theories on the 'visual pyramid', on the 'reception of lights', on the

P. 100/101
Palazzo Pitti, Ammannati's façade, seen from the Boboli Gardens, a typically splendid Italian landscaped garden, designed by Tribolo for Eleanor da Toledo, 1560.

'design that encloses the whole space of the site', and on the 'combination of all the parts arranged together in proportion'. As architect, he confined himself to working out plans and giving directives, leaving to others the task of execution and distinguishing himself with aristocratic complacency from the 'builder' architect—Matteo de Pasti in the case of the Malatesta temple at Rimini, and Bernardo Rossellino at the Palazzo Rucellai. In that building he affirmed another fundamental aspect of the new civic architecture: he abandoned Brunelleschi's method of subdividing façades by means of cornices to mark the storeys, and instead used more solid entablatures, adding the vertical division by slightly projecting pilasters, thus reconstituting for the first time in the façade of a secular building the classical superimposition of the three orders, in an interpretation eminently assimilated to Florentine terms in the broad luminous surfaces, in a clear and harmonious pattern which absorbed at the same time both the influence of study of classical monuments and the relics of medieval tradition, as in the use of the rough-hewn stone which now became a pattern of smooth blocks.

Rucellai also wanted to have his own private loggia, situated on the street beside the house, in accordance with the Florentine custom exemplified in the relics of the loggias of the Frescobaldi (fourteenth century), the Cerchi and the Peruzzi, in the streets of the same names: places in which to meet and rest, open to all like a public annex of the nobleman's house—in fact, for people known as the *nobili di loggia*.

S. Maria Novella. A Dominican church, built on the site of a 10th-century oratory, it was completed in 1360, by Fra Jacopo Talenti.

The Loggia designed by Alberti, outwardly traditional in form, stands in the space in front of the Palazzo Rucellai in Via della Vigna Nuova, with the perfect proportions of its three elegant arches, a measured, open space by comparison with the compact architectonic framework of the nearby palace.

Not far off, in the ancestral chapel of the Rucellai in San Pancrazio, Alberti designed the model of the Holy Sepulchre (1467) with the same dimensions as that in Jerusalem, elaborately adorned like a coffer with inlaid marble in two colours.

This same type of marble covering, adopted from the Florentine Romanesque tradition, from San Miniato to the Baptistry, was more extensively developed by Alberti in those years (between 1458 and 1470; though the plan had already been worked out around 1440) in the magnificent completion of the fourteenth-century façade of Santa Maria Novella, bringing it to the highest geometrical purity in the new, upper part. The secret of the stupendous harmony of this work lies in the fact that the new elements introduced by the architect—the colossal columns, the central portal, the great circular windows, the pediment, and the inlaid volutes—are strictly linked by a single proportional system, in accordance with those simple mathematical relations (in this case of one to two) which Alberti himself had discovered in ancient buildings. And this explains why the arduous enterprise of reconciling the old with the new, the past with the present has produced, not a hybrid result or 'travesty of the Gothic building' (Schlosser), but 'the most imposing façade of the new style' (Wittkower). The original innovation of the two great volutes, which link up with the high central pediment and conceal the different heights of the nave and aisles, creates a new architectonic motif destined to become very popular in the Baroque era.

In every period architecture interprets the dominant characteristic of the day in a particular type of building which becomes almost its symbol: in the Romanesque period the parish church, in the Gothic period the town hall and the great monastic churches, in the Renaissance the houses of the bankers and rich merchants. This new social class acquired its position not, as in the Middle Ages, by arms or privileges but by industry, trade and the skilful management of money. It was a new aristocracy of men who liked to build their own houses, stamped with the splendour of their newly-acquired ease, in the same popular quarters where they had had their origins and toiled to create and consolidate their own fortunes. The oligarchy that was acquiring ever-increasing power, and the craftsman and merchant class slowly on the ascendant in the process of social evolution, did not think about creating great transformations in the old city plan. Where, as constantly happened, empty spaces to occupy became rare, they preferred to fill up and enrich the medieval matrix, as it were sublimating it by replacing old buildings by larger new ones, more regular in appearance and more modern in conception. But the scale was usually still in proportion to the surrounding buildings. This situation furthered a mainly qualitative development in architecture, and it explains why the new Renaissance architecture found its greatest expression and models in Florence.

◁
S. Maria Novella. The magnificent façade, with black and white marble revetment, was begun in 1350. The upper part is Renaissance, designed by Alberti.

The fifteenth-century palace, following the prototypes of Brunelleschi, Alberti and Michelozzo, developed around a porticoed courtyard, a sort of lay cloister, the outward sign of wealth, the centre of the house's life and activity, and a point of convergence for the ground-floor quarters, an island detached from the traffic of the street and the curiosity of neighbours. The façade was for everyone, the courtyard for the family, friends, and customers. You entered from the street by the main portal, through an entrance passage as deep as the thickness of the outer walls themselves. The house, whether flanked by other buildings in the street or isolated on most sides, was generally a single block like a cube, subdivided vertically into three or more storeys, of graduated height, each with its own function (in general, business and services on the ground floor, official life, reception etc. on the first floor where the rooms were larger, and family life on the

S. Spirito. An Augustinian church, it is a masterpiece designed by Brunelleschi, 1444. The building shows the economical style of his late period and the interior is magnificently integrated by a consistent system of proportions.

upper floors). The inner quarters reflected the architectonic divisions of the façade, looking out on to the narrow, irregular streets, but with not much of a view. In compensation there was sometimes at the top a big open loggia with a panorama of the city and the surrounding hills. When there was not much space available, it still continued to be customary right into the fifteenth century for parts of the building to project on to the public street, supported on corbels or small arches (for example, in Brunelleschi's Busini-Quaratesi palace in Piazza Ognis-santi), and sometimes also into the interior of the courtyard in place of porticoes on one or two of the sides. And up above, the rooftops, characteristically projecting and casting a streak of shadow from the eaves, framed a patch of sky amid the Florentine streets.

Beside the Palazzo della Signoria, round the Duomo and the Baptistry, and in front of the big monastic churches there were in olden times

mere open spaces rather than piazzas. The serried ranks of houses and towers in the streets of the historic centre were originally interrupted by little piazzas, open spaces in front of churches, or gardens. It was a far cry from Alberti's idea of the secluded piazza harmonizing into the fabric of the city, a symmetrical space in proportion with the surrounding buildings. Rucellai left hardly any space in front of his palace, and Strozzi only a little more, just enough to merit the name of piazza. Yet Brunelleschi, with the Spedale degli Innocenti, laid the foundations for the modern, Renaissance-type piazza, an architectural feature which Antonio da Sangallo was to bring to completion eighty years later. He had done even more, in the cause of furthering the building enterprises of the Medici: with the new construction of San Lorenzo he had fixed another of the poles (a third one being set at the end of Via Larga, from the piazza and monastery of San Marco, restored by Michelozzo) between which the gradual restructuring of the vast northern quarter of the city was to take place, in the nucleus of which the Medici palace in Via Larga was in turn to become the magnet for more than two centuries of intensive building activity, with the palaces of other great Florentine families, in the Vie Ginori, Ricasoli and Alfani. How intense this fervour of building activity was throughout the city at the time of the Medici can be seen from the account of a local chronicler who records the construction of at least thirty palaces between 1450 and 1478.

Vespasiano da Bisticci, patron of copyists and the last 'publisher' of the hand-written book, an important personage in Florence at the time of Cosimo de' Medici and himself the author of the *Vite di uomini illustri* (Lives of Famous Men) in which he included his own personal recollections, shows his delight at seeing his city becoming more and more beautiful, enriched with new churches, palaces, and works of art; and he tells how Cosimo, himself the enemy of ostentation, confided to him that his passion for building regardless of expense had been inspired and indeed virtually commanded by Pope Eugenius IV, who told him to 'build by way of discharging his duties of conscience'. Cosimo gave lavish hospitality to the Pope and his court for about six years from 1434, and this was the time of the city's greatest prosperity. He also secured the transfer from Ferrara to Florence of the Council which was to try to effect the reunion of the Greek and Latin Churches. It was held in 1439 in the cloisters of Santa Maria Novella, attended by a large number of Greek prelates and monks in their picturesque costumes in the suite of the Patriarch of Constantinople, and also by the Emperor John VII Palaeologus. The presence of so many learned Greeks and the relations they formed with the Florentine intellectual world were among the decisive factors in the spread of interest in classical studies and Platonic philosophy under Cosimo and later under Lorenzo. Florence was then, according to Vespasiano, 'in a most happy state, full of exceptional men of every kind, and the fame of its worthy government extended throughout the world.' Cosimo responded more than magnificently to the Pope's command to spend up to ten thousand florins on reconstruction in the monastery of San Marco (by then transferred from the Silvestrini to the Dominicans), entrusting to Michelozzo the task of enlarging the church and building the cloisters and library (1437-52) on a scale of unusual splendour: in fact, the building in the end cost him many tens of thousands. And this was not because his duties of conscience weighed the more heavily with the years, but because his ambitions grew ever

S. Spirito, façade. This church, completed in 1487, contains many notable works of art. A wooden crucifix by the young Michelangelo was discovered there in recent years, and is now in the Casa Buonarroti.

greater and also latterly his desire to contribute to this remarkable flowering of art and culture. He even, it would seem, in one case himself acted as architect, if we are to attribute to him (as Gombrich and Procacci have suggested) the planning and personal direction of the restoration of the Badia at Fiesole, the monastery and church, later often ascribed by Vasari and others to Brunelleschi.

Cosimo may even also have had some hand in Michelozzo's work when, not satisfied with putting him to build intensively in the city, he charged him no less enthusiastically with the renovation of the castles he acquired in the surroundings of Florence, which became transformed into residential villas to be lived in according to the good Tuscan tradition. The transformation extended not only to the buildings but also to their natural surroundings, where the geometrically planned Italian garden now began to develop. Thus Michelozzo designed for Cosimo de' Medici the villa of Cafaggiolo, in the Mugello,

Palazzo Medici-Riccardi. Built by Michelozzo, 1440-60, it was the home of the Medicis till 1540, and courtyard with statue of Orpheus by Bandinelli.

modernized in 1451 by means of Renaissance additions to the old castle, and also the villa of Careggi, two miles outside Florence, restored in 1457, which while still retaining the massive appearance of a feudal fortress was made less forbidding by the addition of a loggia over the portico. Careggi in fact became the favourite residence of Cosimo and his immediate descendants, who installed works of art there and made it the centre for writers, artists and scholars to meet and carry on learned discussions which became famous under the name of the 'Accademia Charegiana.' From the time of Petrarch onwards, praise of the countryside, an echo of Virgil's bucolic poetry, was accompanied around Florence by the pleasure of possessing a country villa. In the fifteenth century many such villas arose scattered here and there upon the gentle hillsides of Fiesole, and the humanists could satisfy their dreams by building them or receiving them as gifts from the Prince, as happened, for instance, in the case of the young philosopher and humanist Marsilio Ficino, the translator and scholar of Plato and Plotinus, who in 1462 received from Cosimo the little house of Montevecchio, near the Careggi villa, which as reflection of the villa and the reunions held there became known as the 'Academiola' or little Academy. Later on Poliziano loved to frequent the Villa Medici at Fiesole, also built by Michelozzo.

Meanwhile the activities of painters and sculptors were no less in demand than those of architects in Florence. After the death of Masaccio and the departure of Masolino, neither of whom had had

S. Maria Novella, the campanile, by Fra Jacopo Talenti, and a wall forming part of a quadrangle surrounding the tombs beside the church.

time to develop a definite school of followers there, a pause in the flow of renovating ideas might have been expected in the 1430s. But instead the frescoes of the Brancacci chapel carried on their message and soon came to be regarded by all artists as the fountainhead of the new art.

Among the first and readiest to grasp this lesson was a humble friar of the Dominican convent of Fiesole, Fra Giovanni, later to be known as Fra Angelico. When Masaccio died his career had hardly begun, though he was already interested in new ideas, as can be seen, despite subsequent alterations, in his *Madonna with saints* (1428-30) in the church of San Domenico di Fiesole. Within a few years, however, the artist matured rapidly, and his extensive activities soon became coloured by legend. Among the masterpieces of that period which have remained in Florence are: the *Coronation of the Virgin*, painted for the Hospital of Santa Maria Nuova (1434-35), now in the Uffizi, the great *Tabernacolo dei Linaiuoli (Tabernacle of the Flaxworkers)* (1433) within the marble decoration designed by Ghiberti (Museum of San Marco), the *Deposition* (1437-40), executed for the Strozzi chapel in the sacristy of Santa Trinità, and the *Altarpiece* known as '*di Annalena*' (*c.* 1437-40) from its original destination for the Florentine monastery of San Vincenzo, founded by Annalena Malatesta. These last two works (now in the Museum of San Marco) are completely within the Renaissance orbit. A language rich in severe humanistic accents absorbs any excess of religious piety; it reveals, together with some trace of late Gothic cadences and as if with the clear palette of an illuminator, the constructive corporeality of Masaccio and the statuary solemnity of Donatello and Luca della Robbia; and in the architecture, an echo of Michelozzo—a sign that the painter, far from the mystic ecstasies attributed to him by hagiographical tradition, looked clearsightedly around him at the world of living men; and it is not without significance that in the faces of some personages in the *Deposition* a resemblance can be discerned to Michelozzo and to one of the Strozzi, and in the *Pala di Annalena* for the first time the division of the Gothic polyptych is abolished, and the figures of the saints are presented in a single unified setting.

The dates of these pictures all fall within the period of Fra Angelico's closest relations with the Medici. He had meanwhile transferred his workshop from Fiesole to Florence, to the monastery of San Marco, still in a state of confusion owing to the work going on there under Cosimo's orders and Michelozzo's direction. In agreement with them, and at the suggestion of the Prior Fra' Antonino, later Archbishop of Florence and subsequently proclaimed a saint, Fra Angelico executed between 1437 and 1447 (possibly continuing in 1450 after his return from Rome where he had gone to decorate the Cappella Niccolina in the Vatican) the celebrated series of frescoes in the monastery of San Marco: in the corridors (the famous *Annunciation, St Dominic at the foot of the Cross*, and the *Sacra Conversazione*), in the Chapter House (the great *Crucifixion and Saints*), and in a large number of the forty-four cells on the first floor, where frescoes of no great size but harmonious in composition and in delicate and restrained colouring illustrate in each cell a mystery of the Christian faith. Many of them are to be regarded as among the masterpieces of Angelico and of all fifteenth-century painting. In the two cells which Cosimo de' Medici reserved for his private meditations, the frescoes represent *Christ surrounded by Saints* and the *Adoration of the Magi*: this was a subject favoured by the Florentine noblemen as combining devotion to God with the assertion of their own rank. Today this remarkable collection constitutes the greatest museum dedicated to the work of a single painter, for others of Angelico's paintings and altarpieces have now been assembled there. In addition to those already mentioned, those of particular importance are the three Reliquaries of Santa Maria Novella (1434); the great altarpiece of San Marco representing the *Madonna, Saints Cosmas and Damian, and other saints* (the face of Cosmas possibly a portrait of Cosimo de' Medici), painted in 1438-40 for the high altar of the church of the monastery of San Marco (of the dismembered predella, only two panels are here; the other seven are in the museums of the Louvre, Munich and Washington); and the thirty-five panels which, with six others now dispersed, formed the decoration of the doors of the reliquary-cupboard in the oratory of the SS. Annunziata, possibly ordered in 1448 by Piero de' Medici.

A contemporary of Angelico and like him a friar though of very different reputation with regard to character, Filippo Lippi (*c.* 1406-69) at the time of his novitiate in the monastery of the Carmine, was at home with Masaccio's masterpiece in the Brancacci Chapel, had seen it come to birth, and as a novice-painter had derived from it a definite, if not particularly deep, influence towards an essential plasticity, interpreted in flowing style but not lacking in impetus. This can be

▷

Palazzo Pazzi-Quaratesi, designed by Giuliano da Maiano, 1462-72. The decoration of the windows of the first storey is especially lovely.

seen in the fragmentary fresco in the cloister of the Carmine with the *Conferring of the Rule* (1432) and also in the *Trivulzio Madonna*, now in the Museum of the Castello Sforzesco in Milan, in the alternation between Masaccio and Angelico whose clear unshadowed colours he adopts. While the powerful *Madonna di Tarquinia* (1437) suggests the influence of a visit to the Veneto, the *Annunciation* (1437-40) in the Martelli Chapel in San Lorenzo is equally impressive for its heightened colouring and the atmospheric significance of the receding perspective, corresponding more nearly to an empirical vision than to the geometrical standard and optical theory evolved at that time by Alberti and Brunelleschi. In Florence Fra Filippo Lippi left behind no fresco decorations; and his altarpieces and devotional paintings have suffered over the years the removals and dispersion common to so much of the Florentine artistic heritage which has gone to enrich the museums and collections of the world. Most of his remaining works in Florence are in the Uffizi Gallery: the predella of the *Barbadori Altarpiece* (Louvre) painted between 1437 and 1440 for the church of Santo Spirito; the *Madonna enthroned with saints*, painted around 1442 for the Medici, with the Pesellino predella, formerly in Santa Croce; the crowded and effusive *Coronation of the Virgin* (*c.* 1441-47) from the church of Sant'Ambrogio, a fundamental work for its achievement of colour and luminosity, its fluidity of line, its sea-green colouring, its note of worldly exuberance, and its many portraits of contemporary personalities; the *Madonna with the Infant Christ and two Angels* (*c.* 1460), among his happiest creations, pervaded by calm and human lyricism; and from his last period, between the frescoes of Prato Cathedral and his departure for Spoleto, the *Madonna with St Bernard*, commissioned around 1463 by Lucrezia Tornabuoni for the Hermitage of Camaldoli. Apart from the Uffizi Gallery, the Medici Museum in Palazzo Riccardi has a masterpiece of the period 1440-42, the *Madonna with the Infant Christ*, and the Pitti Gallery a tondo of the *Madonna and scenes of the Nativity* (1452), remarkable for its deep perspective, almost like a reflection in a Flemish mirror: another empirical experiment in the problem of the relations between space, light and movement.

A decisive introduction to this topical problem had already been provided at this time by Domenico Veneziano (*c.* 1406-61), who according to recent hypotheses (Kennedy, Longhi) had first arrived in Florence from the North together with Gentile da Fabriano, in time to see Masaccio at work on the Carmine. His first Florentine work, the *Madonna* frescoed in the Tabernacle of the Conto de' Carnesecchi, is in London (National Gallery); a more extensive work, the cycle of stories of the Virgin in the church of Sant'Egidio, on which he had the assistance of the young Piero della Francesca, has been lost; his last known work, the fresco of *St John the Baptist and St Francis* (Museum of Santa Croce), was preserved after the destruction of the Cavalcanti chapel in Santa Croce; and thus the significance of Domenico Veneziano's original vision remains entrusted to the *Altarpiece of Santa Lucia de' Magnoli* (*c.* 1445-48), now in the Uffizi (but the five storeys of the predella are divided among the museums of Washington, Cambridge and Berlin). A silvery morning sun penetrates the short

▷

Palazzo Strozzi. The most famous palace of the Florentine Renaissance, it was begun by Benedetto da Maiano in 1489, and in 1497 Cronaca became the architect and designed this majestic courtyard.

Donatello, La Cantoria, *1433-39. Museo dell'Opera del Duomo.*

space between the portico and the apse, with their fantastic colouring, and determines their perspective sequence, more strictly applied than would have been the case with Lippi, in carrying out the 'optical pyramid' laid down by Alberti. In this space the figures of the Madonna and the four saints take shape with a feeling of rustic energy, tempered by the vibrant luminosity of the clear colours. We have here a clue to the complex development of Piero della Francesca in his early Florentine beginnings, all trace of which has been lost. (Of his masterpieces, the portraits of Federico di Montefeltro and his wife Battista Sforza, now in the Uffizi, came later to Florence from Urbino, where they had been painted in 1465.)

The other link comes with Paolo di Dono, known as Paolo Uccello (1397-1475), and his fanatical interest in perspective as a means of interpretation and fantastic transfiguration of reality. In Florence, on the north wall of Santa Maria del Fiore, his *Equestrian Memorial to Sir John Hawkwood (Giovanni Acuto)*, an English soldier-of-fortune who served as condottiere in the Florentine army from 1377 to 1394, is painted in fresco in grisaille (1436), not so much as a virtuoso imitation or pictorial substitute for a plastic or monumental decoration, still less, as was once thought, as an economic expedient, but rather out of the simple intellectual desire to try out, in the continuity of a wall-surface, a purely visual, immaterial, equivalent between image and reality of spaces and forms. In the same way in the cloister of San Miniato the (now fragmentary) *Scenes of Monastic Life* (1439-40), and in the cloister of Santa Maria Novella the *Stories of the Creation* (1430-50), frescoed in green-toned 'terra verde'—hence its name of Chiostro Verde—unfortunately also much damaged (recently detached, they have revealed interesting *sinopie*), derive hallucinating effects from the dramatic setting within deep perspectives. Accentuated metaphysical abstractions, polemical and ironic significances, and chromatic oddities insinuate themselves into the late Gothic-type narrative vein governing the imaginative formulation and composition of the three episodes of the *Battle of San Romano* (1456-60), painted for the Medici Palace in Via Larga, only one of which is still in Florence (in the Uffizi; the other two are in the Louvre and National Gallery in London).

Villa medicea della Petraia. Built by Buontalenti, 1574-89, it stands in a terrace garden in the Italian style designed by Tribolo.

The influence of Domenico Veneziano, and also, in some more super-ficial ways, of Paolo Uccello and Piero della Francesca, can be seen in Alessio Baldovinetti, who began his career with three panels of the vestments cupboard of the SS. Annunziata (1448, Museum of San Marco) and established himself as a creator of delicate, luminous scenes in the *Nativity* frescoed in the cloister of that church (1460), in the *Annunciation* and *Madonna and Saints* (Uffizi), in the frescoes and the picture of the *Annunciation* in the chapel of the Cardinal of Portugal in San Miniato (1466), and in the frescoes, unfortunately much dam-aged, of the choir chapel of Santa Trinità (*c.* 1471).

Youngest of them all, and short-lived, is Andrea del Castagno (1423-57), who effected a synthesis of the formal and perspective conquests of the early Renaissance in remarkable terms of spectacular monumen-tality and plastic power, as can be seen in the *Equestrian Memorial to Nicolò di Tolentino,* painted in the Duomo twenty years after the similar memorial (to Sir John Hawkwood) by Paolo Uccello; in the youthful, massive and harsh *Crucifixion* (*c.* 1444), detached from the cloister of Santa Maria degli Angeli and now in the Hospital of Santa Maria Nuova; and, superbly, in the great wall of the refectory of

Works by Donatello in the Bargello. Left, David, *1408-9, centre* Athis *or* Bacchus, *c. 1440, and right,* St George, *1416.*

Sant'Apollonia—the first of the Florentine Renaissance series—frescoed with the three stages of the Passion—*Crucifixion, Deposition, and Resurrection*—above the representation of the *Last Supper* (1445-50) contained in a rigid, geometrical, perspective marble room, open like a loggia or a stage-front, beneath a roof, and derived from a theoretical idea of ancient architecture. Within, the figures of the Apostles sitting with Christ at the long table assume a lifelike vitality with their serious, measured gestures and their peasant faces, as if carved in stone, heightened by the graduation of light and charged with an immense moral energy. So, too, to an almost heroic degree are the famous personages represented by Andrea del Castagno in the frescoes of the Villa Pandolfini, at Legnaia, later detached and transferred to the old refectory of the former monastery of Sant'Apollonia with other works of the master to form a museum dedicated to him; the frescoes are now shown in the Uffizi.

Side by side with the main trend embracing the archaic vigour of Andrea del Castagno, another trend existed which appeared to continue, with indifference to novelties that were not merely superficial, the cult of the courtly world revealed by Gentile da Fabriano. This trend furthered the fashion for illustration in the decoration of furniture and wedding-chests, inspired by the legends of chivalry and the tales of Boccaccio: a typical product of the Florentine craftsmen's workshops of the mid-fifteenth century. Outstanding in this field is the delicate art of Francesco Pesellino (1422-57).

With more lively fantasy, Benozzo Gozzoli (1420-98), a former pupil and collaborator of Angelico and translator into prose of his poetic language, established himself as the interpreter of the 'slide' from inwardness to elegance which was an essential feature of Florentine society in the transition from the harshness of the Republic to the refinement of the Medicean Signoria. For its founder, Cosimo de' Medici, and at his son Piero's request, in their new palace in Via Larga Benozzo decorated the family chapel designed by Michelozzo with the luxuriant, crowded scene of the *Journey of the Magi to Bethlehem* (1459-60), transferring to the wall the clarity of colour and meticulous detail of illumination, like the serried composition of Flemish tapestries, in a festive gala parade of heraldic personages moving happy and carefree in gardens of delight. But in the faces are portraits of the Medici family and their friends and guests from other Italian courts, and in their costumes the fabulous, already legendary, recollection of the oriental dignitaries who had taken part in the Council of Florence twenty years before.

A similar coexistence of different trends, less accentuated but equally perceptible, appears in the field of sculpture. Donatello, who as a very young man had made his mark in the sculptures of Or San Michele in the decade following his second stay in Rome (1432-33) showed the influence of his more direct experience of the classical and medieval world. At the beginning, the *Annunciation* in Santa Croce (1433) still has an ample and sustained rhythm, though combined with dramatic movement, within a complex architectonic tabernacle (in collaboration with Michelozzo), in the striking relief of the gold against the grey tone of the *pietra serena*. But the suggestion of the classical appears decisively in the *Cantoria*, or choir gallery parapet, of Santa Maria del Fiore (now in the Museo dell'Opera del Duomo), begun in 1433 and completed in six years, in contrast to the corresponding almost contemporary work of Luca della Robbia (1431-38). A comparison of these two masterpieces is significant. In Luca's *Cantoria*, the same idealized naturalness and tranquil harmony which characterizes the *Bronze Door* of the New Sacristy of the Cathedral (1445-69) is animated by serene joyfulness in the ten finished marble panels, in the attitudes and faces of the youthful musicians intent on singing the last psalm of David, '*Laudate Dominum*', accompanying it with the sound of lutes, drums and triangles: 'a delicious mixture of classicism without pretentiousness, and of a new civilization which still breathes the scent of the countryside' (E. Cecchi). In Donatello's *Cantoria*, on the other hand, the figuration of the reliefs is continuous, punctuated but not interrupted by the pairs of colonnettes, and the train of dancing and singing putti, overwhelmed by wild joy, abandon themselves to unrestrained vitality: it is not so much an interpretation as a translation of the Dionysiac theme, a typical reaction of the artist to the examples of classical sculpture. The *putto* is seen as the fusion of the features of the child, the angel and the classical Cupid to give an appearance which was to be fundamental in the art of the fifteenth century, the discovery of which belongs to Donatello (von Bode).

Around 1440 Donatello modelled for Cosimo the first nude of the Renaissance, the bronze *David*, destined to adorn the courtyard of the Medici palace in Via Larga (and now in the Bargello): a metamorphosis of the King of Israel into a boy Dionysos, an exaltation of the ideal of heroic youth and, at the same time, a revelation of a new sensitivity in the modelling of the forms and the vibration of the light. This masterpiece came to birth in the same rarefied cultural climate that significantly produced another of Donatello's creations of this period: the winged, laughing *Eros* or *Atys*, formerly in Casa Doni (now in the Bargello).

Donatello's Padua period (1443-52, equestrian statue of *Gattamelata* and altar of the basilica of Sant'Antonio) marked a further advance on the road of his restless search for expression. This, on his return to Florence, became translated into fresh masterpieces, inspired by an almost desperate religious lyricism: the harsh, dramatic bronze group of *Judith and Holofernes* (1455-60), transferred in 1495 from the Medici palace to the Palazzo Vecchio as a warning to governments, as the inscription indicates; the shuddering vision of the *Crucifixion* in the bronze bas-relief in the Bargello; the pathetic blood-drained

▷

Villa medicea di Careggi. A medieval manor transformed and enlarged by Michelozzo after 1452. He adapted it to the taste of the time while conserving the machicolation which gives it the appearance of a fortress.

Giambologna, Venus fountain, 1567, in the gardens of the Villa medicea della Petraia.

Gardens of the Villa medicea di Castello with Ammannati's sculpture depicting the Rape of Proserpina.

P. 124/125

S. Marco, façade. Dominican church and convent founded 1249, and renovated by Michelozzo 1437-52. Giambologna designed a funeral chapel and altar tabernacles, 1588. The façade is a late work by Gioachino Pronti, 1777-78.

Benozzo Gozzoli, Journey of the Magi, *1454-60, detail of celebrated fresco in the Cappella di Palazzo Medici, depicting members of the Medici familiy in the guise of the three kings, the procession headed by Piero de' Medici.*

St Mary Magdalen (Baptistry) in the wooden statue, recent restoration of which has uncovered the original polychrome and gold colouring; and lastly the two great pulpits in the church of San Lorenzo (*c.* 1460-65), of incomparable inspiration and intensity in their luxuriant and dynamic compositions and their freedom of modelling, where we find not only an accentuation of the typical Donatello technique of 'flattening' (i.e. the bas-relief graduated to give an effect of perspective) but also the development of the 'unfinished' as an essential value in a completely new principle of style (Martinelli) in the parts that are indisputably by his own hand, as distinct from those entrusted to his pupils, Bartolomeo Bellano of Padua and Bertoldo of Florence.

These works form the link between the activity and ideas of the later Donatello and those of the succeeding generation of sculptors, Pollaiuolo and Verrocchio, in the new dynamic vision of forms, overcoming the gap which seems to occur in those years in the field of art between the death of Cosimo the Elder in 1464 and the advent of Lorenzo the Magnificent in 1469. For it is precisely then that we find in other contemporary artists an attenuation of the hitherto high and austere expressionistic values in favour of a divergence towards eclecticism and preciosity backed up by an increasingly polished mastery of technique.

Exaltation of the individual and his desire for survival finds expression in the portraits and tombs which provide an outlet alike for the Florentine artistic temperament and the new conception of the world.

There is also an understandable tendency towards portraiture in those pictures which the artist presents under mythological or symbolical guise, of ideal personages called upon to represent concepts or sentiments: among the most typical examples is the terracotta bust in the Old Sacristy of the church of San Lorenzo, in which Donatello portrayed the Saint in the likeness of a living person. In the art of portraiture at this time the ceremonial character of the bust becomes accentuated, classical in inspiration like the medal and coinage, with a tendency to analytical precision. Sculptors were already familiar with the use, mentioned by Vasari in relation to Verrocchio, of the plaster cast placed on the face of the dead person, producing a realistic, if sometimes crude and prosaic, incisiveness, as compared with the inward-looking results of psychological research.

The Bargello Museum contains some excellent examples of mid-fifteenth century portraiture: the busts of *Youths* by Donatello, though modern critics have raised doubts as to whether one, the presumed *Niccolò da Uzzano*, popular for its naturalism, in coloured terracotta, is really by him; and busts by Desiderio di Settignano (*Young Gentlewoman and Boy*), Antonio Rossellino (*Francesco Sassetti*, 1464; *Matteo Palmieri*, 1468), Mino da Fiesole (*Piero de' Medici*, 1453; *Rinaldo della Luna*, 1461; *Giovanni di Cosimo de' Medici*), and Benedetto da Maiano (*Pietro Mellini*, 1474).

Alberti attributed a 'civic' importance to tombs inside churches, and he urged that they should be simple, reflecting on a lesser scale the character of the sacred edifice: he himself provided an example —which however was not followed—in the Rucellai Chapel in San Pancrazio. However the more frequent type of tomb was an elaboration of the sarcophagus, supported by brackets or resting on a

◁
Andrea del Castagno, The Holy Trinity, *1454-53,*
with S. Girolamo between two hermits. SS. Annunziata.

base, within a niche crowned by a central arch, the ancient motif of the *arcosolium*. Among the earliest Renaissance examples is the tomb of Onofrio Strozzi, by Piero di Niccolò Lamberti (1421) in Santa Trinità, copied by Bernardo Rossellino for Orlando de' Medici (1456) in the SS. Annunziata and possibly by Desiderio da Settignano for Giannozzo Pandolfi (*c.* 1470) at the Badia. In 1444, with the *Tomb of Leonardo Bruni*, in Santa Croce, Bernardo Rossellino created a new model, in which the role of the architect was closely integrated with that of the sculptor in the composition of the sarcophagus with the recumbent figure of the deceased in an edicule in the form of an arched portal on pilasters. The novelty of the scheme, and especially the new heroic exaltation, at once religious and secular, of human life, had an immediate success and was followed by increasingly ornate elaborations with elegant refinements of carving, by Desiderio da Settignano in the *Tomb of Carlo Marsuppini* (1455), also in Santa Croce; by Antonio Rossellino in the *Monument to the Cardinal of Portugal* (1461), in San Miniato, full of animation and colour, in the ornate chapel built (1461-66) by Antonio Manetti, a pupil of Brunelleschi, and decorated with terracottas by Luca and Andrea della Robbia and paintings by Baldovinetti and Pollaiuolo; and by Mino da Fiesole in the *Tomb of Bishop Leonardo Salutati* (1464) in the Duomo of Fiesole, and in those of *Bernardo Giugni* (*c.* 1468) and *Ugo, Margrave of Tuscany* (1469-81), both in the church of the Badia, where the altarpiece with the *Virgin and two Saints*, in the altar of Diotisalvi Neroni, Councillor of Cosimo the Elder, is also by him.

Another aspect of the same trend towards sculpture of less exacting stylistic demands was the rapid rise to popularity of glazed terracotta, initiated by Luca della Robbia with the important series of tondi in the Pazzi Chapel in Santa Croce and the ceramic insertions in the ciborium done in 1441 for Santa Maria Nuova (now in the church of Peretola) and at once widely diffused from his workshop as a decoration complementary in style to the limpid Florentine architecture, in the form of tabernacles, niches, friezes, lunettes, ceiling-panels, cornices, and coats-of-arms, but also in statues and bas-reliefs, usually in the characteristic white on blue ground, but often with other colours as well. If the naturalistic cornices of leaves, flowers and fruit seem like, and indeed were believed to be, casts from nature, the images they enclose conform to a calm, balanced and harmonious reality, as with the various representations of the Madonna. Outstanding among them are the one in the lunette formerly over the doorway of the church of San Pierino and now in the Palazzo di Parte Guelfa; the *Madonna di via dell'Agnolo*, the *Madonna 'del Roseto'*, and the *Madonna with the apple* (Bargello); and the one preserved in the Spedale degli Innocenti, and that in the coat-of-arms of the Doctors' and Apothecaries' Guild in a tondo on the exterior of Or San Michele. Andrea della Robbia, the nephew and partner of Luca, carried on the work with an extensive production until well beyond the end of the century: in particular the series of swaddled infants in the ten medallions of the portico of the Spedale degli Innocenti won immediate popularity. But later on the quality deteriorated in the innumerable replicas of the more popular models reproduced in the Robbia workshops under Andrea's sons.

After thirty years of control of the Florentine Republic, Cosimo the Elder died in his villa of Careggi on 1 August 1464. On his tomb in the basilica of San Lorenzo was inscribed the ancient title of honour: '*Pater Patriae*'. He had been skilful in associating the

Desiderio da Settignano, Tomb of Carlo Marsuppini,
humanist and secretary of the Republic, 1455. S. Croce.

Mino da Fiesole, Tomb of Bishop Leonardo Salutati,
1464. Fiesole, Duomo.

fortunes of Florence with those of his family, making use of his experience in mercantile affairs and displaying political farsightedness and an unequalled munificence in patronage of the arts. He left behind a revivified city, rich in splendid monuments and unparalleled as a nursery of art and culture. He was succeeded by his son Piero, a bibliophile and friend of scholars and young painters, but weak and tormented by the family malady which earned him the nickname of 'the Gouty' and brought about his early death in 1469. The first of his two sons by Lucrezia Tornabuoni, the twenty-year-old Lorenzo, took his place and contrary to expectations at once revealed beneath the outward guise of a poet and humanist the temper of a ruler and a political genius that astonished the world. After the conspiracy of the Pazzi in 1478 with its tragic epilogue in the murder of his brother Giuliano in Santa Maria del Fiore, he initiated wise reforms to consolidate the instruments of public power and strengthened his own authority and his family's position. He made use of this to extend his influence outside Florence, acting as mediator in agreements between the other Italian states and successfully conducting a skilful policy of peace and equilibrium which caused him to be described as the 'needle-beam between the Princes of Italy'. For his own city, which gave him the name of 'the Magnificent', he reserved all his ambitions and the most stimulating resources of his mind as an artist and man of the Renaissance. In youth he had had a laurel branch painted on his jousting standard, an allusion to his name Laurentius, with the motto '*Le temps revient*'. The destiny of Florence once again became identified with that of the Medici. When he succeeded in getting his thirteen-year-old son Giovanni made a cardinal (he was later to be Pope Leo X) he counselled him to serve the interests of the Church but also those of his city and his family because 'the house and the city go together'. Himself a poet, with his master Angelo Poliziano, among the greatest of his time, he translated into verse the joy of living, as if foreseeing the shortness of his own life, and caused the people to participate in it in the splendid festivals and picturesque masquerades at which they sang his *Canti carnascialeschi* (carnival songs). He extolled the 'vernacular' Tuscan of Dante, Boccaccio and Petrarch as a literary language 'not poor, not crude, but abundant and of great purity'. He rekindled the cult for antiquity and the classical tradition and for Platonic philosophy. With his learning and the versatility and subtlety of his tastes he dominated every field of the intense cultural and artistic activity that made of Florence a new Athens.

Guicciardini, in his *Storia Fiorentina* (History of Florence), shrewdly grasped the personality of Lorenzo, describing his inclination not only for philosophy but also for 'music, architecture, painting, sculpture, indeed for all the arts of talent and industry, so that the city was copiously filled with all these refinements, which emerged the more in as much as he, being universally versed in all things, provided judgement and discriminated between men, so that everyone competed with each other to do his pleasure.'

This was the true aspect of his artistic policy: to arouse by his own enthusiasm that of others, to stand at the centre of the immense beehive that Florence continued to be, and to regulate and dominate its humming activity with the voice of a sage and the infallible judgement of a great connoisseur.

For himself, Lorenzo reserved the more intimate delights of a collector, the satisfaction of augmenting to excess the collection of 'antiquities' inherited from Cosimo and Piero, and nothing seems to have given

Luca della Robbia, Cantoria, *1431-38. Museo dell'Opera del Duomo.*

him greater pleasure than the search for and study of medals, bronzes, cameos and precious stones—everything that spoke to him of the fabulous world of the ancients. He offered the vision, the study and the model of that world to artists and scholars, opening up to them the rooms of his palace in Via Larga, the seat of those extraordinary collections, and creating the new formula of the open-air museum under a portico in the 'Garden of San Marco' where a number of ancient statues and marbles were assembled. The curator and restorer of all these treasures was the sculptor Bertolodo, former assistant of Donatello. Doubts have recently been raised about the historical basis of the legendary fame of this Medicean garden as a school and nursery for young geniuses of this latter half of the century, first and foremost among them Michelangelo. It almost seems as if Vasari wished to exalt it, if not actually to create it from nothing, with the intention of providing an illustrious precedent for the Academy founded by the Grand Duke Cosimo I, on his advice, seventy years later. But there is definite evidence, supported by Michelangelo's biographer, Condivi, of the interest shown by artists and scholars for such important collections and the lessons they could derive from them even indirectly in their ardent search for knowledge of the ancient world in the atmosphere of humanism. In fact the passion for antiquity was part of the situation of Florence, itself a town that was poor in works of the classical period but rich in poetic images and literary and erudite descriptions, in an 'indirect' archaeology, where a faculty of interpretation and imaginative reconstruction could be exercised for which the particular climate created by the philosophical and poetic

133

movement of Careggi was propitious (Chastel). A proof of this can be seen in the custom of Florentine craftsmen of the Quattrocento, and especially of the miniaturists, to have recourse to the most celebrated pieces of the Medicean collections, especially the cameos and medals, to find themes, subjects and forms for their own works. Possibly Donatello himself may have had in mind some small plaque in Cosimo's collection when he composed the four tondi of the Evangelists in the sacristy of San Lorenzo (c. 1440). But there is also a significant example in the courtyard of the Medici palace in Via Larga, where the frieze running above the arches of the square portico is punctuated by a series of tondi—looking back to the shields of the classical era—decorated not only with the Medici arms but also with mythological scenes taken from ancient gems preserved in the palace collections.

The Medici set such store by the gems in their 'museum' that they had them set in valuable mountings by the greatest contemporary artists, like that executed and described by Ghiberti for the famous cornelian of Apollo and Marsyas: a model that became familiar to the Florentine artists, also because the humanists did not fail to attribute a precise symbolical value to its subject of the liberation of the soul from earthly bonds by the divine harmony of Apollo. It is the myth chosen by Raphael to represent Poetry in the ceiling of the Stanza della Signatura in the Vatican.

Today there is a tendency to decry the reputation of a Maecenas traditionally assigned to Lorenzo the Magnificent. To the great and felicitous development of architecture and art in Florence, he in fact contributed rather as a tutelary genius, a refined aesthete soliciting theories and inspiring men, than as the promoter of new buildings or important decorations; moreover many of the undertakings he found had already been started by Cosimo and had to be carried on, thus limiting his possibilities for initiating new ones, except for the villa at Poggio a Caiano, which was entirely his own. But in compensation his presence was prodigious, and his influence decisive in every activity for the glory and prestige of Florence. He always knew how to touch the sensitive chords of pride in his fellow citizens: he promoted a competition to endow Santa Maria del Fiore with its missing façade, and he extolled—as Vasari records in his life of Baldovinetti—the proposal to cover with mosaics and stuccoes the interior of Brunelleschi's immense cupola ('You haven't the artists for it', people objected, and his answer was, 'We have so much money that we'll make them.') And while he aroused the emulation of the great families of the Florentine bourgeoisie (foremost among them the Tornabuoni, the Sassetti, the Gondi, and the Strozzi) in the formation of rich collections and the adornment of churches and palaces, his policy of political expansion gave the city a new primacy as not only the greatest centre of artistic production but also the generous dispenser of the finest energies developing within it. It is difficult to say whether, at a certain point, opportunities for work and local resources dwindled so much as to encourage artists to seek them elsewhere, or whether it was this exodus that caused some dispersal of the workshops and the consequent decline of Florence's productive intensity. Giuliano da Maiano was sent to Alfonso of Aragon, King of Naples, in 1480, as were also, ten years later, Luca Fancelli and Giuliano da Sangallo; Sandro Botticelli, Domenico Ghirlandaio, and Luca Signorelli were lent to Pope Sixtus IV to decorate the Sistine Chapel (1481); and in the course of a few years Leonardo went to Milan (1482), Antonio and Piero del Pollaiuolo to Rome (1488): almost all of them as the result of Lorenzo's recommendation when the potentates turned to him because of the reputation he had acquired as promoter of the arts and a shrewd judge of artists.

There was no pause in civic building activity during the second half of the fifteenth century, and indeed it even intensified during the last two decades. As happened with the figurative and decorative arts, there was much copying of chosen prototypes, with interpretations adapted to the places, needs, tastes and economic possibilities of the various classes, within the framework of homogeneity constantly maintained between major and minor works, and between town and country, which gives an unmistakeable character to Florence and its surrounding countryside. Among the Medicean architects, Benedetto da Maiano and Giuliano da Sangallo were occupied on important new buildings.

Filippo di Matteo Strozzi, who had been exiled to Naples in 1458 because of disputes with the Medici family, became finally reconciled with Lorenzo the Magnificent. On his return home, anxious to re-establish his fortune and power, he decided to build a palace which would stand comparison with those of the Medici, the Pitti, and the Rucellai. He turned to Giuliano da Sangallo, the favourite architect

Luca della Robbia, Madonna, *Bargello.*

of Lorenzo, and obtained from him a model in wood, which still exists, reflecting the tradition of Michelozzo. But the building, begun in 1489, assumed different dimensions and became more imposing in proportions as a results of the intervention of Benedetto da Maiano (who, according to Salmi's theory, interpreted Strozzi's ideas and possibly brought him into it personally) and later of Simone del Pollaiuolo, known as Cronaca, who in 1497 took over the direction of the work left in suspense because of the architect's death and completed it, on the outside with the last storey and the beautiful cornice, unfortunately left unfinished, and on the inside with the harmonious courtyard. Despite the different interventions, it is the most grandiose and imposing of the Florentine palaces of the Renaissance: open on three sides and with three symmetrical prospects, clearly articulated, it combines the plastic strength of the rough-hewn stone walls with the free fantasy and delicate technical elaboration of the decorative carving of the capitals and corbels, which reveal the architect Benedetto da Maiano's own preferences as a sculptor, as can also be seen in the pulpit of Santa Croce and the Porta dei Gigli in Palazzo Vecchio. To his older brother Giuliano da Maiano, who probably carried on the building (1462-65) of the Strozzino Palace begun by Michelozzo in 1458, is attributed the Palazzo Antinori, formerly Martelli, of a noble simplicity with its façade of smooth ashlar and its elegant courtyard (*c.* 1465); and in recent times, after careful restoration, Giuliano has also been reaccorded the credit, hitherto given to Brunelleschi, for the plan of the Palazzo Pazzi-Quaratesi, at the corner of Via del Proconsolo and Borgo degli Albizi, built around 1470 for Jacopo de' Pazzi, who subsequently was implicated and killed in the famous conspiracy against the Medici in 1478.

More rigorous rationality and desire for innovation is shown by Giuliano da Sangallo, the most learned and best all-rounder of the architects working in Lorenzo's time and the dominant personality in the artistic world, in contact with Botticelli, Filippino Lippi, Ghirlandaio, Leonardo and Michelangelo. Much of his time and work was carried on outside Florence. In 1479 he brought back from Rome memories of the Early Christian basilicas which inspired one of his first works, the quadriportico of the church of Santa Maria Maddalena dei Pazzi, recently restored. In Prato he created his masterpiece with the church of Santa Maria delle Carceri (1485-92), in the form of a Greek cross. In Florence he reiterated the motif of the central plan with original inspiration in the spacious octagon of the Sacristy of Santo Spirito (1489-92). The entrance portico (completed by Cronaca in 1495-96) recalls a similar solution adopted in the Villa Medici at Poggio a Caiano, built for Lorenzo the Magnificent between 1480 and 1485: the first and most splendid model of a new type of country house, in the union of the two wings of the building by a great *salone*, and in the original enclosure by a colonnade which forms the basis for the simple, powerful structure, on whose smooth clear walls the texture of the *pietra serena* stands out and also, through the addition made by Pope Leo X, the entrance loggia with the great tympanum above the Sansovinesque frieze in glazed terracotta. Other Florentine works of Sangallo (this name was given to his family, the Giamberti and the Cordiani, because they lived near Porta S. Gallo) are, apart from the

▷

Villa del Poggio a Caiano. Built by Sangallo, c. 1480-85, for Lorenzo de' Medici.

Piero della Francesca, a double panel depicting Federigo da Montefeltro on the right, and, left, his wife Battista Sforza, 1465. On the back of each panel the couple can be seen riding in triumphal chariots. Uffizi.

already mentioned model for the Strozzi palace, the palace formerly belonging to Bartolomeo Scala, secretary of the Medicis, the house 'of Apollo' in Borgo Pinti (1490) later incorporated in the Palazzo Gherardesco, Palazzo di Borgo Pinti, now Panciatichi-Ximenes, which the Sangallos built for themselves at the end of the century, and the Palazzo Gondi (1490-1501) in Piazza San Firenze, in which the reference to the Medicean prototype in Via Larga is substantially reabsorbed in a freer form of structure, both outside (despite the alterations made in 1874 by Poggi's restorations with the addition of the left wing) with the three great arched doorways and the belvedere with columns crowning it, and inside with the elegant courtyard, the staircase, and in a room on the first floor the ceiling and a chimneypiece, also carved by Sangallo. The noble Gondi chapel in Santa Maria Novella and the severe tombs in the Sassetti chapel in Santa Trinità (1486) are also

by him. He proposed numerous designs for the façade of S. Lorenzo
on the occasion of the competition for it in 1515.

Towards the end of the century, Simone da Pollaiuolo, known as Cronaca, seems to bring to an end the formal style created by Brunelleschi:
he built the vestibule of the sacristy of Santo Spirito, accentuating in
a plastic sense the free elegance of Giuliano da Maiano's project; he
planned and completed the enlargement of the Palazzo della Signoria
with the grandiose Salone dei Cinquecento (1495, later altered by
Bandinelli and Giuliano di Baccio d'Agnolo); and while carrying on
the work on Palazzo Strozzi he created his own masterpiece with the
church of San Salvatore al Monte (also known as San Francesco al
Monte alle Croci), which for its elegant and genuine simplicity was to
please Michelangelo and earn from him the name of the '*bella villanel-
la*': almost like a gem of the early Mannerist style of the new century.

Sandro Botticelli, The birth of Venus,
detail c. 1483/84. *Uffizi.*

Sandro Botticelli, St Augustine in his cell,
1480. *Ognissanti.*

Domenico Ghirlandaio, Birth of the Virgin, *1484-90. S. Maria Novella.*

In the development of the figurative arts in Florence between 1460 and 1470, coinciding with the rising star of Lorenzo the Magnificent, the personality of Donatello marked out a course and provided an impetus which was followed and extended by Pollaiuolo and Verrocchio. It was no mere chance that both of them practised painting and sculpture at the same time: the distinction was becoming increasingly rare. An essential force was proving stronger than the professional categories and overstepping their traditional rules. In a certain sense, there was already a hint of anti-classicism in this search for an energy to be

found in the devotion to form: it was the discovery of a new vitality, even if it seemed to be derived from the 'dionysiac' agitation of the ancients: for the original intuition was movement, as the expressive element of the individual inner force in the tension of the plastic form, giving rise to a freedom that extended to all the arts. Marsilio Ficino declared that 'since the mind is the source of movement, a free and universal animation results from it.' This, one can say, is the element that preserves the renewed attraction of antiquity from the danger of being merely a matter of cold exterior imitation. Antonio Pollaiuolo,

in his workshop of a goldsmith, engraver and inlay-worker (cf. his early silver *Crucifix*, of 1457, in the Museo dell'Opera del Duomo), was already moving over from the influences of the 'courtly' style to the harsh realistic vision of Donatello in the series of twenty-seven panels with *Scenes from the Life of St John the Baptist* (Museo dell'Opera); and he at once showed a predilection, almost an obsession, for the theme of the nude in all its resources of movement, vigour and febrile tension verging on the physical sense of violence. And while in his paintings he used great incisive force to emphasise line, as in the frenzied nude *Dancers* frescoed in the Villa della Gallina at Arcetri, in bronze he implacably modelled the movement of muscles and tendons in the vibration of the form, giving a sense of ferment to his material. The theme of the labours of Hercules—but it is the man who is transfigured in the legend—recurs repeatedly in the works done for the Medici palace: in the famous bronze group in the Bargello, with *Hercules suffocating Antaeus*, and in the two splendid panels in the Uffizi, again with *Hercules and Antaeus* and *Hercules struggling with the Hydra*, a reminder of the lost paintings of the same subject done around 1460 for the Palazzo Medici.

Andrea del Verrocchio, too, was attracted by the search for hidden vivifying energies in human forms and in every natural thing, attaining in his own development as a goldsmith a superb command of his material. In the bronze group of the *Incredulity of St Thomas* in Or San Michele the grandiose compositional structure which coordinates in counterpart the solemn gestures of the two figures is combined with the skill and technical refinement of the modelling of the draperies in rhythmic cadence. But in the *Funeral Monument of Piero and Giovanni de' Medici* (1472), in the Old Sacristy of San Lorenzo, human figures and religious symbols are excluded, and everything is resolved into a pure decorative abstraction, in the original motif of the empty arched space over the sarcophagus and the bronze cord network that fills it, in the firm modelling of the powerful lions' paws, the thorny acanthus and oak branches and the cornucopias, and in the crowns and flowered border-frames. Porphyry and bronze are united with masterly skill, worked on with an impressive formal clarity and a restless vitality in the apparent coldness of the minutely detailed chiselling. (In the same Old Sacristy Verrocchio also sculptured the beautiful *Fountain*.) · The *David* in the Bargello, sold by Lorenzo and Giuliano de' Medici to the Signoria in 1476, is generally compared with the no less famous *David* of Donatello (1440, Bargello) from which it undoubtedly takes the motif of the youthful hero, but with less absorbed expression and more calculated formal contrasts.

For a fountain at the Medici villa at Careggi, Verrocchio executed in 1476 the *Winged Putto with Dolphin*, which in 1565 was placed in the courtyard of the Palazzo Vecchio on the fountain designed by Vasari.

Other works of Verrocchio preserved in Florence, of varying character, are: in the Museo dell'Opera del Duomo, the silver relief for the altar of the Baptistry, with the *Beheading of St John the Baptist* (1477-80); in the Bargello Museum, the *Madonna and Child*, an original terracotta from Santa Maria Nuova (the marble version is from his workshop), the delicate marble bust of the *Lady with a bouquet*, and the terracotta

◁
Palazzo Vecchio, the Sala de Lys. The fine carved ceiling is by Giuliano da Maiano, and the architecture by Benedetto da Maiano.

of the *Resurrection of Christ* from Careggi. An unusual case is that of the most famous of Verrocchio's few paintings: the *Baptism of Christ*, done for San Salvi and now in the Uffizi. The plan of the composition is traditional, recalling Baldovinetti's *Baptism* in the SS. Annunziata. But the execution presents uncertainties and interest concerning the insertion of the figure of the kneeling angel in the foreground, which since Vasari has been recognized—possibly with a part of the landscape—as being by the young Leonardo da Vinci and a proof of his apprenticeship in Verrocchio's workshop. Thus we find a link of continuity in one of the strongest trends in Florentine painting in the last decades of the Quattrocento.

Sandro Botticelli brings the century to an end with a pathos which, though with varying accents, finds expressive essence in a coherent poetic world, matured in a complex spiritual situation in which recollections of the medieval and neo-Gothic can even be discerned in the contrast between the exaltation of humanism in the cultural circle of Lorenzo, Ficino and Poliziano and the dramatic religious crisis of Savonarola.

In Florence, most of Botticelli's masterpieces are preserved in the galleries of the Uffizi, the Pitti Palace, and the Accademia and in a few churches. In the Uffizi it is possible to follow the development, in its essential stages, of Botticelli's creative genius and complex inspiration, amid speculative elements both mystical and literary. From his early period, after his youthful apprenticeship in the workshops of Filippo Lippi, Pollaiuolo and Verrocchio, are the *Madonna della Loggia* and the *Madonna of the Rose-bush* (before 1470), the *Fortitude* (1470) in the series of the 'Virtues' executed by Piero del Pollaiuolo for the Tribunale della Mercanzia (the Merchants' Guild); the *Sacra Conversazione* with the portraits of Lorenzo and Giuliano de' Medici in the figures of SS. Cosmas and Damian kneeling before the Virgin; the beautiful *Portrait of an unknown man* (supposedly the author of the medal, possibly Antonio Filipepi, brother of the painter) *with the Medal of Cosimo the Elder;* the two fine panels, perhaps originally forming a diptych, representing *Judith returning from the camp of Holofernes* and *Holofernes found dead in his tent,* composed with a lively sense of the flexibility of forms and with great refinement of detail; the *Adoration of the Magi,* a masterpiece of early maturity painted around 1475 for the Lama chapel in Santa Maria Novella, with portraits of the main contemporary personalities, among them all the Medici from Cosimo the Elder to Lorenzo the Magnificent, and the self-portrait of the artist, in the original conception of the broad and open symmetrical composition the plan of which is not ignored a few years later by Leonardo when dealing with the same subject (all in the Uffizi).

To the following years, before and immediately after Botticelli's stay in Rome for the frescoes of the Sistine Chapel (1481-82), belong the three masterpieces that originally adorned the villa of Castello, acquired in 1477 by Lorenzo and Giovanni di Pierfrancesco de Medici: the *Primavera,* the *Birth of Venus,* and *Pallas taming the Centaur*: works of supreme beauty, saturated in a liquid poetry which both dissolves and heightens the allegorical elements which modern criticism has discerned with the aid of contemporary neo-Platonic texts. The *Primavera* (1477-78) celebrates the virtues of universal love in the vision of an ideal world in which beauty, courtesy and reason live together, symbolized by Venus, by Spring in a flowered robe, Eolus and Flora, and by the Graces and Mercury. The *Birth of Venus* (1486) breathes

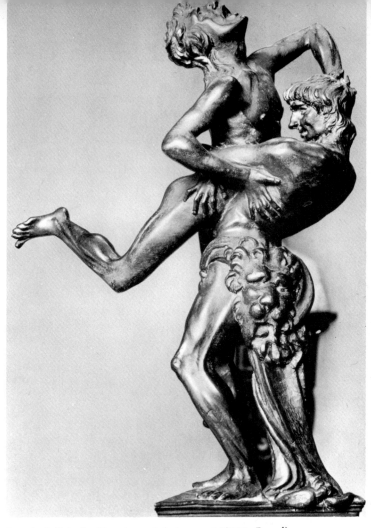

Antonio Pollaiuolo, Hercules and Anteus, c. *1465-70.* Bargello.

the incarnation of beauty in the vivifying spirit of the Zephyrs and the protection of nature; this picture has a recognizable relationship with Poliziano's *Stanze,* written for the joust of 1475. In the myth of the *Centaur tamed by Pallas* (*c.* 1482) the neo-Platonic ideal is evoked of the balance between instinct and reason in the mind of men; the languor of the dreaming faces, the grace of the gestures, the lightness of the figures are linked in a single continuous undulating rhythm, abstract as a pure musical modulation. The same occurs in the famous tondo of the same period with the *Madonna of the Magnificat* (1481-82), permeated by trembling sensuality in the swirling linear link of the composition within the circle: a favourite motif of Botticelli and one that evidently met with an immediate response, seeing that it recurs not only in the *Madonna with the Pomegranate,* possibly executed in 1487 for the Magistrato dei Massai di camera (Magistrate of House hold Stewards), also in the Uffizi, but also in the numerous tondi that emerged from Botticelli's busy workshop and are now scattered among the museums of the world (among originals and replicas reckoned to number about thirty). Other works of the last period preserved in the Uffizi are: the splendid *Altarpiece of San Barnaba* (Madonna with Child and four angels and six saints), executed around 1486 for the church of San Barnaba, under the patronage of the consuls of the

Physicians' and Apothecaries' Guild; the great *Altarpiece of San Marco* with the Coronation of the Virgin and four saints, and the beautiful predella with five scenes, executed between 1488 and 1490 for the chapel of the Goldsmiths' Corporation in the church of San Marco; the *Annunciation,* painted around 1489 for the Guardi chapel of the church of Santa Maria Maddalena de' Pazzi; *St Augustine in his study* (after 1490), in the exquisite style suitable to its small dimensions; and another superb creation, impregnated with turbulent energies: *Calumny,* inspired by Lucian's account of a picture by Apelles, and extraordinarily packed with mythological symbolism in the highly ornate architectonic scene. It is a concluding work of the artist's career in the last decade of the century, possibly coinciding with the excommunication of Savonarola (1497).

Botticelli's works in the Pitti Gallery include a *Portrait of a Youth* (*c.* 1470), the *Madonna and Child with the Infant St John,* a work of the painter's late maturity, and the delicate *Portrait of a Young Woman,* still the subject of dispute as to the identity of the original shown in profile (? Simonetta Vespucci) and also as to the attribution (Berenson first assigned it to the 'Friend of Sandro', later to Ghirlandaio) but now recognised by the majority of scholars as by Botticelli, around 1475. In the Gallery of the Accademia there is the *Madonna and Child and Infant St John,* formerly in the church of Santa Maria Nuova, an early work under the influence of Lippi and Verrocchio; in the Uffizi the *Annunciation,* recently removed from the Ospedale di San Martino alla Scala, where it was painted in 1481, the year after the stupendous *St Augustine,* in the church of Ognissanti, was done in fresco in competition with Ghirlandaio who painted *St Jerome.*

From the school of Verrocchio, the recognized master, as a contemporary wrote, 'of all those whose names are known throughout the towns of Italy', came also Lorenzo di Credi, who carried on into the new century the fifteenth-century tradition enriched by elements from Leonardo. By him there is in San Domenico di Fiesole a *Baptism of Christ,* derived from that of Verrocchio, and in the Uffizi the stages of his youthful career are marked by the *Annunciation,* the tondo with the *Madonna, St John and two angels,* the *Adoration of the Shepherds,* in which the influence of Flemish painting is evident, and the *Venus* from the Medici villa of Cafaggiolo, a version of the Botticelli model already in sixteenth-century style.

In 1483 the Florentine artistic world had been excited by the arrival in the church of Sant'Egidio of the great triptych of the *Adoration of the Shepherds* (now in the Uffizi) commissioned from the Flemish painter Ugo van der Goes by the rich Florentine banker and agent of the Medici in Flanders, Tommaso Portinari, who had wished to be portrayed in it with his wife and children, kneeling in prayer under the protection of four saints. The unusual way, both iconographically and in perspective, in which the legend of the Birth and the angels' presence is combined with the peasant realism of the shepherds, and the penetrating acuteness of the portraits with the fresh naturalness of the flowers in the vase and the jug, must have seemed daring in Renaissance Florence; but it also satisfied certain inclinations towards empirical objectivity among the Florentine bourgeoisie and caused the Medicean artists to approve it.

The narrative vein that had inspired Benozzo Gozzoli's painting had never been entirely interrupted; and now Domenico Ghirlandaio took it up again. His whirlwind activities ranged from the youthful frescoes of Sant'Andrea at Cércina to the *Madonna della Misericordia* (1472) for the altar of the Vespucci in the Ognissanti, the altarpiece of San Giusto alle Mura, now in the Uffizi, and the great *Last Supper* painted in 1480 at the same time as *St Jerome* in the Ognissanti; and after the frescoes in the Sistine Chapel in Rome (1481) he revived the narrative treatment in the figures of the *Saints* and *Famous Men* frescoed in the Sala dei Gigli in the Palazzo Vecchio (1482) and in the cycles of the *Stories of St Francis* in the Sassetti Chapel in Santa Trinità (1482-85) and the *Stories of the Virgin and St John* in the Sanctuary of Santa Maria Novella (1485-90), commissioned by Giovanni Tornabuoni. In the first cycle, the Franciscan story becomes a chronicle transferred to Piazza della Signoria and played out by contemporary personalities among the Florentine nobility, from Lorenzo the Magnificent to Poliziano, with the young Giuliano, Piero and Lorenzo de' Medici, Luigi Pulci, Matteo Franchi, and Antonio Pucci welcomed and accompanied by Francesco Sassetti with his son: like a stupendous documentary showing the costumes of the day, topical events, the trusting homage accorded to the powerful, and familiar places, as in the panel of the *Resurrection of the boy* where among those present are Sassetti and

Verrocchio, Bust of an unknown woman, *mid-15th century. Bargello.*

Verrocchio, Baptism of Christ,
c. *1470-75. Uffizi.*

all his family along the road (the present Via Tornabuoni) leading to the old bridge over the Arno, between Palazzo Spini on the left and the church of Santa Trinità with its original Romanesque façade. In the altarpiece of the same date, the *Adoration of the Magi* shows recollections, almost like textual quotations, of the Portinari triptych of Ugo van der Goes in the rude realism of the group of shepherds. More flowing narrative and a wider range of expression, from the intimate to the eloquent, and spontaneous sureness of scenic touch and detail, can be seen in the frescoes of Santa Maria Novella, which, unusually, run from bottom to top of the walls in portraying the succession of events in the life of the Virgin and St John the Baptist. Here too in the varied scenes frequent portraits occur: on the further wall those of the kneeling figures of the commissioning patrons, Giovanni Tornabuoni and his wife Francesca Pitti. But the family concern which associated Domenico Ghirlandaio's brothers Benedetto and David in the work also brought in, especially for the ceiling and the upper panels, other pupils and collaborators, Bastiano Mainardi, Giuliano Bugiardini, and a certain Francesco Granacci who had just then introduced to the Master a thirteen-year-old apprentice, Michelangelo Buonarroti; he is believed to have made his first attempts at trying his hand on some of the figures in the *Death of the Virgin* and the *Baptism bestowed by St John*. Ghirlandaio's last work remaining in Florence is the *Adoration of the Magi* (1488) in the Spedale degli Innocenti, among his most felicitous creations for its unity and intimate balance of values.

In the same church of Santa Maria Novella, some years after Ghirlandaio, Filippino Lippi came to paint in the nearby chapel of the Strozzi family, commissioned by Filippo Strozzi, who at that time was perhaps the greatest of the Florentine magnates and was then building his palace. The decoration with the *Lives of St Philip and St James,* begun in 1487, was carried on sporadically owing to the artist's alternations between Florence and Rome (for the Carafa chapel in the Minerva) and was finished in 1502. From the biblical figures in the vault to the compositions on the walls, the artist's Roman experiences of the classical world show their influence in a bizarre and exuberant interpretation of the scenography, and in a whimsical figurative liveliness and sense of pathos which seem like precursors of the Mannerist style. Yet a few years before he had been judged worthy to complete the *Life of St Peter,* left unfinished by Masaccio in the Brancacci chapel. And his early days, clouded in uncertainty for modern historiography until the pictures grouped by Berenson under the attribution of 'Friend of Sandro' were recognised as his, are documented in Florence by the *Five Virtues,* in the Corsini Gallery, the *Stories of Lucretia,* in the Pitti, one of the stories of *Esther,* formerly in the Torrigiani collection, now in the Horne Museum, and the *Nativity* in the Uffizi. The great altarpiece of the *Madonna enthroned and four saints* shows the influence of Botticelli and the young Leonardo, while Flemish influence, especially in the colour, can be seen in the *Madonna appearing to St Bernard* (1480), in the church of the Badia. From his mature period there are in Florence two *Saints* (Accademia), the *Madonna and Child with two saints and the patrons Tanai de' Nerli and his wife* (Santo Spirito, c. 1490), the *Adoration of the Magi* and *St Jerome* in the Uffizi, and the *Deposition* (Accademia) finished by Perugino.

▷

Domenico Ghirlandaio, The Visitation, *1484-90, detail. S. Maria Novella.*

Perugino, Crucifixion, *1493-96. A triptych in the Chapter House of the S. Maria Maddalena dei Pazzi. Above, central panel showing Mary Magdalene at the feet of Christ, and right-hand panel showing St John the Evangelist and St Benedict.*

Piero di Cosimo, akin to Filippino and influenced by Ugo van der Goes, also belonged to the group of artists who were aware of crisis in the air, going in for extravagance and whimsicality in the search for

unusual themes, sometimes taken from Ovid and often from a wild imaginary mythology, situated in fantastic landscapes, and steeped in transparent, luminous atmospheres, as in the *Perseus liberating*

Andromeda (Uffizi), while in the *Immaculate Conception* (Uffizi) a 'return to order' in the cold symmetry of the traditional altarpiece is redeemed by the depth of colouring and the incidence of light.

In Verrocchio's crowded workshop, Leonardo da Vinci for long remained in the background, first as pupil, then as collaborator. In the part attributed to him in the Master's *Baptism of Christ* and in the *Annunciation* (Uffizi), which is of that period and entirely by his hand, the stamp of his extraordinary talent appears in the expressive force, in the naturalness of the figures moving in different directions, while the countryside, still detailed in the flowering meadow, is rendered in the distance with a new sensitivity to the transparency of the atmosphere. Becoming independent in 1478, the young artist took on various works, among them the great picture of the *Adoration of the Magi* for the church of the Monastery of San Donato at Scopeto; this was soon interrupted when the artist was called to Milan to the Sforza court (1481), and it thus remained permanently unfinished (Uffizi). But (as numerous preparatory sketches show), already in the tormented search for movement within the rigorous compositional plan, there is the essence of modelling in light and shadow, the '*sfumato*', on which Leonardo was to base his own original vision of a poetically interpreted reality. This novelty was not without influence on some contemporary Florentine painters.

Towards the end of the century Luca Signorelli and Pietro Vannucci, known as Perugino, were working for the Medici. Of Signorelli we recall with regret the lost *Education of Pan* (formerly in Berlin), but in the Uffizi there are the *Holy Family,* painted for the Udienza dei Capitani di parte Guelfa (Audience of leaders of the Guelph party), and the *Madonna and Child,* done for Lorenzo di Pierfrancesco de' Medici; in both these tondi, the figures with their strong modelling are curved to fit in to the circular space, and especially in the second, with the nudes in the background, we seem to see an anticipation of Michelangelo's idea for the *Doni Tondo.* The tone of melancholy always present in Signorelli's representations of figures is accentuated to the point of tragedy in the later painting of the *Crucifixion with St Mary Magdalen* in the Uffizi. Perugino worked in Florence particularly during the last decade of the century, in his most fruitful period; he established his workshop there in 1493, having married the daughter of the architect Luca Fancelli, and he was always held in high regard there, being called upon to act as one of the judges on the most important artistic questions, for example the competition for the façade and restoration of the lantern of the Duomo, and the placing of Michelangelo's *David.*

In the altarpieces by him now in the Uffizi (*Madonna with St John the Baptist and St Sebastian,* of 1493, formerly in San Domenico di Fiesole; the *Altarpiece of Vallombrosa,* 1500) and in the Pitti (*Lamentation over the dead Christ,* 1495, formerly in Santa Chiara), his insinuating compositional harmony, the expressions of the faces and the luminosity of space have not yet reached the point of sentimentality of his later works. Also in his portraits in the Uffizi, especially those of *Francesco delle Opere,* 1494, and of Don Biagio Milanesi, and in the *Self-portrait,* if such it be (though the general tendency is to attribute it to Raffaello Sanzio), there is spiritual penetration and solidity of pictorial substance. In the refectory of the Convent of Sant'Onofrio

◁

Perugino, triptych, left-hand panel showing St Bernard and the Virgin.

Filippo Lippi, Virgin and Child, *1452. Galleria Pitti.*

of the Franciscans of Foligno, Perugino directed his pupils in the painting of the great *Last Supper* (known as the Cenacolo di Foligno), adapting the composition to the style then traditional in Florence but introducing innovations in the scenography of the background, where a vast luminous countryside is seen through a Renaissance portico. He treated in a similar way the subject of the Crucifixion in the fresco, completed in 1496, in the chapter house of the monastery of Santa Maria Maddalena de' Pazzi. Looking at the dates and recalling the events which were maturing in Florentine society in those years, it must be admitted that such contemplative calm, such sure implication of the gentle trend of life, had about it something superficial and contradictory, not to say illusory, in a world already destined to encounter great changes.

After 1480 the neo-Platonic movement in Florence became one of the great driving forces of Italian culture. It helped not so much to solve as to propound and elaborate the fundamental ideas and central problems governing the intellectual climate of the period: the rediscovery of antiquity as an experience of civilization, and the conception of man as the centre and measure of the world; and also too the ideas of the soul, of nature and of history, which were to nourish the art of Leonardo, Michelangelo and Raphael. The splendours of the Renaissance were not born in an atmosphere of serene felicity. Restlessness of spirit was always latent in the immense creative workings of that privileged city.

On 8 April 1492 Lorenzo the Magnificent died. Two years later a clumsy move by his son Piero, which humiliated the city before Charles VIII of France, aroused afresh the opponents of the

Filippo Lippi, Virgin and Child, *detail.*

Medicean Signoria, angered the people, and brought about the end of the Medicis' power, which had lasted exactly sixty years. The family was banished from the city and its houses were plundered. The Dominican friar Gerolamo Savonarola from the monastery of San Marco had for years castigated laymen and clergy, the Medici government and the Roman Curia, in his ardent preaching, medieval in tone and apocalyptic in spirit. Now at the head of the popular movement he inspired the constitution of the new republic and demanded reforms extending from policy to religious practices and habits of life, in a blaze of collective asceticism opposed to luxury, festivals, literature and the arts. It seemed to be the end of Florence as a centre of

humanism, wealth, industry and power. The old factions revived, divided now between 'Whites' and 'Greys', between 'Piagnoni', or snivellers, and 'Arrabiati', or fanatics, the scornful appellations given to the followers of Savonarola and those of the Medici. Finally, the Pope, after showing tolerance for a long time, excommunicated the rebel friar. The Florentine Republic tried him and sentenced him to death on the pyre in Piazza della Signoria on 23 May 1498. Four years later Pio Soderini was elected Gonfalonier for life. Niccolò Machiavelli became Secretary of the Republic. But in 1512 Pope Julius II supported the restoration of the Medici in the persons of Cardinal Giovanni and Giuliano, sons of Lorenzo the Magnificent, and a cousin of theirs, Giulio, a natural son of the victim of the Pazzi conspiracy, who also soon became a cardinal. The second Medicean Signoria (1512-27) coincided with the ascent of the Medici to the pontifical throne: Cardinal Giovanni became Pope Leo X (1513-21), followed by Cardinal Giulio as Clement VII (1523-34). The name of Leo X is associated with the period of greatest artistic splendour in Rome, that of Clement VII with the failure of his policy, which led to the sack of Rome (1527) and the restoration of a last short-lived republic in Florence (1527-30). Following the death of Macchiavelli, the spirit of Savonarola returned in triumph, as can be seen from the decision, in February 1528, to elect Jesus Christ King of the city and engrave his monogram above the doorway of the Palazzo della Signoria with an inscription declaring Him 'King elected by decree of the Florentine people' (it was altered to the present inscription by Cosimo I in 1551). The peace agreement between the Emperor Charles V and Pope Clement VII provided for a fresh restoration of the Medici in Florence; and after a year of siege and resistance (1530), for which Michelangelo prepared fortified bastions on the hill of San Miniato, this came about in July 1531 with the arrival in Florence of Alessandro de' Medici, natural son of Lorenzo Duke of Urbino. Ironically, the imperial decree appointed him 'Duke of the Florentine Republic'—which no longer existed. Alessandro governed for six years amid disputes and accusations of tyranny which brought him up against his cousin Lorenzo di Pierfrancesco de' Medici who, on a January night in 1537, had him assassinated.

Forty years had gone by since the death of Lorenzo the Magnificent, and Florence despite all these vicissitudes had not lost its primacy in the arts, though now it had to contest this with Rome, whither Florentine artists had gone to carry the conquests of Tuscan art. Moreover the fame of the Florentines throughout the world did not rest on artistic activities alone. The names of two Florentines were linked with the discoveries of Christopher Columbus: Amerigo Vespucci, who lived in Borgo Ognissanti and had been agent of the Medici bank in Seville at the beginning of the century, went to seek the New World which was later to take its name from him; and some twenty years later Giovanni da Verazzano, a relative of the Rucellai, sailed forth on behalf of Francis I, aided financially by Florentine merchants of Lyons, and landed in the northern territories of the continent, where he left the memory of his city in the names of various Florentine places and buildings.

Before the death of Lorenzo the Magnificent Michelangelo had been

◁
Filippino Lippi, Abraham, *completed c. 1502. S. Maria Novella.*

Michelangelo, Battle between Lapiths and Centaurs, c. *1490, Casa Buonarroti.*

working in Ghirlandaio's workshop and later, as guest of Lorenzo, in the Garden of San Marco; and he had begun to work on sculpture. The *Madonna of the Steps* and the *Battle of the Centaurs* (Casa Buonarroti) belong to this early period and fully express, in the grandeur and movement of the figures and the detachment of the naked bodies from any reference to place and time, the high ideals of the young sculptor. The gigantic statue of *David,* commissioned in 1501 by the Opera di Santa Maria del Fiore, kept him occupied for eighteen months, almost in challenge to all past achievements in sculpture. Before it was finished, the Florentines in an access of enthusiasm, in contrast to their usual dislike of over-emphasis which had caused them in the past to reject all gigantic statues, decided to place it in front of the Palazzo della Signoria as a symbol of liberty beside the bronze group of Donatello representing *Judith and Holofernes,* which had been taken from the Medici palace after the eviction of Piero. The 'Giant', as it was at once called, seemed to be the sign of the new times. 'In his austere and uncompromising nudity the *David* states for the first time the essence of Michelangelo's ideal. As a piece of modelling the torso is equal to the finest work of antiquity, both in science and plastic vitality. Cut out the head and the hands, and you have one of the most perfect classical works of the Renaissance. Put them back and you put back the rough Tuscan accent, which was part of his birthright.' (Kenneth Clark)

While he was working on this statue, Michelangelo accepted among other commissions one from the Consuls of the Woolmerchants' Guild for the statues of twelve Apostles for the Duomo; but between 1503 and possibly 1506 he worked on only one of them, *St Matthew* (Accademia), the first expression of the powerful twisting of the human body and the 'unfinished' treatment of the carved surfaces. Other masterpieces belong to the same period: the painted tondo of the *Holy Family,* known as the *Doni Tondo* (1503, Uffizi) and the sculptured tondo of the *Pitti Madonna* (1505, Bargello), examples of a monumental conception of the human form contorted and pregnant with energy. In the new Salone dei Cinquecento, built by Cronaca (1495) in the Palazzo Vecchio for the assemblies of the General Council of the People established by the new republican administration inspired by Savonarola, the Gonfalonier Pier Soderini in 1504 entrusted to Michelangelo and Leonardo in competition the task of representing two historical events linked with the freedom of Florence, the battles of Cascina and Anghiari. The cartoons prepared for the frescoes and the parts of them that were finished were destroyed half a century later. Cellini wrote of them that they had been 'the school of the world'.

In 1504 Raffaello Sanzio (Raphael) came to Florence from Urbino and made a longer stay there from 1505 to 1508. While working intensively for the great Florentine families, he studied and absorbed with wonderful intelligence the essence of the Florentine artistic language, going back from Leonardo and Michelangelo to Pollaiuolo and Donatello. But he consumed every experience in the fire of his own genius and poetic intuition and in the stupendous faculty of synthesis which he exercised in his inexhaustible capacity for research and invention and compositional variations on the favourite themes of the Virgin, the Child and St John; and in his portraits, where a veil of thoughtful

▷

Michelangelo, David, *1501-4. Galleria dell'Accademia.*

Michelangelo, Brutus, c. *1540. Bargello.*

melancholy contrasts with the intellectualized insistence on physio-
gnomical features, and where refinements of colouring unknown to
the Tuscans soften the strict modelling of forms and symmetries into
a higher harmony. The collections in the Pitti Palace and the Uffizi
contain most of Raphael's masterpieces done in Florence, and also some
from his subsequent Roman period which later came into the Medici collections. To his Florence years belong, in the Pitti, the *Madonna del Granduca* (so called because it belonged after 1799 to the
Grand Duke Ferdinand III of Lorraine), the portraits of *Angelo Doni*
and *Maddalena Doni,* and the *Portrait of a Woman* (The Pregnant
Woman), and also the unfinished altarpiece known as the *Madonna del
Baldacchino,* designed for the chapel of the Dei family in the church
of Santo Spirito. In the Uffizi is the *Madonna of the Goldfinch.* To
his Roman period belong the famous *Madonna dell'Impannata,* the
Portrait of Inghirami, and the *Donna Velata* (Pitti); and also the portraits of *Julius II* and *Leo X* (Uffizi). A reminder of Raphael's activity
as an architect is in the Palazzo Pandolfini, in Via San Gallo, built
from his design (of the Roman period) by Giovan Francesco and Aristotile da Sangallo and completed around 1520. Raphael is also known
to have taken part in the competition for the façade of San Lorenzo.

It was not easy for Florentine artists to accept with equanimity the
new ideas advanced by Leonardo, Michelangelo and Raphael during
the time when by good fortune they all coincided in Florence. Each
of the three seemed in his own way to have interpreted and heightened that Florentine tradition which had gone on uninterruptedly and

Michelangelo, Madonna of the steps, c. *1490-92. Casa Buonarroti.*

consistently for the past two hundred years; but in fact each had opened up wider perspectives of new problems, anxious research, and sharp contrasts in their ever-increasing perception of ideal aims of which they also made others aware. Some painters found a solution in a synthesis of the new trends or more frequently in a compromise between tradition and innovation, in unitary and imposing compositions and in balanced and solemn landscapes which it would be easy, but incorrect, to place in the category of sixteenth-century 'classicism'. Such is the case with Bartolomeo della Porta, a Dominican friar of San Marco and follower of Savonarola, whose anti-pagan austerity seems to be translated into dignified figures pervaded with devotional ardour and animated by strength of conviction. After the fresco of the *Last Judgement* (1499), transferred from the cemetery of Santa Maria Nuova to the refectory of San Marco—a composition recalled by Raphael in the *Disputa del Sacramento*—the *Apparition of the Virgin to St Bernard* (1504, Accademia) achieves a masterly combination of the contributions to figurative art from Leonardo to the Flemish painters and from Raphael to the Venetians. More elaborate scenography, where the buildings melt into the shadows or canopies of Raphaelesque inspiration arise, is to be seen in the *Madonna and Saints* in the church of San Marco (1509), in the picture on the same subject in the Uffizi, and, among his works in the Pitti, in the theatrical *Risen Christ* (1516) and the well-known *Deposition from the Cross,* of a harmonious and calculated unity. Similar in trend to Fra Bartolomeo but with greater outward eclecticism is his companion Mariotto Albertinelli in the *Visitation* (1503, Uffizi) and the *Annunciation* (1510, Accademia).

The first decades of the sixteenth century were dominated in Florence by the outstanding artistic personality of Andrea del Sarto. This was the time when Michelangelo and Raphael were bringing the 'grand manner' to Rome in the ceiling of the Sistine Chapel and the Stanze. Vasari called del Sarto a 'painter who made no mistakes', though he reproached him for 'a certain timidity of mind' which today people are more inclined to recognize in the restricted character of his themes and the balance of his eclecticism rather than in the extraordinary fertility of his production. His field of work was in Florence, where there are many examples of it. In the church of the SS. Annunziata, in the Chiostrino dei Voti, adorned with a series of frescoes that embraces the major masterpieces of the early Florentine sixteenth century, those by Andrea del Sarto, done from 1509 onwards, mark a crescendo in the skilful use of Leonardesque *'sfumato'* and in the direction of a purely sixteenth-century compositional inclusiveness, as can be seen in the beautiful scene of the *Nativity of Mary* (1514), depicted in the rich surroundings of a contemporary Florentine house. And in the nearby Cloister of the Dead there is another masterpiece, the fresco of the *Holy Family,* known as the *Madonna del Sacco.* The cycle of the *Life of St John the Baptist,* painted in chiaroscuro (1514-26), in the Chiostro dello Scalzo, has a concise strength of solutions which is exceptional even in the higher classicism (Ragghianti). In the numerous altarpieces now assembled in the Pitti and Uffizi galleries— among which it will suffice to mention the famous *Madonna of the Harpies* (1517), a monument of human melancholy—the feeling for design, colour, light, and relationships in a deeply vibrant texture of light and shade touches exceptional heights of communicative gentleness and subtle poetry. Andrea del Sarto was asked by the Medici in 1521 to collaborate in the pictorial decoration of the Salone of the villa at Poggio a Caiano, and he painted in one of the larger compartments a fresco of *Julius Caesar receiving tributes from Egypt,* an allusion to the gifts sent to Lorenzo by the Sultan: in its general composition and in the part by the artist's own hand (it was completed sixty years later by Alessandro Allori) this is a ceremonial picture in descriptive, prosaic style which seems to anticipate the Florentine painters of the seventeenth century. An important work undertaken by Andrea at the beginning and finished at the end of his career is the *Cenacolo di San Salvi* (*c.* 1527), splendidly animated in composition and delicate in colouring.

The Florentine sculptors who were active during the first decades of

Raphael, Lady with the veil, c. *1516. Galleria Pitti.*

the sixteenth century also sought to find a balance between tradition and the new ideas. Andrea Contucci, known as Sansovino, sculptured in marble the *Baptism of Christ,* commissioned in 1502 to go above the east door of the Baptistry (it was however finished and placed there later by Vincenzo Danti, who in 1571 modelled for the south door the three bronze figures of *The Baptist, Salome,* and *The Executioner*). Giovan Francesco Rustici was the author of another group showing *St John the Baptist Preaching* (1506-11), above the north door, executed with 'terrifying bravura', according to Vasari. In those years Baccio da Montelupo modelled the bronze statue of *St John the Evangelist* (1515) for a tabernacle in Or San Michele; and Benedetto da Rovezzano sculptured the Crucifix of the high altar and the statue of *St John* for Santa Maria del Fiore, and altars, tombs and portals with

classical ornamentation for Santa Trinità, the SS. Apostoli, the Carmine, and the Badia.

Florentine architecture in the early sixteenth century remained faithful to the style consolidated in the preceding century, for example in the works of Cronaca, if we are to attribute to him the Palazzetto Horne, formerly of the Alberti, in Via dei Benci, and the Palazzo Guadagni (1503-06), in Piazza Santo Spirito, one of the most typical examples of the Renaissance nobleman's house. The measured sobriety of the fifteenth-century designs—with smooth surfaces, rows

P. 170/171
The Ponte S. Trinità over the River Arno.

of arched windows, and heavily projecting roofs—continued to be preferred by the rich Florentine bourgeoisie, in contrast to the grandiloquence of the Roman models represented, if only timidly, by the Raphaelesque designs for the Pandolfini and Uguccioni palaces. The most outstanding personality at this time was the architect Baccio d'Agnolo, partly because of his extensive activity.

This met with misfortune when he initiated (1506) the gallery above the drum of the cupola of Santa Maria del Fiore, which was halted in 1515 because of the severe judgement of Michelangelo, who called

Leonardo da Vinci, The Annunciation, *1470-75, detail. An early work, usually attributed to the Master, painted during his apprenticeship to Verrocchio.*

Bronzino, Lucrezia Panciatichi, c. 1470-75. *Uffizi.*

it a 'cage of crickets'; but otherwise his work was varied and lively, as in the typical Palazzo Taddei (1504), in Via Ginori, in the Villa Belvedere, formerly Borgherini, at Bellosguardo, and in various other palaces—the Torrigiani in Via Porta Rossa and Piazza dei Mozzi, the Ginori in Via Ginori, the Borgherini, later Rosselli del Turco, in Borgo SS. Apostoli, the Cocchi-Serristori in Piazza Santa Croce, and most of all the Palazzo Bartolini Salimbeni (1520), at Santa Trinità, where Baccio d'Agnolo became converted to the classical and Raphael-esque styles, arousing the criticism of the Florentines, who accused him of having built 'the façade of a temple rather than a palazzo'. But he nevertheless marked a turning-point in Florentine civic building of the sixteenth century.

In the years preceding the Sack of Rome (1527) and the siege of Florence (1529-30), art too reflected a general situation of crisis, a

Pontormo, Cosimo il Vecchio, *1518-20. Uffizi.*

widespread state of dissatisfaction and unrest. The movement expressing this became known as Mannerism. It had to await modern times
before achieving full recognition; up to the beginning of the present
century it was granted at most, according to Wöfflin's views, an intermediary and transitional position between Renaissance classicism and
Baroque. The young artists Pontormo and Rosso, its daring and isolated protagonists, shared in the same moral torment that assailed Michelangelo and disturbed his faith in the universal harmony of which
Raphael had become the symbol. The 'Mannerists' felt the same dissatisfaction, exasperated to the point of rupture, born of a conscious cultural
saturation. Thus they could be anti-classical even within the framework of classicism. The complexities of an ambiguous and tormented
moral world were at work within them, finding expression both in
heightened sensuality and in rigorous formal intellectualism, in the
search for calculated stylistic subtleties, and for that 'lively and spiritual

grace' in which Lomazzo discerned the new form of beauty. It was more than a fashion and less than a school—more of a trend, an attitude that insinuated itself like a leaven or ferment into the otherwise moribund classical patterns.

Jacopo Carrucci, known as Pontormo, began with powerful expressive works such as the frescoes in the chapel of the Popes (1515) in the monastery of Santa Maria Novella, the *Visitation* (1516) in the Chiostrino dei Voti of the SS. Annunziata, and the *Holy Family and Saints* (1518), in the church of S. Michele Visdomini, known as San Michelino. For the Medici, in 1521, he painted with sensual abandon and new intonations of colour one of the side lunettes of the Salone in the villa at Poggio a Caiano, showing the pastoral legend of *Vertumnus and Pomona*.

He accentuated the touching and expressionistic note in the frescoes of the *Scenes from the Passion* in the Certosa del Galluzzo and in their composition showed his familiarity with Dürer's engravings. There are also a considerable number of altarpieces, today in the Uffizi and the Pitti, in which he heightens still further the unreal atmosphere and the restless torment of his figures. The church of Santa Felicità contains one of his masterpieces, the stupendous *Deposition* (1528), 'an incredible cluster of figures without weight or shadow, entrancing in their extreme unreal beauty' (L. Berti), and also the powerful tondi with the *Evangelists* (one done by his young pupil Agnolo Bronzino) and another masterpiece, the fresco of the *Annunciation*. The same vein of originality is found in his portraits (important among those in the Uffizi are *Cosimo the Elder* and *Maria Salviati*), and certainly too in the frescoes in the choir of San Lorenzo, on which he worked with high ambitions during the last ten years of his life, depicting scenes from the Last Judgement almost as if in emulation of Michelangelo—unhappily they were destroyed in the nineteenth century.

Less tormented but no less whimsical and inclined to the refinements of a subtle intellectualism is Giovanni Battista di Jacopo, known as Rosso Fiorentino, whom we also find making his début in the cloister of the SS. Annunziata (*Assumption,* 1517). In the five years he spent in Florence before going to Rome and then to the court of Fontainebleau, which was to be the scene of his triumphs, he gave the best of himself in a short period between 1521 and 1523, in the *Doni Altarpiece,* formerly in Santo Spirito, now in the Pitti, in the *Marriage of the Virgin,* in San Lorenzo, and in *Moses defending the daughters of Jethro,* in the Uffizi, a fascinating painting for the tragic atmosphere in which its ghostly personages exist, of Michelangelesque descent but as if petrified in the moment of heightened tension, in the abstract coldness of an inlaid pattern.

Thus Michelangelo is always the demiurge, ever present even when far away or making only solitary, shy appearances: he who impersonates the drama of the world and interprets its universal values in tension and suffering, in the tragic sense of life, of its immense solitude and the inexorable end of all things. Yet three times in the course of his life he fled from Florence, seized by irrational fears strange in a man of his immense moral courage and supreme indifference to physical adversities. When he returned in 1520 he had still on his shoulders the

◁

Fortezza del Belvedere, built by Buontalenti from plans by Giovanni de' Medici, 1590-95.

Michelangelo, Dawn, *one of the sculptures surmounting the magnificent tomb, 1520-34, built for Lorenzo de' Medici in the Sagrestia Nuova, S. Lorenzo.*

fifteen-year-old burden of his first great Roman undertaking, the tomb of Julius II, for which he made fresh projects and contracts, quarried marble from Carrara, and planned and possibly roughed out the first statues. The 'tragedy of the Tomb', he called his never-to-be-finished monument. It is not known precisely when he executed the four unfinished *Slaves* left in Florence (Accademia), while the two in the Louvre, given in 1544 by Michelangelo himself to Roberto Strozzi,

Michelangelo, Victory. *Designed in Rome about 1552 for the tomb of Julius II which remained unfinished, it was brought to Florence in 1565. Palazzo Vecchio.*

then in exile in Lyons, are recorded as in process in a document of 1513. The statues of the *Slaves,* in their incomplete state and in the unfinished' treatment of the surfaces as compared with the naturalistic definition of certain details, admirably express the creative process of the image in its twisted movement revealing its dynamic violence. In 1519-20, at the request of Cardinal Giulio de' Medici and Pope Leo X himself, Michelangelo accepted the task of building in San

Lorenzo a chapel destined to receive the tombs of Lorenzo, Duke of Urbino, and Giuliano, Duke of Nemours. He was new to the profession of architect; he had merely taken part with enthusiasm, five years before, in the competition for the façade of the church of San Lorenzo, and had won it, but the work was never carried out (the model in wood, made in accordance with his designs by Baccio d'Agnolo, is in the Casa Buonarroti). For the Medici chapel (known as the 'New Sacristy' because it symmetrically balanced the Old Sacristy, built by Brunelleschi, on the opposite side of the chancel) he introduced a complete innovation in relation to all preceding traditions of Tuscan architecture, articulating and moulding the space into a composite framework repeated in the four walls with the coordination of every element—arches, entablatures, niches, and windows—thus creating a new reality which superseded and eliminated the actual shape of the walks. According to Tolnay, 'The whole chapel was intended to be an abbreviated image of the universe, with its spheres hierarchically arranged one above the other. The lowest zone, with the tombs, is the dwelling place of departed souls, the realm of Hades. The intermediate zone, with its rational architecture, was intended to incarnate the terrestrial sphere. The zone of the lunettes and of the cupola was intended to represent the celestial sphere. The gradation of the lighting which is admitted in largest quantity in the celestial zone and penetrates the terrestrial zone through smaller openings, while the zone of Hades has absolutely no direct source of light, can also be best understood in connection with this content.' In this ideal space, the pagan apotheosis of the heroes in the Christian view of death, the tomb of Lorenzo and that of Giuliano on opposite walls, with the solemn and thoughtful statues—the figures are not recumbent, as was traditional in Florentine tombs, and are not likenesses of the originals— and the allegories of Dawn and Twilight, Night and Day, unite in symbolical significance of the inexorable flow of time and the relationship between man and eternity and in a subtle rigorous formal link of stupendous harmony. The third tomb, intended for Lorenzo the Magnificent, is unfinished, but the statue of the *Madonna and Child* remains, a poetic transfiguration of a profoundly human vision of fatalistic melancholy resignation in contrast with the vitality of the impetuous Child. This statue and that of Giuliano, which were done last, reflect in their lengthened, 'serpentine' form the influence of a Mannerism which was developing in Florentine circles in those years.

In 1523 the first negotiations began to endow the monastery of San Lorenzo with a new library to accomodate the wealth of books and manuscripts of Leo X and the Medici family. The work on the Biblioteca Laurenziana, or Laurentian Library, begun in 1524, did not escape the fate common to so many other works of Michelangelo, and for ten years it was alternately suspended and resumed. Between the vestibule (the *Ricetto*) and the great hall of the library there is an intentional contrast, an impressive jump from the dynamic sense of compressed forces in the highly original architecture of the vestibule to the impression of calm and harmony in the simplicity and dimensions of the great library hall. In the vestibule the architectonic subdivision accentuates the narrowness of the room with the blind windows, the twin columns attached to the walls, and the curving brackets: motifs which were soon to become general in sixteenth-century architecture.

In the last years of Michelangelo's stay in Florence he sculptured the statue of *David* which was at once placed in the Medici collection

*Model of a project by Michelangelo
for the façade of S. Lorenzo. Casa Buonarroti.*

(now in the Bargello), and probably between 1532 and 1534 the group of the *Genius of Victory,* possibly intended for the tomb of Julius II, and subsequently placed in the Palazzo Vecchio. Among his lesser architectural works are the designs for the pavement around the choir of Santa Maria del Fiore and for the kneeling windows of Palazzo Medici (Casa Buonarroti). Michelangelo also gave advice to Ammannati about the new bridge of Santa Trinità. The other sculptures preserved today in Florence were executed in Rome: after 1539 the bust of *Brutus* (Bargello), which was partly finished off by his pupil Tiberio Calcagni and which, according to Portheim, was an idealized portrait of Lorenzo de' Medici, the murderer of Duke Alessandro (the contemporary epigraph, attributed to Bembo, justifies the unfinished state of the work: 'while the sculptor was extracting from the marble the effigy of Brutus, he recalled his crime, and ceased from work'); and the group of the *Pietà,* brought to Florence by Cosimo III and since 1722 placed in Santa Maria del Fiore. The so-called *Pietà di Palestrina* (Accademia), whose attribution to Michelangelo is regarded as dubious, also came from Rome.

Unlike what he accomplished in Rome, where as architect he laid the stamp of his genius on the city from St Peter's to the Campidoglio, Michelangelo had no opportunity to participate in the great architectural works of Florence, where the main buildings are essentially medieval or Renaissance in character. In compensation, within some of its most important buildings he enriched the city with splendid monuments which, above all, exercised a reactive and stimulating influence that was decisive for subsequent developments in art.

The City of the Grand Dukes

After the death of Duke Alessandro de' Medici in 1537 the succession passed to a descendant of a collateral branch of the Medici, by name Cosimo, son of Giovanni delle Bande Nere and Maria Salviati. Not yet twenty years old, he at once revealed the intelligence, daring and ruthlessness necessary for a policy of absolutism. He had the assistance of Francesco Guicciardini but drew his inspiration from Niccolò Machiavelli. He thus succeeded in concentrating all power in his own hands, and exercised it with wisdom, justice and farsightedness. With him the story of a city ends and that of a state begins, the state of Tuscany with Florence as its capital. Duke Cosimo imposed a sound administration on the new state, doubled its territory, raised its prestige, and increased its political importance, making it first among the states of Italy. He was given the title of Grand Duke in 1569, but it was the confirmation of a sovereignty already exercised for the past thirty years.

In 1539 he married Eleonora of Toledo, the rich and beautiful daughter of the Spanish Viceroy of Naples, and he at once offered her a more luxurious (and also safer) dwelling than the ancestral palace in Via Larga was now thought to be. He transformed the severe Palazzo della Signoria into the ducal residence, carrying out extensive alterations and internal decorations and assembling numerous art treasures there. When in 1549 his wife acquired the Pitti palace he had it enlarged and transferred the official residence of the principate to it. On the occasion of the marriage of his son Francesco, he connected it with the Palazzo della Signoria (now known as the Palazzo Vecchio) by an immensely long corridor passing above the house and crossing the Arno by Ponte Vecchio (where he turned out the butchers and put in instead the goldsmiths with their characteristic workshops). He revived the pomp of the great days of Medicean patronage, obscured since the death of Lorenzo the Magnificent: he finished the Laurentian Library begun by Michelangelo, built the Uffizi and rebuilt the Ponte Santa Trinità, founded the Botanical Garden, known as the Giardino dei Semplici (herb garden), established the Florentine tapestry-weaving workshop, calling in weavers from Flanders, and founded the Florentine Academy from which the Accademia della Crusca later developed, and also the Academy of Design, where he welcomed and honoured the great artistis who worked for him. Among painters he chose Agnolo Bronzino from the outset as official portraitist of the ducal family; Bronzino was one of the first Mannerists, a friend and pupil of Pontormo but inclined to a colder and more restrained reproduction of statuesque likenesses with a suave abstraction and formal polish to which the portrait lent itself more readily than compositions of a more complex character. His ability as an artist can be clearly seen from the numerous portraits of the Medici family, most of them still in Florence, in the Pitti and the Uffizi (where, among others, are the two admirable portraits of Bartolomeo and Lucrezia Panciatichi, and in Palazzo Vecchio (in particular the splendid *Battiferro,* in the Loeser collection). In the long period of Cosimo I's government many important artistic undertakings were entrusted to a generation of artists called upon to carry on the difficult heritage of Michelangelo. A few years earlier there had been the ambitious attempt of Baccio Bandinelli to compete with the master's fame in the field of colossal statuary, though with a polemical respect for more balanced and traditional formal values: his laborious and infelicitous marble group of *Hercules*

Palazzo Vecchio. The courtyard, remodelled by Michelozzo in 1470, was redecorated in 1565 for the wedding of Francesco de' Medici.

and Cacus, placed in front of the Palazzo della Signoria in imprudent confrontation with the *David,* was greeted by the derision of the Florentines and by Cellini's mocking comparison with a 'sack of melons set up straight, leaning against the wall'. He was no more fortunate with his statue of *Giovanni delle Bande Nere* (1540), commissioned by Duke Cosimo in honour of his father and placed in Piazza San Lorenzo. But his bas-relief figures on the choir screen of Santa Maria del Fiore (1555) were deservedly more appreciated for the delicacy of the modelling and the skilful effects of light and shade.

A very different personality was Benvenuto Cellini, who, around the middle of the century, returned from that great centre of Mannerist ideas, Fontainebleau, and modelled the fine *Bust of Duke Cosimo* (1548) and the famous *Perseus* (1553), the casting of which is described in a page of his no less famous autobiography. His technical skill, revealing the goldsmith's feeling for detail and displayed in the pedestal of the statue showing *Perseus rescuing Andromeda* (a copy—the original is in the Bargello), is supported by exceptional vitality and a richness of invention not wholly free from whimsicalities (such as, for instance, the probable self-portrait in the back of Perseus' helmet). The placing of the statue in the Loggia dei Lanzi (1554) marked the revival of the old Florentine custom of open-air sculpture, which was more widely adopted in Cosimo's time: for it was not until then that fountains (hitherto impossible because of water shortage) and commemorative monuments began to appear in the principal piazzas. The most spectacular example came a few years later, also in Piazza della Signoria, with the *Fountain of Neptune* (1563-75), the work of Bartolomeo Ammannati with the collaboration of Giambologna, Danti and others: a composition of typically Mannerist style with the fantastic posture and balancing in space of the elegant bronze figures, voluptuous nymphs, restless fauns and satyrs, and sea-horses around the massive marble statue of the sea-god—another proof of emulation of Michelangelo's *David* and a source of sarcasm from the Florentines, who called it 'il biancone', the big white fellow, and went about chanting 'Ammannato, Ammannato, che bel marmo hai rovinato' (Oh Ammannato, what fine marble you've ruined). Ammannati worked on another fountain between 1550 and 1555, intended for the Salone dei Cinquecento in Palazzo Vecchio, but it was never finished and the sculptures for it were put in the Boboli Gardens, the Villa of Pratolino, and one, *Ceres*, in the Bargello.

Ammannati was more fortunate in his activities as architect for Cosimo I, with the enlargement of the Pitti Palace and the creation of the two interior wings to form the solemn courtyard, a powerful structure with three tiers of half-columns, effecting with its rusticated stone blocks 'like rock' a transition between the building itself and the natural surroundings of the Boboli Gardens. There too are masterpieces full of novelties, in the general layout due to the fantasy of Niccolò Pericoli, known as Tribolo (1550), in the combination of architecture and sculpture in the grotto designed by Buontalenti (1583-88), in the method of clipping the trees and hedges, and in the variety of ornamental statues scattered about everywhere: from the basin of the pool with the bronze statue of *Neptune* by Stoldo Lorenzi (1565) to the curious *Fountain of Bacchus*, in which the sculptor Valerio Cioli portrayed Cosimo I's famous dwarf, Pietro Barbino. Another great work of Ammannati's, the Ponte a Santa Trinità (1567-69), built to replace the bridge destroyed in the floods of 1557, may have been derived from a suggestion of Michelangelo's but reveals the architect's mastery in the elegant tension of the arches and the style of the sculptural insertions of scrolls and statues. His versatility appears in the variety and novelty of the methods adopted for the palaces built for important families—the most stately and spectacular example is the Ramirez Montalvo palace, in Borgo degli Albizi (1568) —by comparison with that prototype of the ordinary house, the building constructed for the Wool Merchants' Guild in Via degli Alfani and Via della Pergola, which is already an intermediary solution between the nobleman's palace and the modest house lived in by the

▷

Baccio Bandinelli, Hercules and Cacus, *1534, standing at the entrance to the Palazzo Vecchio.*

Benvenuto Cellini, Cosimo I de' Medici, *1555-57. Bargello.*

workman or craftsman, with the workshop on the ground floor or in the semi-basement, in accordance with the usual type of residential housing in Florence, still visible today in the old centre of the town.

The true protagonist of this time is Giorgio Vasari, first interpreter of Duke Cosimo's artistic policy, architect and painter, executant and coordinator of great decorative undertakings, inventor and constructor of all the apparatus of festivals and ceremonies, a man of inexhaustible energy, many-sided culture, and prodigious activity—and he found time, moreover, to collect the necessary material and write the *Lives of the most excellent architects, painters and sculptors*, a key work in the history of art.

In Palazzo Vecchio, the Duke had the Salone dei Cinquecento adapted for public audiences by Bandinelli and Giuliano di Baccio d'Agnolo and built the new Quartiere degli Elementi on Via della Ninna under the direction of Battista del Tasso; he also had the chapel of Eleonora da Toledo decorated (1541-46) by Bronzino with frescoes, representing

▷

Benvenuto Cellini, Perseus, *1553. Loggia dei Lanzi, Piazza della Signoria.*

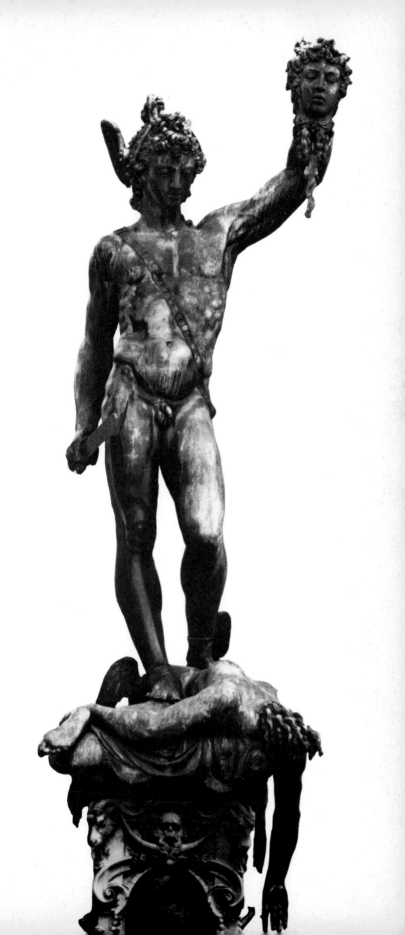

four saints in the ceiling and the life of Moses on the walls, which are remarkably representative of the evolution of Mannerism towards classicism, and towards a 'superbly glacial plastic idealism' (Longhi). Bronzino, with Pontormo and Salviati, also supplied the cartoons for the tapestries with the *Life of Joseph* for the Sala dei Duecento, woven in the new Medici workshops by the Flemings Roast and Karcher (1546-49). On the death of Battista del Tasso, Vasari succeeded him as official architect to the Palazzo, and he at once embarked on an impressive overall programme of work affecting its whole interior. Thus, on the second floor, the Quartiere degli Elementi and the Quartiere di Eleonora di Toledo (the consort's apartments) were completed, with great wealth of decorations and allegorical paintings designed by

Ponte S. Trinità, the present construction is a replica
of the former bridge, built by Ammannati 1566-69, after it had been
destroyed in World War II. Most of the original
material which lay at the bottom of the river was used again.

Vasari and later described by him in his *Ragionamenti* as the most difficult problem he had to solve: the Audience Chamber, which already had Giuliano da Maiano's beautiful ceiling, was further enriched with fine wall-frescoes by Francesco Salviati showing the *Life of Camillus* and various allegories (*c.* 1550-60); and the Guardaroba was furnished with inlaid cupboards by Dionigi Nigotti and with geographical maps painted by the Olivetan cosmographs Egnazio Danti (1562-75) and Stefano Buonsignori (1575-84), the famous author of the most important perspective plan of Florence. On the first floor the new Quartiere di Leone X was created, with six rooms decorated by Vasari and his assistants with frescoes illustrating the enterprises and achievements of the Medici family down to Duke Cosimo I, shown in the

midst of his friends and artists, in celebration of his victories; and lastly the adjacent huge Salone dei Cinquecento was decorated on walls and ceiling with tremendous paintings of subjects celebrating the glories of the Medici, done by Vasari and his assistants: the whole history of Florence is there, from the Roman era to the most recent enterprises and the apotheosis of the Prince. This was a ten-year-long undertaking, a new concentration of eager endeavour to carry out an overall scheme devised by Vincenzo Borghini and Giovambattista Adriani covering both the ceiling (1563-65), divided into compartments of varying size to avoid an over-strict geometrical pattern, and the immense rectangles of the walls (1568-72). 'A tasteful, skilful gradation of colouring harmonizes the darker oils with the warmer golds on the blue frameworks of the ceiling, giving the frescoes a light intonation like tapestry.' (P. Barocchi). Vasari was inexhaustible in the face of these immense tasks and seems to have known no limits in proposing and undertaking them. Also in Palazzo Vecchio, on the occasion of the marriage of Cosimo's eldest son Francesco to Giovanna of Austria (1565), he planned and directed the transformation of the imposing mass of Michelozzo's courtyard (of 1470) into a flowered, picturesque elegance of Mannerist style, covering the columns with stuccoes and gilding and the ceilings and walls with frescoes. Five years later, in a small space at the end of the Salone dei Cinquecento he created the Studiolo del Duca Francesco, decorating it sumptuously and putting in the walls cupboards, rendered invisible by the framed paintings, as in a little gallery, a secret storeroom of the artistic and natural treasures that the prince loved to collect. A team of artists was called upon to collaborate on this work which, while fantastic and whimsical, was also of great refinement because of the learning and culture that inspired it. For the cycle of paintings illustrating human activities, treated as fables rather than allegorically, the artists were Alessandro Allori, Macchietti, Cavalori, Battista Naldini, Maso da San Friano, Stradano, Poppi, Santi di Tito and others with Vasari himself; and for the little bronzes Giambologna, Ammannati, Vincenzo Danti, Stoldo Lorenzi, Bandini, Elia Candido, Poggini and De Rossi.

Vasari also gave outstanding proof of his talent both as architect and, as we would now say, town-planner in the planning of the great Palazzo degli Uffizi and its surroundings, begun in 1560 to provide a headquarters for all the administrative and judicial offices of the state of Tuscany. It is an imposing complex of two matching buildings facing each other and joined together at one end by a triumphal arch surmounted by a loggia. The space within—more like a courtyard than a piazza—thus connects the Palazzo Vecchio with the right bank of the Arno, affording remarkable visual scenographic perspectives with the oblique view it gives of the fourteenth-century mass of the Palazzo and its tall tower. The formal dignity of the architecture contributes to these effects, with its two separate wings and the continuity of the openings. The building of the Uffizi, on Vasari's designs, was continued and completed by Bernardo Buontalenti, an architect who displayed his ardent and whimsical fantasy not so much in his architectonic forms, which remained simple and adhered to traditional rules if freely interpreted (as in the Medicean villas built or altered by him, Artimino, Petraia, Pratolino etc.), but rather in the ornamentation and the decorative inventions of naturalistic derivation which covered them profusely, as in the Casino Mediceo di San Marco (1574), on the ground floor of the Palazzo Nonfinito, in the façade of Santa Trinità,

Palazzo Vecchio, ceiling over staircase to first floor, decorated by Vasari.

and the 'Tribune' of the Uffizi with its cupola encrusted with mother-of-pearl shells. This vein of naturalism can perhaps be attributed to the revival in the sixteenth century of the Florentine trend towards country life and its close association with life in the city. (Incidentally Buontalenti, in the Villa of Artimino, built for the Grand Duke Ferdinando I in 1594 at the extreme end of the range of hills on which the old fortified borgo lay, may have provided the first example of 'reorganization' of the countryside within the framework of a replanning of Medicean farmlands.) The same vein of naturalism also pervaded sculpture towards the end of the century, when sculptors were called in by architects to collaborate with them on parks and gardens in the increasingly numerous wealthy villas. Tribolo adorned the gardens of Castello and Petraia with fountains and statues. Here and in the Boboli Gardens the charming Venuses sculptured and modelled by Giambologna with subtle grace and virtuoso skill found rustic surroundings. A rival of Cellini with his famous *Mercury* in the Bargello and possibly a collaborator of Ammannati in the sinuous naiads of the *Neptune* fountain, Giambologna, born in Flanders but Florentine by adoption after 1553, was a channel for international culture within the orbit of late Mannerism, with a balance of his own between academic elegance and naturalistic vitality, in works ranging from the classical recollections of *Virtue overcoming Vice* (1567, Bargello) and *Hercules struggling with the Centaur Nessus* (1599, Loggia dei Lanzi) to the daring composition of the *Rape of the Sabines* (1583, Loggia dei Lanzi), which in the three intertwined figures expresses the idea of the spiral, a development of Michelangelo's 'serpentine' form, and the restraint of the statue of *St Luke* (1601) in Or San Michele and the colder effects of the commemorative equestrian monuments of the Grand Duke Cosimo I (1581, Piazza della Signoria) and the Grand Duke Ferdinando I (completed by Tacca in 1608, Piazza della SS. Annunziata).

Now, at the end of the century, the different artistic activities came together in sharing an eclecticism receptive of outside influences on a permanent foundation of traditional restraint in design, as seen in the architects Giovanni Antonio Dosio and Giambattista Caccini and the painters Alessandro Allori, Santi di Tito (also architect of San Michele at Doccia and the villa 'I Collazzi'), Poccetti, Empoli, and Cigoli (also an architect, in the rhythmic, airy courtyard of the Palazzo Nonfinito). Thus here the transition to the new century passed almost unnoticed, while elsewhere it was to mark more definite trends in art towards new aspects of sensibility.

It is not without significance that Florence should have consigned to music 'the last relic of that form which had been revealed by the Renaissance as the eternal principle of all created things' (L. Becherucci). There was an ancient and noble tradition in this field too, if we think back to the Florentine composers of the fourteenth century revealed by the Squarcialupi (Bibl. Laurenziana) and Panciatichi (Bibl. Nazionale) codices and promoters of the *ars nuova*. Musical culture in Florence had a history which in the fifteenth century and the first half of the sixteenth saw maturing, in the same atmosphere of humanistic

▷

Bartolomeo Ammannati, Neptune Fountain, *1560-75, detail, in the Piazza della Signoria, a popular style of ornament of the type where a plinth set in the middle of a basin supported a mythological or historical figure.*

*Giambologna, equestrian monument
of Ferdinand I, 1608, which
was completed by Pietro Tacca,
in the Piazza SS. Annunziata.*

◁
Detail from Ammannati's
Neptune Fountain.

Vasari, Lorenzo de' Medici, *1533. Uffizi.*

▷

*The Boboli Gardens, a beautifully landscaped park, in which the Palazzo Pitti
stands. Originally laid out by Tribolo, it was embellished by Ammannati, and
contains fountains and romantic grottos among the lawns and shrubbery.*

intelligence and idealism, the foundations for the birth of opera, in
other words for a new form of expression, both musical and visual,
which would open up new horizons for instrumental music. The invention of 'recitar cantando' was born in the Florentine Camerata dei
Bardi (a society so called from the name of the host, Conte Bardi di
Vernio, in the palazzo built by Brunelleschi in Via dei Benci 5)
among a group of intellectuals among whom, in addition to Vincenzo
Galilei, father of the scientist, were the musicians Jacopo Peri (1561-
1633) and Giulio Caccini (1550-1618) and the poet Ottavio Rinuccini
(1564-1621), to whom we owe the first 'operas' in music, in the new
'recitative' style, given in 1594 at Palazzo Corsini in Via Tornabuoni
and in 1600 in Palazzo Pitti. This great novelty found a generally
favourable atmosphere in the Florentine tradition for theatrical representations, public and social festivities (Vasari speaks of 'ingenious
displays' for the latter) and carnival parades which flourished especially in the sixteenth century: weddings and funerals were the most

196

Pietro Tacca, Fontana della Taccanella, *1629, in the Piazza SS. Annunziata.
Above and right.*

frequent occasions for such displays, whose remarkable inventor and renowned impresario at the Grand Ducal court was the architect Buontalenti. The ceremonial decorations in the Church of San Lorenzo, ordered in 1564 from the Academy of Design for the funeral of the church's tutelary deity Michelangelo, have remained famous; their magnificence was in sharp contrast to the modest character of the monument erected to him a few years later in Santa Croce, taken from a project of Vasari's and executed by minor artists such as Lorenzi, Cioli and Baldini. Even more magnificent decorations, displays and scenarios in various parts of the town greeted in the following year the marriage of Francesco I with Giovanna of Austria. Even the most important buildings housed theatrical spectacles and installations: in 1579 mimic jousts and a sham sea battle were given in the courtyard of the Palazzo Pitti, and in 1585 Buontalenti constructed on the first floor of the Palazzo degli Uffizi the Medicean Theatre, where he himself organized fantasmagorical 'choreographic intermezzi'. Drawings and engravings in the Department of Prints and Drawings in the Uffizi and in the Biblioteca Marucelliana and the Biblioteca Riccardiana fully document these ephemeral but extremely elaborate scenographies. They provide the source for baroque staging in the seventeenth and eighteenth centuries.

It was in this atmosphere that the Medici Grand Dukes gradually evolved the ambitious idea of adding to the splendid architectonic complex of San Lorenzo, like an enormous protuberance developed on

its longitudinal axis, the huge mausoleum that was to be known as the Chapel of the Princes. The idea seems to have originated with Cosimo I, but it was revived in 1602 by his son Ferdinando I (1549-1609) who succeeded Francesco I (1541-87) as Grand Duke. Planned in 1602 by a prince, Don Giovanni de' Medici, with the aid of the indispensable Buontalenti, conceived in extraordinary proportions, executed by Matteo Nigetti with a hitherto unknown profusion of semi-precious stones and rare dark-coloured marbles worked by skilled craftsmen under enormous difficulties and at a vast cost which for over a century was to involve the Medicis' resources and employ a specially created workshop, it seemed to express in those outer elements themselves that adherence to the new aesthetic of the striking and sumptuous which was lacking in the intimate conception of its plan and architectonic form.

Giovanni de' Medici had already collaborated with Buontalenti in the creation of a sort of fortified villa in the Fortezza di Belvedere or San Giorgio (1590-95). This is an elegant little palazzo at the top of an imposing fortified construction built in the form of a star. It was to serve when needed for the personal safety of the Grand Duke Ferdinando I, who was himself a man experienced in business affairs and politics and promoted land reclamation, road construction and building improvements in the Tuscan towns, which testified their gratitude by erecting monuments to him in Livorno (by Giovanni Bandini, with the 'Four Moors' of Pietro Tacca) and at Arezzo and Pisa (by Francavilla)

as well as that by Giambologna in Piazza della SS. Annunziata in Florence. He was also a lover of antiquities and had made a collection of them in Rome, at Villa Medici, when he was Cardinal before succeeding his brother as Grand Duke. Thus we owe to him many of the ancient statues preserved today in the Uffizi. But he merely carried on the work of his brother Francesco I and their father Cosimo I. Cosimo had been active in reconstituting and adding to the splendid Medicean collections which had been plundered and dispersed in the stormy days after the death of Lorenzo the Magnificent. Francesco I wanted to have in the new building of the Uffizi a series of rooms in which to assemble the most valuable works of art preserved in the Guardaroba of the Palazzo Vecchio. And it was, as usual, Buontalenti who carried out the Grand Duke's wishes, building the rooms and the octagonal Tribune flanking Vasari's loggia and having them decorated by the most expert craftsmen of the day, led by Alessandro Allori (1581). Thus came into being the Uffizi Gallery, a product and testimony of Mannerist culture and a first example of the structures and functions of the modern museum. 'The Principality ensured its continuity and development. All the Grand Dukes, of whatever political attitude or personal qualifications, realised that the Gallery was the most valuable contribution that their little state, increasingly isolated in the struggle for power of the great European States, could yet give to the civilization of the world.' (L. Becherucci). Thus though the great season of the Renaissance closed with the end of the sixteenth century, some autumnal leaves nevertheless still remained on the trees. The Grand Duchy of Ferdinando I already witnesses the coexistence of outdated ideas and of foreshadowings of modern rationalism and interesting cultural crosscurrents. His son Cosimo II is remembered not only for the enlargement of Palazzo Pitti (carried out in 1620 by Giulio Parigi, who extended the façade by three windows on each side) and the rebuilding of the Villa Imperiale (by the same architect) but also for having recalled from exile and protected Galileo Galilei, offering him the position of 'Head Mathematician' of the Grand Duke and giving him the villa of Arcetri, where he was able to make many of his most important astronomical discoveries, destined to transform man's knowledge of the universe. This interest in science was a new departure for the Medicean Grand Dukes, which did not replace but complemented their more traditional interest in art and culture, as was especially shown by Ferdinando II (1610-70). He succeeded his father in 1621 at the age of ten under the regency of his mother and grandmother, and was invested with full powers when he was eighteen. Seven years later he married the young Vittoria della Rovere, last descendant of the Dukes of Urbino, whose dowry considerably enriched the Medicean collections. For the Uffizi Gallery now received therefrom the famous portraits of the *Dukes of Montefeltro*, by Piero della Francesca, the youthful small portrait of *Francesco Maria della Rovere* and the *Self-portrait* by Raphael as well as the portrait of *Julius II* (an old copy), and the portraits of *Francesco I della Rovere, Duke of Urbino* and of *Eleonora Gonzaga, Duchess of Urbino* by Titian, the *Venus*, by Titian, the *Judith* by Palmo Vecchio, and a series of pictures by Federico Barocci; while to the Pitti went the *Portrait of the grey-eyed nobleman* and the *Magdalen* by

◁

Villa 'la Ferdinanda' at Artimio, 5 miles from Florence. Built by Buontalenti for Ferdinand I de' Medici in 1594.

Palazzo Vecchio, Salone dei Cinquecento, constructed by Cronaca in 1495 from designs by Leonardo da Vinci. The ceilings are painted with frescoes by Vasari and pupils, and the walls are hung with Florentine tapestries.

P. 202/203
The Uffizi and Palazzo Vecchio.

Casa Buonarroti, built by Michelangelo and now a museum devoted mainly to his works.

Titian and the portrait of *Guidobaldo II della Rovere* by Barocci; and there were also various other art treasures and a collection of Urbino maiolica (now in the Bargello). This event doubtless influenced the Grand Duke Ferdinando II's decision to embellish the Palazzo Pitti with new pictorial decorations. The Medicean myth thus received fresh affirmation. Born with the return of the family to power and strengthened with the rise of the Grand Duchy, it had been first celebrated in the Salone of the villa at Poggio a Caiano with the series of frescoes begun by Andrea del Sarto and completed by Alessandro Allori, and then, in spectacular fashion, in the skies painted by Vasari in the Salone and the state apartments of Palazzo Vecchio; it was resumed in the Pitti palace in the great Sala degli Argenti, in other words of the treasure (from which later all that part of the palace, including the museum, took its name), and again, after some years and under the same patron, in the courtyard of the Medici villa at Petraia, in the lively frescoes of Volterrano (1636-48). At Palazzo Pitti the work was entrusted to the painter Giovanni da San Giovanni (1635), who exalted the splendour of the house of Medici in the person of its most illustrious son, Lorenzo the Magnificent, in a complex series of symbolical representations inspired by the poet and court librarian Francesco Rondinelli, evoking the mythology of the Harpies and Satyrs, the Muses and Apollo, and by the lives of the philosophers and Mahomet to glorify the restorer of civilization, thought and the arts. The frescoes, executed for the most part by Giovanni da San

Works by Giambologna.

Above,
Tacchino.
Bargello.

Left above,
Rape of the Sabines, *1583.*
Loggia dei Lanzi.

Left below,
Fontana Diavoletta
Vie Ventrietti e Strozzi.

▷
Buontalenti fountain in
Borgo S. Jacopo, Oltrarno.

Giovanni and completed after his death (1636) by Francesco Furini, Cecco Bravo (Francesco Montelatici) and Ottavio Vannini, are regarded as a fundamental witness to Florentine and Tuscan painting of the first half of the seventeenth century, an example of freedom and novelty of composition in 'gorgeous, rich chromatic garb; with a sense of air, of gentle Tuscan countryside and fresh, clear light.' (A.M. Francini Ciaranfi). Three more rooms were decorated in 1636 to 1641 by Angelo Michele Colonna and Agostino Mitelli, both from Bologna and 'quadraturist' painters, or painters of sham architecture and fantastic prospects derived from scenography, much in vogue from the sixteenth to the eighteenth century. At about the same time Ferdinando II also wished to have decorated some of the big rooms on the *piano nobile* of his apartments and of the floor on which since his father's time the most important of the pictures scattered throughout the palace had begun to be collected, thus forming the family gallery. The new decoration was entrusted to a 'modern' painter, Pietro da Cortona. The Sala della Stufa, which was frescoed first (1637-40) with the *Four Ages of the World* (the Ages of Gold, Silver, Bronze and Iron), is considered his masterpiece, 'not only because his fantasy created the purest image there, drawing on that adventurous seventeenth-century feeling which was opening up towards a hardly-discovered world, but also for the quality of the painting, full of feeling, dissolved in light, rich and gay' (C. Briganti). There followed, with various long interruptions, the frescoes in the Halls of Venus (1641-42), with a new experiment in the use and abundance of refined stucco-work, certainly by the hand of the same painter, in the medallions with portraits of personages of the Medici family, and then, more slowly, in the Halls of Jupiter and Mars, while the Hall of Apollo, left unfinished in 1647 because of the final departure of the artist from Florence, was completed only eighteen years later by Ciro Ferri. Meanwhile local painters had been called in to decorate other rooms, such as that known as the 'Room of the Allegories' in honour of the Grand Duchess Vittoria della Rovere, wife of Ferdinando II, with frescoes by Volterrano.

The presence of Pietro da Cortona produced various effects in Florentine artistic circles: people noted with some disquiet the difference in trend and quality from local figurative art, but none of the better artists, Matteo Rosselli, Furini, Volterrano, Dolci, Martinelli, or Lorenzo Lippi, appeared to be much influenced by him. During his stays in Florence Pietro da Cortona had been in contact with many of these artists, having been the guest of Michelangelo's grandnephew in Casa Buonarroti in Via Ghibellina, that strange monument characteristic of this period where a few years earlier the 'gallery' had been installed with paintings and frescoes showing the main episodes in Michelangelo's life, done by Rosselli, Furini, Giovanni da San Giovanni, Empoli, Passignano, Cristofano Allori, Bilivert, and other lesser artists.

But the fact that Pietro da Cortona was working in Florence and in the Grand Duke's palace seemed symptomatic of the process of gradual exhaustion of those local energies which for centuries had been the pride of the city. More and more artists from outside were coming in,

▷

Palazzo Pitti, Galleria Palatina.

P. 210/211

S. Lorenzo, Capella dei Principi. Begun in 1604 by Nigetti, from a plan by Giovanni de' Medici, it holds the sarcophagi of six grand dukes.

Palazzo Pitti,
Sala di Marte,
Galleria Palatina.

P. 214/215
Palazzo Pitti,
Museo
degli Argenti.

from the Frenchman Jacques Callot to the Neapolitan Salvator Rosa and, among the most important of them, the Flemish painter Giusto Sustermans, for forty years active as official portraitist of the Grand Ducal court.

Around the middle of the century interest in music and science intensified in Florence. The year 1657 marked two important events: the first representation of a music-drama in the theatre which the talented Ferdinando Tacca had constructed for the Accademia degli Immobili in the building of the Wool Merchants' Guild in Via della Pergola (hence the name of the famous theatre, later frequently renovated); and the first session of the Accademia del Cimento, founded in the Pitti Palace by Prince Leopoldo de' Medici, brother of the Grand Duke, to further scientific research according to the experimental methods demonstrated by Galileo. *I Saggi di naturali esperienze* (Essays on Natural Experiments), published by Lorenzo Magalotti as secretary of the Academy, give an idea of the extent and importance of its work. Both the theatre and the Academy were taken as models in the main cities of Europe, the theatre as an example of modern theatrical technique and the Academy as a new form of association among experimental scientists. To Prince Leopoldo, who later became a cardinal and moved to Rome, also belongs the initiative of first forming the collections of self-portraits, drawings and gems which, together with the collections of miniatures assembled by his brother Cardinal Giovan Carlo, are now the pride of the Uffizi Gallery. During the same period there were some significant achievements in the artistic field, though nothing to compare with those of the preceding centuries. The workshop of semi-precious stones and the Medicean tapestry factory produced some notable work. The Pitti palace was again enlarged on the ground floor and first floor with the addition of five windows on each side of the façade (1640-50). The church of San Gaetano, reconstructed by Matteo Nigetti in 1604, was completed by Gherardo and Piero Francesco Silvani between 1633 and 1648 with an imposing façade modelled on the Roman baroque, though in the restrained interpretation compatible with the tenacious Florentine Renaissance tradition. Antonio Ferri and the two Silvanis (who were also active in modernizing old palazzi in various parts of the city) built the Palazzo Corsini on the Lungarno (1648-56), of grandiose sixteenth-century design but with new features in the articulation of the various parts of the building, the balustraded pavilions topped by statuary, and the monumental interior staircases. The sculptor Ferdinando Tacca renovated (1649-55) the interior of the Romanesque church of Santo Stefano al Ponte and nobly modelled the bas-relief of the bronze altar-frontal with the *Stoning of St Stephen* (1656). Later on in the century the lengthy process of redecorating the interior of SS. Annunziata was continued, with paintings and stuccoes and the ornate wooden ceiling designed by Volterrano, who painted the fresco of the great cupola with the *Coronation of the Virgin* (1681-83). Antonio Ferri, following a design of the Roman architect Cerruti, rebuilt in Baroque form the church of San Frediano in Cestello (1680-89) and added a new cupola to the profile of the city on the far bank of the Arno (1698). P.F. Silvani after a design of Ciro Ferri covered with

◁

S. Maria del Fiore (Duomo), The façade in neo-Gothic style built by Emilio de Fabris, 1868-87, which has as its theme the greatness of Christianity and contains many busts of popes, bishops and Florentine citizens.

rich marbles the choir chapel (1675-1701) of the church of Santa Maria Maddalena dei Pazzi, and he built the splendid Corsini chapel in the church of the Carmine (1675-83), enriched with three great marble high-reliefs by Giambattista Foggini and with *Sant'Andrea Corsini in Glory*, frescoed in the cupola by Luca Giordano. The skill shown by the Neapolitan artist in this glittering, crowded composition procured him other commissions in Florence including one exceptional undertaking. Marchese Francesco Riccardi was then enlarging the famous Medici palace in Via Larga, which he had acquired from the family in 1659, and he entrusted to Luca Giordano the task of painting the ceiling of the new great gallery. The subject, suggested by the writer Alessandro Segni, allegorical and mythological in conception, dealt with the *Vicissitudes of Human Life* at the same time doing honour to the Medici, the house's former owners. The painter's lively but thoughtful interpretation, as seen in the elaboration of the detailed sketches (Mahon Collection, London), resulted in a highly expressive representation of poetic quality in the festive animation of an airy, fluent narrative, as if sustained by a musical rhythm.

This masterpiece by a non-Florentine painter seemed to set the seal on the end of the long and luminous era of Florence's conquest of civilization and of her role as transmitter of the highest values of art. What came after rarely rose above the level of everyday events. As an introduction to the eighteenth century, the last explosion of decorative craftsmanship, Foggini's exuberant Baroque décor in the Feroni chapel (1692) of the church of the SS. Annunziata, was less significant than the delicious frescoed decorations done by the Venetian Sebastiano Ricci in a little room of Prince Ferdinando's apartment in the Pitti palace (now the office of the Superintendant of Monuments) and in two rooms in Palazzo Marucelli, in Via S. Gallo (1706-7). This lesson in fantasy and narrative felicity found an echo in the unconstrained frescoes of Alessandro Gherardini in the cupola of San Marco (1717) and in some rooms of Palazzo Corsini and of the villa of Poggio Imperiale, while other artists inclined towards easier decorative methods when employed during the first half of the eighteenth century, particularly in frescoing cupolas: Anton Domenico Gabbiani, in San Frediano in Cestello (1718), Gian Domenico Ferretti, in the Badia (1734), and Vincenzo Meucci, in San Lorenzo (1742). Ferretti and Giovanni Camillo Sagrestani also did some interesting frescoes in Florentine palaces and churches. Among sculptors, the Roman sculptor Innocenzo Spinazzi is noted for the monument to Niccolò Machiavelli (1787) in Santa Croce and for the *Angel* (1792) placed beside Sansovino's statues above one of the doors of the Baptistry. Among the relatively small number of building works were those of the architect Ferdinando Ruggieri, of timidly rococo inspiration: the remodelling of the church of Santa Felicità (1736), the Palazzo Bastogi (1740), the slender campanile of San Lorenzo, and the beginning of what was to become the most important and original Florentine building of that century, the Palazzo San Firenze. Standing in the scenographic Piazza San Firenze formed by the Bargello, the Badia and the Palazzo Gondi, it consists of the façades of two similar churches linked by that of a palazzo (formerly the monastery of the Philippine fathers and today the seat of the Tribunal). The façade on the left was designed and built in 1715 by Ruggieri, with a single storey and a curiously composed upper part; the right-hand façade symmetrically corresponding to it and the palazzo were built sixty years later by Zanobi dei Rosso. In the second half of the eighteenth century, in Piazza San Marco the Palazzina della

Livia was built by the architect Bernardo Fallani (1775) and the new façade of the church of San Marco by Gioacchino Pronti (1780); the headquarters of the confraternity of the Misericordia was renovated (Stefano Diletti, 1781); the old Ospedale di Bonifacio was remodelled with the addition of the porticoes (Giuseppe Salvetti, 1787); and further important works were done in the Pitti Palace, with the beginning of the two lateral wings looking on to the piazza, with porticoes and terraces, and of the Palazzina della Meridiana and new rooms, among them the ballroom ('Sala Bianca'), the work of the architect Gaspare Maria Paoletti, who confirmed his neo-classical orientation with the Sala Niobe in the Uffizi Palace.

A mediocre and somewhat pretentious building of the middle of the century commemorated the end of the Medici dynasty with the death of the last Grand Duke, Gian Gastone (1737) and the succession of the Dukes of Lorraine to the throne of Tuscany: this was the triumphal arch built in 1745 by I.N. Jadot, from Lorraine, in memory of the entry of Francis of Lorraine as the new Grand Duke of Tuscany. It stands opposite the old Porta San Gallo, a survival of the walls of medieval Florence. The two monuments thus mark the beginning and end of a glorious period of history that had lasted for five centuries.

A last ray of grandeur was given to this twilight scene by Anna Maria Ludovica de' Medici, widow of the Elector Palatine, the last legitimate heir of the Medici dynasty, who in 1737 under the 'Family Pact' bequeathed to the state of Tuscany the immense patrimony of the Medici family, its villas and art collections—including those in the Uffizi and Pitti Galleries and the Laurentian and Palatine Libraries, and the collection of gems and of Etruscan and Egyptian antiquities—on condition that these treasures should remain 'an ornament of the State, for the use of the public and to attract the curiosity of outsiders.'

The years that followed, from the long period of enlightened and innovating government under the Grand Duke Leopold (1765-90) to the period of French rule (1799-1815), left little mark in a city which remained virtually unchanged, unlike the other capitals of Europe which during the Baroque era were transformed by new town-planning and the building of palaces and residences for their monarchs. Comparing the numerous plans and panoramic views of the city published during the eighteenth century with Buonsignori's plan of 1584, the fabric of its buildings and the green spaces within the great circle of the walls appear almost unaltered. On the other hand, in the course of two centuries the villas in the surroundings and countryside had multiplied or been enlarged or renovated, those villas where the Florentine nobility and patricians, emulating the luxury of the Medicean residences, gave intellectual and worldly animation to their old and new dwellings—among them the Salviati at Ponte della Badia, the Ferroni at Bellavista, the Corsini at Castello, the Palmieri at Tre Visi, the Gorini at Montughi, the Guadagni at La Luna, the Ricasoli at Tana, the Dini at Collazzi, and many others.

It was the beginning of that cosmopolitan life of which Florence was to be the unparalleled centre long after the eighteenth century and almost into our own times, the 'cultural salon' of the world to which have come—not just out of 'the curiosity of outsiders' but summoned thither by the most sublime thoughts and finest creations of man—poets, writers, artists and men of every branch of knowledge and every country, whose names and memories now form part of the spiritual patrimony of this city.

The Modern City

At the beginning of the nineteenth century, Florence did not escape the general isolation of figurative culture and its progressive decline towards a theoretical imitation of antiquity which the neoclassical movement had produced in the last decades of the preceding century. This situation, which Florence shared with the more active centres of Rome, Milan and Venice, was in her case aggravated by the lassitude of the political environment and, in the field of art, by the continued persistence of works of traditional and sixteenth-century style and influence—as has already been mentioned with reference to the works of the Grand Ducal architect Gaspare Maria Paoletti (see p.   ) and as can be seen in those of his pupil Giuseppe Cacialli (restoration of the villa at Poggio Imperiale, rooms in the Pitti palace) and of Pasquale Poccianti (projecting part of the façade of the villa at Poggio Imperiale, staircase and rooms in the Pitti palace). The Palazzo Borghese in Via Ghibellina was planned for Prince Camillo Borghese, Caroline Bonaparte's husband, by Gaetano Baccani (1823) on a simple but academic neoclassical design above the massive, archaic rustication of the ground floor; to the same architect belongs the design for the even colder Palazzo dei Canonici (1825) behind the Duomo; not to mention his sortie into Gothic style in the campanile of Santa Croce (1847).

In sculpture, Antonio Canova's great reputation was enhanced by his monument to Vittorio Alfieri (1810), executed for the Countess of Albany—a great sarcophagus of white marble resting on a dual base and with the figure of a grieving Italy—and was confirmed in the *Venus Italica* (1812, Pitti), done to replace the so-called Medici Venus, taken to France by Napoleon. Lorenzo Bartolini, who had been trained in Paris in David's studio side by side with Ingres, tried to react against neoclassical influences by a chilly mixture of naturalism and purism. Protected by Napoleon, who sent him to direct the Fine Arts Academy in Carrara from which he moved on to the Florentine Academy in 1837, he was a prolific and influential artist, famous throughout Italy. Florence has a number of his works, among the best known of which are the *Carità Educatrice* (1824) in the Pitti Gallery, the grandiose monument to Nicola Demidoff, in Piazza Demidoff, and three tombs in Santa Croce (that of the Princess Sofia Zamoyski on her deathbed shows greater insistence on realism); but he appears freer and more penetrating in his many busts, especially those preserved in the original casts in the gallery of San Salvi. Heir of his school, Giovanni Dupré aroused controversy for the lively realism of his recumbent figure of *Abel* (1842, Gallery of Modern Art in the Pitti Palace), which was even suspected of having been taken from the cast of a live model, and which was accompanied by the gesticulating and rhetorical *Cain* (1843). He held an important position in the official art world of his day; many of his sketches are preserved in the Villa Dupré at Fiesole.

◁

Giambologna. Child with Fish *Bargello.*

Another pupil of Bartolini's, Pio Fedi, continued his methods throughout the century and is remembered for his marble group of the *Rape of Polyxena* (1866), which was accorded the honour of being placed in the Loggia dei Lanzi.

Painting, too, between neoclassicism, romanticism and purism was mainly of a secondary and provincial character in Florence at this time. Mythological and historical subjects invaded every space, leaving no room for problems of style. The Palazzo Pitti demonstrates the complex application of this trend in the decorations of the rooms: the populous Olympus and the festive mythology of the Sala dell'Iliade (1825) by Luigi Sabatelli, the stories in the Salone d'Ercole, by Pietro Benvenuti (1828); and the ceilings of the Sala di Berenice, by Giuseppe Bezzuoli, the Sala delle Belle Arti, by Domenico Podestà, and the Sala d'Aurora, by Gaspare Martellini and others.

Outside this dignified and official setting, the vogue for compositions on historical and religious themes continued until well past the middle of the century, while new ideas were maturing. They were pursued with varying and ephemeral fortune by Antonio Ciseri, whose *Ecce Homo* (Gallery of Modern Art) is impressive for its elaborate composition, while his *Martyrdom of the Maccabees* (1863) bears unequal comparison with Pontormo's *Entombment* in the church of Santa Felicità; by Amos Cassioli, author of the crowded *Battle of Legnano* (1870, Gallery of Modern Art); and by Stefano Ussi, the acclaimed author of the theatrical *Eviction of the Duke of Athens*, which received an award at the Paris Exhibition of 1867 (Gallery of Modern Art).

It must, however, be admitted that these same painters, Benvenuti, Sabatelli, Bezzuoli, Ciseri and the rest, when they left behind the mythology and fake medievalism of their enormous canvasses, proved more convincing in their sketches and landscapes and especially in portraiture, which offered them more immediate resources of expression, of a more authentic kind, in the interpretation of character and in refinement of pictorial design.

The break with the conventionalities that had stultified painting, and not in Tuscany alone, in the early nineteenth century came with the development of the 'Macchiaioli' movement which emerged in Florence between 1850 and 1860 in search of a new figurative language. This, once again, was to be 'Tuscan', and was to recover the ancient gifts of simplicity and conciseness, rejecting all oratorical and emotive effusiveness. There was also a political aspect, influenced by the Risorgimento, in the new awareness of a cultural unification on the national plane and of events in progress in other countries outside Italy.

The motives inspiring the essentially realistic artistic theories of the Macchiaioli were not unlike the widespread aspirations towards a new freedom and immediacy of expression that animated the Impressionists in France, though the two movements are otherwise not comparable since their respective problems arose from historical and other experiences which had little in common.

The fact remains that the Macchiaioli were the most advanced and vital of the artistic trends in Italy in the nineteenth century. Shortly after the middle of the century, Florence became the meeting-point, with the Caffè Michelangelo as headquarters, for fiery discussions between artists who were more open-minded towards the new ideas. Centring round Telemaco Signorini, Odoardo Borrani, Cristiano Banti, and Diego Martelli (a young writer and future patron of the arts, and a serious and shrewd critic of the Tuscan Macchiaioli movement and the French Impressionists), there came from other regions of Italy,

Palazzo Riccardi-Manelli. Begun in 1557 and completed 1575 by Ammannati. Today it holds the Riccardiana-Moreniana, rich in manuscripts and incunabula.

making longer or shorter stays in Florence possibly en route for Paris, Vincenzo Cabianca from Verona, Nino Costa from Rome, Giovanni Boldini from Ferrara, Federico Zandomeneghi from Venice, Vito d'Ancona from Pesaro, and a whole lively troop of southerners, Giuseppe Abbati, Saverio Altamura (who is said to have introduced the study of 'macchia'), Domenico Morelli, Bernardo Celentano, and Michele Cammarano.

It was a courageous reanimation of the vein of realism which had never been completely interrupted in Florence and was now renewed with fresh conviction. A contributing factor was the presence in Florence from 1856 to 1860 of the young Degas, who painted there the *Bellelli family* (Louvre), one of the most significant pictures in modern painting.

The advance of photography also played some part, associated locally with the first activities of the firm of Alinari; and another influence was the first National Exhibition, held in Florence in 1861, at which artists from all over Italy of every trend from the romantic to the revolutionary were able to meet.

The group of Florentines became stronger and demonstrated its weight in the search for a freer and more subjective style of painting whose aim and ambition was to return, if with cautious archaisms, to the inexhaustible felicity of simple nature in the poetic atmosphere of everyday rural surroundings and of detailed narrative descriptions heightened by clear intensity of vision.

The painters Giovanni Fattori and Silvestro Lega and the sculptor and critic Adriano Cecioni by their forceful personalities and untiring activity by the end of the century ensured the avant-garde position of Tuscany in Italian art of the nineteenth century.

In the first decades of the twentieth century, with the return from a long stay in Paris (1900-07) of the vivid and many-sided young painter and writer Ardengo Soffici, Florence acquired a clearer and more direct idea of Impressionism and its protagonists through some tentative exhibitions of their works and through controversial articles in the review *La Voce*. That review, together with *Leonardo*, was then at the centre of the literary and cultural movement which had arisen around a small group of Florentines headed by the writers Giuseppe Prezzolini and Giovanni Papini. Once again a new message came from Florence to stimulate the reawakening; and once again a Florence café, the 'Giubbe Rosse', became the scene of literary and artistic battles and encounters.

In *La Voce* Soffici made known the most advanced European artistic movements such as Cubism under the apocalyptic acceptation of Futurism. He was also among the champions of the 'Strapaese' movement, to which Ottone Rosai belonged, advocating a return to the values of local tradition. Literary advances in various directions centred round the new reviews *Lacerba* (1913) and *Il Selvaggio* (1924). They were followed by *Solaria* (1925), *Il Frontespizio* (1929) and *Letteratura* (1937), expressing the ideas and experiences of an élite literary society of great vitality and pronounced temperament, with stimulating participation from the artist world.

In the succeeding decades and down to our own times, this cultural liveliness, alternating between mordant sarcasm and a cold capacity for expressive synthesis, continued to characterize the Florentine literary and artistic world. Its role in the increasingly expanding and varied panorama of international art and literature tends nowadays, however, towards a retreat to orthodox ideas and traditional balance, forming areas of resistance to the more impulsive and open-minded voices of the modern avant-garde movements, almost as if 'Toscanità' wished to exercise a moderating or restraining influence. But there are many outstanding Florentine or Tuscan personalities among the writers— novelists, poets, essayists and critics—of the last two generations: Emilio Cecchi, Aldo Palazzeschi, Bruno Cicognani, Nicola Lisi, Arturo Loria, Alessandro Bonsanti, Carlo Betocchi, Mario Luzi, Romano Bilenchi, and Vasco Pratolini; among the painters, Primo Conti, Gianni Vagnetti, Arturo Checci, Mino Maccari, and Giovanni Colacicchi; and

▷
The Duomo seen from the Campanile.

among the sculptors Libero Andreotti, Romano Romanelli, Bruno Innocenti, Piero Bigonciari, Antonio Berti, Corrado Vigni, and Quinto Martini. But now the artistic trends most typical of our times have definitely overstepped regional bounds to embrace a wider cultural scope and become more open to international circles, where Florentine representation, with the precedent of Massimo Campigli's exodus to Paris, reckons in the forefront Alberto Magnelli and Marino Marini.

In considering developments in architecture we must revert to the second half of the nineteenth century.
When, in 1865, Florence unwillingly became the provisional capital of the new united Italy, she disguised with seemingly sceptical indifference the obscure presentiment of the upheaval that this new status would mean for her, representing as it did a violation of her centuries-long equilibrium and her old, simple, parsimonious and somewhat detached way of life.

The Ponte Vecchio, the oldest bridge in Florence, dating from the 10th century. Rebuilt 1345, it was severely damaged in the floods of 1966. It has now been restored and multitudinous shops still flourish there.

Many problems, especially in connection with town-planning, had remained unsolved for centuries and even after the upheavals of the French revolution, except for some limited and misguided attempts to widen streets in the centre such as Via Cerretani and Via Calzaioli. These problems now suddenly came to the fore together with new ones of unpredictable magnitude: the installation of the Royal House, the Court, the Parliament and the Government; the housing of 30,000 newcomers to be added to a population of less than 120,000; the provision and regulation of the city's inevitable and immediate expansion; the adaptation of structures, services and communications to meet the new situation; slum clearance in the old centre of the town; and defence of the inhabitants against recurrent flooding.

The main palazzi and monasteries were occupied, from Palazzo Pitti, which became the royal residence, to Palazzo Vecchio, the seat of Parliament (with trepidation on the part of the Florentines as to the fate

of Vasari's frescoes in the Salone dei Cinquecento, transformed into the assembly hall), from Santa Maria Novella to San Firenze, and from the Medici palace to the Palazzo Nonfinito.

The task of planning and carrying out the expansion of Florence as capital was entrusted to the architect Giuseppe Poggi. He devoted himself to it with immense energy if with disputed success. His plan was not without a feeling for moderation and respect for the human side, though his job was to give the scope of a metropolis to a city whose medieval framework still remained intact. The outer areas were tackled intelligently and in the course of a few years the surroundings of the historic centre were completely changed. The hitherto intact walls marking the boundary between the town nucleus and the country-side were demolished and in their place broad surrounding avenues were constructed running from gate to gate and providing ample arteries for traffic and expanded communications. More than 51,000 houses were built. New piazzas were opened up and the old piazzas enlarged—from Piazza Cavour to Piazza Beccaria, from Piazza San Gallo to Piazza Indipendenza and Piazza Azeglio—to include old and new converging street-entrances; and they were surrounded by buildings and arcades of correct but cold architectural style—based on Renaissance or neoclassical models. Outside the surrounding belt of avenues a network of new roads was designed to cope with suburban building developments and new districts, thus adding parts of the surrounding communes to the city itself.

It was a great town-planning reform, breaking through the ring within which Florence had remained immobile for three centuries. Despite facile regrets and justifiable objections (destruction of the walls could have been avoided without harm to the surrounding avenues) it can now, at a distance of a hundred years, be recognized that the life of the modern city owes much to Poggi's farsighted vision. The great examples of Valadier and Haussmann were present in his mind, even though, as has rightly been said, Piazza Beccaria is not the Etoile.

The most successful part of Poggi's great replanning is undoubtedly the creation of the Viale dei Colli. A courageous plan on broad, free lines follows the natural contour of the ground, respecting the character and treed areas of the surroundings and exploiting the ups and downs with slopes that shorten distances and facilitate the route; it gives new access, almost like an invitation to discovery, to the ancient churches of San Miniato and San Salvatore and to the other monumental buildings of Monte alle Croci; and the inevitable structural features are carried out on the model of the 'picturesque' and the 'rustic' Baroque with which Ammannati had experimented in the Boboli Gardens. And at the top, to crown it all comes the Piazzale Michelangelo. It is a monumental climax to the restructuring of the hillside, and something more than a spectacular viewpoint over the city: it is the apex of the city's extension and penetration into the nearby southern outskirts of its wonderful surrounding countryside.

After Poggi's efforts two further matters of concern to the city were tackled: the façade of the Duomo and slum clearance in the historic centre.

For thirty years Florentine artistic life was involved in the problem of

◁
The Lungarno Corsini, named after the palace which houses the most important private collection in Florence.

the façade of Santa Maria del Fiore. There had been talk of it ever since 1822. More concrete proposals began to be made after work started in 1857 on the façade of Santa Croce under the architect Nicola Matas: here too it was a question of completing in the appropriate style a most important part of an ancient monument.

For the Duomo, it was decided to do what no one had dared to attempt in the golden days of art. Then, the first competition for the façade, announced in 1491, in which Pollaiuolo Maiano, Sangallo and Francesco di Giorgio took part, was called off through the wisdom of Lorenzo the Magnificent; and a second attempt in 1586, in which Giovanni de' Medici, Buontalenti and Dosio entered the lists, dragged on for half a century without reaching any conclusion.

The new competition, which was held in 1862 and 1865, was won by the Florentine architect Emilio De Fabris. His plan was naturally in the neo-Gothic style then fashionable. It envisaged three gables, as at Santa Croce, but in the end the side ones were reducd to the horizontal.

In this case too there were interminable debates and disagreements among the major architects and art critics of the day, including even the great Viollet-le-Duc.

The undertaking reflected a critical stage in nineteenth-century architecture, where the romantic conception of the work of art still persisted, and it involved among other things the great problem of completing unfinished ancient buildings and monuments in accordance with the morphology of styles. There were numerous such cases in Italy: those in Florence—the façade (1853-63) and campanile (1847) of Santa Croce, by Matas and Gaetano Baccani respectively, and the façade of Santa Maria del Fiore (1871-87)—had the privilege of opening and giving the stamp of approval to a series of historical fakes.

De Fabris's plan was even then regarded as a northern-Gothic 'transplant': a meticulous, academic, formalistic solution in the train of the Gothic Revival, like a wedding-cake, as Diego Martelli sarcastically described it, obtained by 'turning the flanks of the church on the façade, aligning its appearance with the different stages of the campanile, and stealing one line from Siena and another from Orvieto'; and overwhelming the whole with a superabundance of inlaid marbles and sculptures in the most barefaced imitation of style.

The other great undertaking of the century's latter years was the clearance of the historic centre, which an ostentatious tablet proclaims to have been 'da secolare squallore a vita nuova restituito' (restored from centuries-old squalor to new life). The present Piazza della Repubblica, with its great open space surrounded by pallid examples of eclectic architecture, has made a poor job of healing the violent onslaught dealt to the exhausted but still living body of the medieval city. Around the Piazza del Mercato Vecchio were the old houses of the Amieri, the Lamberti, the Sassetti, and the Castiglioni, the primitive little churches of S. Andrea, S. Tommaso and S. Pier Buonconsiglio, the Loggia del Pesce, built by Vasari, and the column with the statue of Abundance which marked the exact centre of the city amid an intricate network of alleyways and crowded slums: a whole seething, picturesque world the memory of which would have been lost but for numerous artists, foremost among them Telemaco Signorini, who before its destruction documented it on the spot in drawings, water-colours and engravings now collected in the Museum of 'Firenze com'era' (Florence of the past). Some coats of arms and other fragments of decoration from the demolished houses were put in the Museo di San Marco, and a large number of them were also preserved and bequeathed to the city by the antiquarian Stefano Bardini and his son Ugo. The Loggia del Pesce was later reconstructed in the Santa Croce quarter, in a space off Via Pietrapiana. The *Abundance* column was put in the Piazza della Repubblica (the original statue being replaced by a copy).

Time has not healed the mistake of so radical an urban upheaval, which modern civilization would now condemn as inopportune in any town but which was absolutely inadmissible in a city like Florence. These episodes, which cut into the very face of the city, cannot be passed over here; but it must also be said that at the time they occurred they fell below the general cultural level of the city, which was by no means purely provincial. Among the outstanding men living and working there were Giosuè Carducci, before he went in 1860 to take up a chair at Bologna university; Nicolò Tommaseo, who returned to live in Florence in that year; Gian Pietro Vieusseux, from Geneva, with his soon to be famous literary circle in Largo Santa Trinità; and Marchese Gino Capponi, one of the chief figures in that cultural and moral world, author of the *History of the Republic of Florence* and founder with Vieusseux of the Italian Historical Archives. In that cultural climate the review *L'Antologia*, founded in 1832, resumed in 1841, and reissued in 1866 with the title of *Nuova Antologia*, represented a powerful affirmation of the Italian national spirit.

In the first two or three decades of the present century the florid *art nouveau* style of architecture arrived late in Italy at a time when it was already dying out in Austria, France and England. In Florence its chief exponent was Giovanni Michelazzi, who had studied in Otto Wagner's school in Vienna. Few of his works have survived demolition, among them the villas in Via Scipione Ammirato and Via Giano della Bella, notable for their originality of construction and skilful decoration, worthy to stand comparison with the best foreign examples of this trend, which modern opinion has reinstated after earlier disapproval. It is doubtful whether the same will happen with regard to the contemporary and subsequent invasion of academic eclecticism, an indiscriminate, hybrid mixture of every style, Romanesque, Gothic and Renaissance, a vogue of which Florence retains undesirable examples in various streets and whose chief representatives were the Coppedé brothers, then active in building here and elsewhere. A building that qualifies under this head is the Biblioteca Nazionale, constructed between 1911 and 1935 on plans of the Roman architect Cesare Bazzani.

Around 1930 the development of football offered an exceptional opportunity to Florentine architecture in the construction of the town stadium. The work was entrusted to Pier Luigi Nervi, then only a young technician experimenting in the use of reinforced concrete. It aroused violent scepticism and disapproval; but when finished its daring construction and spirit of innovation, graceful Marathon tower, bold awning-roof and elliptical hanging staircase at once won general acclaim, and it still remains a masterpiece of modern architecture.

Soon afterwards another important event was the opening, in 1935, of the new railway station of S. Maria Novella. Its plan, conceived, contrary to experctations, in a rational and anti-decorative style which aroused bitter arguments, represented a contrast and break with the then current and often confused ideas entertained about modern architecture by a good many critics and by the general public.

The plan was drawn up by the architect Giovanni Michelucci, who shared its paternity with a group of young pupils (P.N. Berardi, Italo

Gamberini, Nello Baroni, Sarre Guarnieri, and Leonardo Lusanna) who entered the competition under the collective name of the 'Tuscan Group'. It did not easily overcome the resistance of those who thought it quite unsuited to the exceptional surroundings, conditioned by the dominating presence of the church of Santa Maria Novella. Today it is recognized that the individual character of that monument is much better ensured by the structural nature of the new architecture, 'organic' under a semblance of 'rationalism', as Frank Lloyd Wright acutely put it, than it could have been by a sterile stylistic imitation. The sure articulation of the masses, the firm rhythm of volumes and surfaces, the perfect proportion and sequence of the spaces, and the resistance of every form, even in the smallest details, to the changes of fashion after many years confirm the aesthetic validity of this original example of modern architecture in Florence.

Subsequent years did not bring the sequel that might have been hoped for after so propitious a beginning. In this the trend towards classicism widespread in official architecture under the Fascist regime, with its predilection for the monumental, probably had an influence.

The Rex Cinema, now the Apollo, by Nello Baroni (1936), renovated by Gamberini after the flood of 1966, and the Military Aeronautical Academy in the park of the Cascine, by Raffaello Fagnoni (1937-38) are among the more important constructions carried out in the period immediately preceding the Second World War.

On 4 August 1944 the centre of the town was devastated by the retreating German army. All the bridges were blown up except the Ponte Vecchio, and the streets leading to it, Porta Santa Maria, Via de' Bardi and Via Guicciardini, were reduced to a heap of rubble, from which some of the medieval towers incorporated in the old blocks of houses emerged miraculously spared.

The problem of reconstruction brought with it a revival of the passionate disputes and division of views which had arisen ten years before about the railway station. Opinions fell into two opposite camps, one side advocating faithful restoration while the other asserted the claims of modernity.

The outcome was substantially negative, as usual in such compromises, especially when hastened, as in this case, by the obvious pressure of the economic interests concerned; and it was revelatory in relation both to the particular cultural crisis caused by the war and also to the increasing tendency in the world today to pay less attention to the interests of art in favour of other more pressing and powerful needs of social life.

The rebuilding of the bridges over the Arno was also preceded and accompanied by lively disputes. The public competitions for them were won by the plans of the architects Baroni, Bartoli, Gamberini and Maggiora for the Ponte della Vittoria (1946); by Riccardo Morandi for the Ponte a San Niccolò (1951); by Ettore Fagioli for the Ponte alla Carraia (1952); by the Michelucci, Detti, Gizdulich, Santi and Melucci group for the Ponte alle Grazie; by the Gori, Nelli and Morandi group for the new Ponte Amerigo Vespucci (1957); and by the Savioli, Damerini, Scalese and Santi group for the new Ponte Da Verrazzano (1970).

The more serious and delicate problem of the rebuilding of the Ponte Santa Trinità was solved by deciding, this time by almost unanimous consent, to rebuilt it 'as it was', on the basis of the reliable and detailed evidence that the architect Riccardo Gizdulich was able to

Bargello. Loggia on the first floor.

assemble from Ammannati's original masterpiece, and by salvaging from the water and recomposing as far as possible the fragments of the statues, mouldings, cornices and ornamental scrolls and of the stones themselves. To supplement them the old *pietra forte* quarry in the Boboli Gardens was opened up again, from which the stone for the original bridge had been taken.

Post-war reconstruction involved a resumption of building activity which kept busy the new, young and lively Florentine school of architects which had been reactivated under the guidance of Michelucci and made aware of the implications of town-planning.

Present-day architecture, as we know, like every other artistic language shares in the process of osmosis and the tendency to a form of Esperanto which is typical of our times. The spread of means of communication and, even more, the trend towards uniformity in necessities and ways of life induced by mass civilization have had the effect of abolishing the traditional frontiers in art.

Tuscan architectonic culture has nevertheless preserved, even in the new languages, those characteristics of syntactic clarity and formal distinction which have always been traditional to it. The phenomenon of the more or less disorderly but always depressing spread of suburbs seems in Florence, as compared with other large Italian towns, to have been fairly restrained and in tune with the sense of moderation and the general architectonic characteristics typical of the city. True, here the inevitable tendency to expansion showed itself almost unexpectedly between the last decades of the nineteenth century and the early years of the twentieth, with an enormous expansion of building of anonymous character in the area outside the surrounding avenues of the northern quarter, from Ponte San Niccolò to the park of the Cascine in the spaces still unoccupied at the foot of the Bellosguardo hillside, from Porta Romana to Porta San Frediano and the slopes of the surrounding hills.

Greater awareness of town-planning needs was slow to find expression. Following an earlier plan of 1942, the new post-war plan did not appear until 1962 and after modifications only became law in 1968. It was thus too late to remedy past errors and situations already compromised and now made more complex by the economic and other difficulties, common to all the historic centres of Italy, of reconciling an ancient urban framework with the needs of modern technological and social progress.

Such conditions, in an exceptional city like Florence, involve more difficult and delicate problems than elsewhere, for a whole variety of reasons: the great number of historic buildings and works of art in the centre of the city, and its nearness to and centuries-long association with its unparalleled framework of the surrounding countryside, where a marvellous, conscious balance has been attained between the gentle architecture of the hundreds of villas and farms and unspoilt nature itself, made fruitful over the centuries by man's assiduous toil.

During the last decades, architectural planning and building in Florence has had the help of a number of important personalities. Foremost among them is the architect Giovanni Michelucci, who after the success of his plan for the railway station became the city's leading architect and town-planner, moving on from the rationalism of the houses in Via Guicciardini (1956) and the new headquarters of the Florence Savings Bank (1957) to the freedom of expression and imaginative intensity of the church of San Giovanni Battista on the Autostrada del Sole in the plain between Sesto and Campi Bisenzio, a work regarded by international opinion as among the most important of our time. The inspired motif of the tent, like a reversion to biblical times and an evocation of nomadic peoples in an era that boasts of the machine civilization, is here translated into a gigantic plastic plume, in a form that winds in on itself and includes dynamic, articulated spaces modulated with stupendous intuition and original and daring solutions of form and technique.

The architects Rolando Pagnini, Emilio Isotta, Giuseppe G. Gori, Leonardo Savioli, Leonardo Ricci and others have all contributed in various ways to modern trends in architecture, undertaking the difficult task of inserting new buildings, residential blocks, and villas into the delicate fabric of the Florentine city and countryside—not without an occasional inevitable clash of style.

Other buildings important for their dignity and artistic and technological originality are the new RAI-TV headquarters (1968), the offices of the Florence daily *La Nazione* (1966), and the modern and functional Congress Centre (1967-69), carried out by means of the interior transformation and creation of a large underground hall in the former Villa Contini Bonacossi, done by the architect Pierluigi Spadolini.

An activity in a specialized technical field which nevertheless closely concerns Florence's cultural inheritance is the restoration of historic buildings and works of art. A number of problems involving reconstruction and repair following damage done during the last war have been solved during the intervening years. Mention has already been made of the Ponte Santa Trinità and the quarters at the end of the Ponte Vecchio. But the disastrous flood of 4 November 1966 raised new problems of quite unaccustomed proportions. Some thousands of paintings on wood and canvas, frescoes, sculptures, furniture, art treasures and antiquities of every kind were submerged in water and mud with grave danger of complete destruction. Immediate salvage work was carried out with great devotion and with successful results under the guidance of Ugo Procacci. The work of rescue was also at once set on foot and carried on by the technical, scientific and advisory bodies of the State Fine Arts department, with the generous aid of international committees and institutions, who together conducted the greatest restoration operation ever known in human experience, thanks to which an artistic heritage of incalculable importance can today be said to have been saved. The work of restoration and conservation has also been expanded with the aid of modern techniques. The most important centre for this is the big Restoration Laboratory (director Umberto Baldini) which has been set up in the Fortezza da Basso, with modern equipment for scientific research and practice, which should certainly be well fitted to ensure the care needd to maintain Florence's immense artistic heritage.

A similar work of preservation was done with regard to historic buildings. The most immediate and urgent measures were taken at once, and then the Soprintendenza of Monuments, under the direction of Guido Morozzi, carried out a full programme of new research, restoration and re-evaluation of the most important and famous buildings and monuments of the historic centre, reclaiming them from alterations and damage sustained in the past. Thus the remains of the original Franciscan construction of 1228 in Santa Croce were discovered; the foundations of the ancient cathedral of San Reparata beneath the floor of Santa Maria del Fiore were brought to light; Brunelleschi's original structures in the cloisters of the Spedale degli Innocenti were uncovered and restored; the huge underground vaults of the church of San Lorenzo were opened up; the walled-up side of Sangallo's cloister at Santa Maria Maddalena dei Pazzi has been reopened; restoration of the Renaissance cloister of Santa Apollonia and of Andrea del Castagno's muralled refectory has been completed; the two great rooms of Or San Michele have been opened up again; and Vasari's Corridor, impassible since the last war, has been restored.

The preservation and restoration of Florence's artistic treasures are among the most significant aspects of the vitality and resilience shown after the disaster of the floods in all the activities of fundamental importance for the city's economic life. Thus tourism now has adequate facilities to cope with the growing influx of visitors carrying on the centuries-old tradition which has made Florence, 'the city of the spirit', an obligatory stage in every ideal journey from every part of the world. The typical specialities of handicrafts, from everyday objects to the most delicate examples of the craftsman's skill, bear witness to an unparalleled tradition of taste and experience. The antiques market finds in Florence one of its main international centres and meeting-points. Contemporary artists find hospitality in numerous private exhibition galleries and in collective shows, among which the 'Premio del Fiorino' has been important for the past twenty years. It is interesting to recall that the exhibitions of earlier art now so frequent in Italy and abroad had their origin in Florence, with the exhibition of Italian Portraiture in 1911 and that of Seventeenth- and Eighteenth-century Painting in 1922. Now such exhibitions are held periodically on suitable subjects of cultural interest, while there are also regular exhibitions of the drawings of old masters, organized with excellent annotated catalogues by the Prints and Drawings Department of the Uffizi. Florence can also claim to have been the first in the field of international musical festivals, with the Maggio Musicale Fiorentino initiated in 1933 by Vittorio Gui with the Stabile orchestra which he founded in 1928; it has acquired great prestige for its excellent presentations of orchestral concerts and operas, old and new, with fine scenography and production.

Numerous institutions play an active part in the city's cultural life. Many of these are of ancient origin or long standing, such as the University, the Fine Arts Academy, the Art Institute of Porta Romana, the 'Luigi Cherubini' Music Conservatoire (whose directors in recent years have included such famous musicians as Oldebrando Pizzetti, Luigi Dallapiccola, Adriano Lualdi, and Antonio Veretti), the Accademia della Crusca, the Tuscan Academy of Science and Letters ('La Colombaria'), the Accademia dei Georgofili, the Gabinetto Vieusseux, the Military Geographical Institute, the National Institute for Renaissance Studies, and, recently, the International University of Art. Foreign cultural institutes and their librairies also play an important part (the Institut Français, the British Institute, the Kunsthistorisches Institut, and the Dutch Institute). A recent addition is the Villa of 'I Tatti' (with its extensive library and collection of pictures and art treasures), which the well-known art critic and writer Bernard Berenson arranged and lived in for over fifty years and then left in his will to the university of Harvard (1959) as a foundation for the study of Italian art history. This is only a recent example of the many similar acts of generosity on Florence's behalf over the past century: they include the Buonarroti bequest (1858), in the Casa Buonarroti; the Carrand (1888), Ressmann (1896) and Franchetti (1916) bequests, all in the Bargello Museum; the Stibbert (1906), Horne (1916) and Bardini (1923) bequests, each in its own premises; and, more lately, the Fondazione di Salvatore Romano, in the refectory of Santo Spirito, and gifts of numerous works by Italian and foreign artists under the auspices of C.L. Ragghianti after the floods to build up a new Gallery of Contemporary Art, to which Ettore della Ragione in 1970 promised his rich and valuable collection of pictures and sculpture by contemporary artists.

Another recent and particularly valuable acquisition is the munificent donation of the Contini Bonacossi heirs, destined for the Uffizi Gallery and consisting of twenty-seven pictures by great masters and numerous art treasures, selected on the principle of supplementing the main historical periods of the artistic heritage preserved in Florentine museums.

▷
Scenic view of the hills of Fiesole.

P. 238/239
Map of Florence.

P. 240
View of Florence from the Viale dei Colli.

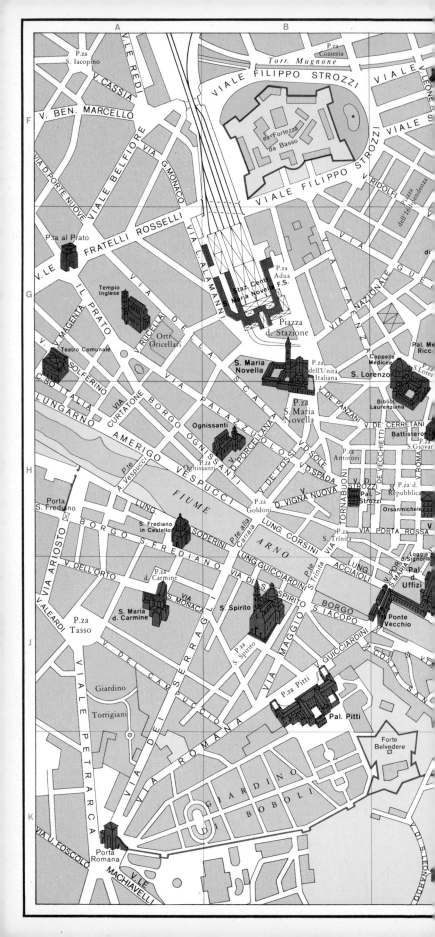

Museums and Galleries

Bargello - see **Museo Nazionale**

Galleria dell'Accademia

Via Ricasoli 52 [GD]. *Open in summer from 9.30 to 4.30, and in winter from 9.30 to 4, Sundays and public holidays, 9 to 1. Closed on Mondays.*
The collection was begun in 1784 by Grand Duke Pietro Leopoldo, and later considerably enlarged. It contains paintings of the Tuscan school of the 13th to the 16th centuries and sculptures by Michelangelo. The entrance leads into the large hall hung with 16th-century tapestries woven in Brussels and Florence. Works by Michelangelo: four of the unfinished *Prisoners* designed for the tomb of Julius II in Rome (*c.* 1518), a project that was never completed; *St Matthew* (*c.* 1504), also unfinished, designed for S. Maria del Fiore; the *Palestrina Pietà*, formerly in the church of S. Rosalia at Palestrina; *David,* originally in front of the Palazzo Vecchio (1504) and later removed to protect it from the weather. Alongside the main hall are the rooms of the Pinacoteca. *Room I.* Florentine primitives of the 13th and early 14th centuries. *Crucifixion,* Sienese school, possibly by Duccio; the *Tree of the Cross* by Pacino di Buonaguida, of the school of Giotto; *S. Mary Magdalen* by the 'Maestro della Maddalena'. *Room II.* Florentine painting of the 14th century. Works by Daddi and his school, Agnolo Gaddi, and a polyptych by Andrea Orcagna of the *Madonna and Child with angels and saints. Room III.* Florentine painting of the 14th century. *Pietà* by Giovanni da Milano (1365); *Coronation of the Virgin* by Jacopo di Cione; the *Life of Christ* and *Life of St Francis* by Taddeo Gaddi, cupboard doors from the sacristy of S. Croce. *Room IV.* Florentine painting of the late 14th and early 15th centuries. *Crucifixion* by Lorenzo Monaco, and *Annunciation* by the 'Maestro dell'Annunciazione dell'Accademia'. *Room V.* Florentine painting of the early Renaissance. Front of a cassone by an unknown Florentine painter of the 15th century known as the 'Maestro del Cassone Adimari'; *Nativity* by the 'Maestro della Natività di Castello'. *Rooms VI* and *VII.* Florentine

painting of the later 15th century. *Madonna of the sea,* attributed to Botticelli; *Trinity and saints* by Alessio Baldovinetti; *Thebaid,* attributed to Paolo Uccello; *Madonna and Child with angels and the infant St John Baptist* by Botticelli; *Adoration of Christ* by Lorenzo di Credi. *Room VIII,* called the 'Colosso'. Works of the early 16th century. *Assumption with saints* by Francesco Granacci; *Assumption with saints* by Perugino; *Deposition* (1504) by Filippino Lippi; *Apparition of the Virgin to St Bernard* by Fra Bartolomeo (1504/7); *Removal of the body of St Zenobius* by Ridolfo del Ghirlandaio (1517); *Madonna and Child with angels and saints* by Fra Bartolomeo (1584); *Annunciation* by M. Albertinelli (1510); *Madonna of the well* by Franciabigio. *Room IX,* called the 'Anticolosso'. Paintings from the second half of the 16th century. Works by Bronzino, A. Allori (*Annunciation,* 1603), Ridolfo del Ghirlandaio, Daniele da Volterra, *St John in the desert* attributed to Raphael but possibly by Giulio Romano; *Venus and Cupid* by Pontormo, after a cartoon by Michelangelo 49, 146, 148, 152, 164, *164,* 168, 178, 181.

Galleria d'Arte Moderna
Palazzo Pitti [JB]. *Open from 9.30 to 4. Closed on Tuesdays.*
Founded *c.* 1860. Its twenty-seven rooms contain representative works of 19th-and 20th-century Tuscan painting, also works of the same period by other Italian schools and by foreign artists. 221, 222.

Galleria Corsini
Via di Parione 11, Palazzo Corsini [HB]. *Open on Saturdays from 12 to 1, closed in August.*
The most important private collection in Florence, it was begun in the 18th century. Works by Italian and foreign artists. 152.

Galleria Palatina, or Galleria Pitti
Piazza Pitti [JB]. *Open in summer from 9.30 to 4.30, and in winter from 9.30 to 4. Sundays and public holidays from 9 to 1. Closed on Tuesdays.*
Started by Cosimo II in 1620 as the Palace picture gallery, and additions made subsequently by the Medici

grand dukes and princes. It comprises Italian and foreign works of the 15th to the 18th centuries, including some masterpieces by Raphael and Titian. A staircase in the style of Brunelleschi leads to the Vestibule with a 15th-century fountain and statue by Tribolo, and then on to the Sala della Tazza containing Luca Giordano's *Triumph of Galatea*. This leads to the Sala dell'Iliade, so called on account of the subject matter of its 19th-century frescoes: Raphael's *Pregnant woman* (*c.* 1506) reveals the influence of Florentine masters; *Assumption with apostles and saints* by Andrea del Sarto; *Portrait of Count Valdemaro Cristiano* by Sustermans (*c.* 1662); *Philip IV of Spain,* equestrian portrait by Velazquez. *Room II,* 'Sala di Saturno' contains most of the works by Raphael in this collection: *Madonna del Granduca* (1504-5), which receives its name from the Grand Duke Ferdinando III; portrait of *Tommaso Inghirami* (*c.* 1514); *Madonna del Baldacchino,* a large picture painted in 1506, at the end of his Florentine period; portrait of *Agnolo Doni,* a Florentine portrait in an Umbrian type landscape; *Ezekiel's vision,* a small picture of his Roman period; portrait of *Maddalena Doni,* reminiscent of the Mona Lisa; portrait of *Cardinal Bernardo Dovizi da Bibbiena* (*c.* 1516); *Madonna della Seggiola* (*c.* 1515), the most famous painting of his Roman period. The two works by Perugino are the *Deposition,* signed and dated 1495, and *Mary Magdalen. Room III,* 'Sala di Giove'. *St John Baptist* by Andrea del Sarto (1523); *Deposition* by Fra Bartolomeo (*c.* 1516), one of his latest and best works; portrait of *Guidobaldo della Rovere* by Bronzino; *Annunciation,* an early work by Andrea del Sarto; *St Jerome* by Piero del Pollaiuolo; *The veiled woman,* also known as 'La Fornarina', one of Raphael's greatest works (*c.* 1516); *The Three Ages of Man,* (*c.* 1510), Venetian school, has been attributed to Giorgione and Giovanni Bellini; *Madonna della Rondinella* by Guercino; *Madonna del Sacco* by Perugino. *Room IV,* 'Sala di Marte'. *Madonna and Child* and *Madonna of the Rosary* by Murillo; *Four philosophers* and *The consequences of war* by Rubens; portrait of *Daniele Barbaro* by Paolo Veronese (1570); portrait of *Cardinal Ippolito de Medici,* and portrait of *Andrea Vesalio* by Titian; portrait of Cardinal *Guido Bentivoglio* (*c.* 1623) by Van Dyck; portrait of *Luigi Cornaro* by Tintoretto. *Room V,* 'Sala di Apollo'. *Portrait of a gentleman,* known as *The Englishman* (*c.* 1540) one of Titian's finest portraits; *Deposition* by Andrea del Sarto; *Nymph pursued by a satyr,* influenced by Giorgione; portrait of *Vincenzo Zeno* by Tintoretto; *Madonna and Child enthroned with saints* painted by Rosso Fiorentino, for the church of S. Spirito; *St Peter raising Tabitha to life* by Guercino (1618); portrait of *Vittoria della Rovere* by Sustermans; *Hospitality of St Julian* by Cristofano Allori; portrait of *Arnolfo dei Bardi,* a good early work of Carlo Dolci; *Charles I and Henrietta Maria* by Van Dyck; *Mary Magdalen* (1530-40) by Titian, painted for the Duke of Urbino. *Room VI,* 'Sala di Venere'. Works by Titian: the famous portrait of *La Bella* (1536-37); *Julius II,* after Raphael; *The Concert,* an early work, once attributed to Giorgione. *Sacred conversation* by Bonifacio de' Pitati; *Peasants returning from work* and *Ulysses on the island of the Phaeacians* by Rubens; *Seascape* by Salvator Rosa. *Room VII,* 'Sala del Castagnoli', which takes its name from the artist who decorated it. In the centre, the *Round Tables of the Muses,* made in precious marble by the Opificio delle Pietre Dure; two easel paintings, *Bacchus* by Guido Reni and the *Banner for a Sienese confraternity with St Sebastian* by Sodoma (1525). *Room VIII,* 'Sala delle Allegorie', also known as the 'Quartiere del Volterrano' takes its name from the artist who decorated it. The allegories incorporate the figure of Vittoria della Rovere, the wife of Ferdinando II. Also by Volterrano is the painting of *Arlotto of Pieve's practical joke.* Paintings by Sustermans, Alessandro Allori and Giovanni da S. Giovanni. *Room IX,* 'Sala delle Belle Arti'. Works by Matteo Rosselli, Cristofano Allori and Carlo Dolci. *Room X,* 'Sala d'Ercole', 19th-century frescoes and an enormous Sèvres vase given by Napoleon to Ferdinando III. *Room XI,* 'Sala dell'Aurora'. Works of the 16th and 17th centuries. *Room XII,* 'Sala di Berenice'. Devoted to the works of Salvator Rosa: *Seascape with towers,* and the *Forest of the philosophers. Room XIII,* 'Sala di Psiche'. Early 19th-century ceiling. *Room XIV,* 'Gabinetto Rotondo'. *Room XV.* The bath of Maria Luisa, with fine neoclassical architecture. *Room XVI,* 'Sala dell'Arca'. Contains a precious Sèvres vase. *Room XVII,* reliquary chapel with paintings by Carlo Dolci. Going back through the 'Quartiere del Volterrano' we come to the music room, known as the 'Sala dei Tamburi' (*Room XVIII*) because it contains some curious furniture shaped like drums. The room is done in an elegant neoclassical style, with paintings by Guido Reni, Pontormo and Baroccio. *Room XIX,* 'Galleria del Poccetti', named after the painter who executed the frescoes which depict an allegorical triumph of the Medici. Works by Pontormo, Rubens, Matteo Rosselli, Gaspard Dughet and Ribera. The table against the wall is inlaid with precious marbles. *Room XX,* 'Sala di Prometeo'. Early 19th-century decorations. *Madonna in Adoration* by Jacopo del Sellaio; *Holy Family,* tondo by Luca Signorelli (1452); *Apollo and the Muses* by Giulio Romano. *Room XXI,* 'Corridoio delle Colonne', so-called on account of the two alabaster columns with small paintings of the Flemish and Dutch schools. *Room XXII,* 'Sala della Giustizia'. Venetian school. *Venus, Vulcan and Cupid* and *Madonna of the Conception* by Tintoretto; *Baptism of Christ* by Veronese; *Portrait of a man* by G. B. Moroni; *The Saviour* and portrait of *Vincenzo Mosti,* an early work of Titian. *Room XXIII,* 'Sala di Flora'. *Venus Italica* by Canova, (*c.* 1810); *Adoration of the Magi* by Pontormo; *Martyrdom of St Agatha* by Sebastiano del Piombo, (signed and dated 1520); *Joseph the Jew* by Andrea del Sarto (1520-23). *Room XXIV,* 'Sala dei Putti'. Works of the Flemish and Dutch schools, including the *Flowers* by Rachel Ruysch. *Room XXV,* 'Sala di Ulisse'. *Madonna dell'Impannata* by Raphael (1514); *Death of Lucrezia* by Filippino Lippi. *Room XXVI.* Bathroom in the Empire style. *Room XXVII,* 'Sala dell'Educazione di Giove'. *Sleeping Cupid* by Caravaggio, painted in Malta (1608); *Judith* by Cristofano Allori. *Room XXVIII,* 'Sala della Stufa', completely decorated in pure 17th-century Florentine style. 114, 146, 148, 152, 157, *158,* 164, 166, 168, *169,* 177, 182, 201, *208, 213,* 219, 221.

Galleria degli Uffizi and **Gabinetto dei Disegni e delle Stampe** - *see also* **Palazzo degli Uffizi**
Loggiato degli Uffizi, 6 [JC]. *Open in summer from 9.30 to 4.30 and in winter from 9.30 to 4. Sundays 9 to 1. Closed on Mondays.*
The most important art collection in Italy, it comprises the most outstanding works of the Florentine school, groups of paintings from the other Italian schools (especially the Venetian) some very fine Flemish pictures, a collection of self-portraits, and much antique sculpture. *Ground floor. Entrance:* tapestries from the Medici workshops; *Mars and Venus,*

classical group in marble; Medici busts. *Salone dello Ascensore*; Remains of columns from S. Pietro in Scheraggio; tapestries from the Medici workshops; Medici portraits and busts. Vasari's staircase, decorated with Roman sculpture and 16th-century bronzes, leads to the first floor and the entrance to the *Gabinetto dei Disegni e delle Stampe,* and continues on to the second floor. *First Vestibule*: Roman busts and detached frescoes by Giovanni da S. Giovanni. *Second Vestibule*: statues of Caesar and Augustus of the Imperial age, and two Hellenistic Molossian dogs. The *Gallery* is divided into two wings. The first gallery has a ceiling decorated with 16th-century grotesques, and the walls are covered with groups of tapestries: *Hunting scenes,* designed by Stradano, and the *Months,* woven in Flanders; *Festivities at the court of Catherine de' Medici,* woven in Brussels in the 16th century. Among the classical sculptures are *Hercules and the Centaur,* Hellenistic, restored in the 16th century; *Persephone,* Roman copy of a Greek original, and *Apollo,* also copied from a Greek original. The ceiling of the second gallery is painted as a pergola with 17th-century grotesques. This gallery contains antique sculptures on 16th-century pedestals. *Wild boar,* Roman copy in marble of a Hellenistic bronze; *Dancing girl,* copy of a Hellenistic original. The third gallery is decorated with 17th-century allegorical paintings and portraits of famous men on the ceiling, and groups of tapestries: *The Passion of Christ,* designed by A. Allori and Cigoli; *Jacob,* woven in Brussels in the 16th century; *Battle scenes,* woven in Flanders. Imperial busts and copies of classical sculptures. Two statues of *Marsyas,* copied from Hellenistic originals of the 3rd century B.C., the first restored by Verrocchio, the second by Donatello; bust of *Cicero; Pothos,* after a bronze attributed to Scopas: *Room I.* Antique reliefs. The rooms alongside the first and third galleries contain the collection of paintings. *Room II.* Giotto and the 13th century: *St Luke* by the Maestro della Maddalena; *Madonna and Child enthroned with angels,* known as the *Madonna Rucellai* by Duccio di Buoninsegna; *Madonna and Child enthroned with angels and saints* by Giotto (*c.* 1310); *Madonna and Child enthroned,* by Cimabue, formerly on the high altar of S. Trinita; *Room III.* Sienese school of the 14th century. *Annunciation with saints* by Simone Martini, triptych signed and dated 1333; *Madonna in Glory* by Pietro Lorenzetti, signed and dated 1340; *Room IV.* 14th-century Florentine school. *St Matthew* by Andrea Orcagna and Jacopo di Cione, triptych with predella designed for Or San Michele; *Pietà* by Giottino; *S. Nicholas of Bari, Madonna with child and saints* by Ambrogio Lorenzetti, triptych of c. 1332. *Rooms V and VI.* Late Gothic. *Adoration of the Magi* by Lorenzo Monaco (c. 1420); *Crucifixion* by Agnolo Gaddi; *Madonna and Child* by Jacopo Bellini; *Adoration of the Magi* by Gentile da Fabriano, signed and dated 1423, painted for the Cappella Strozzi in S. Trinita; *Coronation of the Virgin,* triptych by Lorenzo Monaco signed and dated 1413, formerly in S. Maria degli Angeli; *The Thebaid* by Gherardo Starnina. *Room VII.* Florentine painting of the early 15th century. *Battle of S. Romano* by Paolo Uccello. Portraits of the *Duke of Urbino* and his wife *Battista Sforza,* by Piero della Francesca (c. 1465) with the *Triumph* of the duke and duchess on the back, inspired by the 'Trionfi' of Petrarch; *Madonna and Child with St Anne* by Masaccio and Masolino da Panicale (1420-24); *Madonna and Child enthroned with four saints,* altarpiece from S. Lucia dei Magnoli, by Domenico Veneziano (c. 1445-48); *S. Frediano, Annunciation of the death of the Virgin,* and *St Augustine in his study* (predella of the Barbadori altarpiece, now in the Louvre) by Filippo Lippi (1437-42). *Room VIII.* Filippo Lippi and Pollaiuolo. Altarpiece with *SS. Vincent, James and Eustace,* by Antonio and Piero del Pollaiuolo (1467); *Madonna and Child with two angels* by Filippo Lippi (c. 1465); *Annunciation* by Alessio Baldovinetti; *Coronation of the Virgin* by Filippo Lippi (1441-47), formerly in the church of S. Ambrogio; *Madonna and Child* by Angelico (c. 1445). *Room IX.* Pollaiuolo and Botticelli. *Portrait of an unknown man with a medal of Cosimo il Vecchio,* by Botticelli (c. 1470). *Judith's return from the camp of Holofernes, The dead Holofernes,* and *Fortitude,* by Botticelli. *Virtue* by Piero del Pollaiuolo (1470, executed for the Tribunale di Mercanzia; the series was completed by Botticelli's *Fortitude*). Two small pictures by Antonio del Pollaiuolo, *Hercules* and *Anteus,* and *Hercules and the Hydra. Rooms X and XI.* Botticelli. *Madonna with the pomegranate* (1487), tondo corresponding to the *Madonna of the Magnificat; Primavera* (1477-78) painted for Lorenzo di Pierfrancesco de' Medici, and inspired by Poliziano. *Birth of Venus* (1486) painted for the Medi-

ci villa at Castello; *Adoration of the Magi* (1475) painted for the Cappella Lama in S. Maria Novella, and containing contemporary portraits. *Pallas and the Centaur* (1485) painted for the villa at Castello; *Calumny,* a late work evoking Lucian's description of the painting of Apelles; *St Augustine in his cell* (c. 1495). *Room XII.* 15th-century Flemish painting. *Portrait of a young man, Portrait of a man, Portrait of Benedetto Portinari, St Benedict,* by Hans Memling; *Deposition* by Rogier van der Weyden, possibly painted in Florence. *Room XIII.* Florentine painters. Works by Filippo Lippi, Bartolomeo di Giovanni, Botticelli, Filippino Lippi; *Venus* by Lorenzo di Credi, formerly in the Medici villa at Cafaggiolo. *Room XIV.* Called the Van der Goes room since it contains his masterpiece, the *Portinari triptych,* painted in Bruges 1476-78, and commissioned by Tommaso Portinari; *Tobias and the three archangels* by Francesco Botticini (c. 1470); works by Domenico del Ghirlandaio, Filippino Lippi and Lorenzo di Credi. *Room XV.* Umbrian school and Leonardo. Works by Lorenzo di Credi, Piero di Cosimo, Luca Signorelli (including his *Holy Family* and *Madonna and Child*); *Baptism of Christ* by Andrea Verrocchio (c. 1470), in which the landscape and the angel are by Leonardo; *Adoration of the Magi* by Leonardo da Vinci, commissioned in 1481 by the monks of S. Donato a Scopeto; *Madonna with St John the Baptist and Sebastian* by Pietro Perugino (signed and dated 1493). *Room XVI.* Maps of Tuscany painted in 1589 by Stefano Bonsignori; *Annunciation,* an early work of Leonardo da Vinci, formerly in the convent of Monte Oliveto; *Young man in a red cap,* attributed to Lorenzo di Credi. *Room XVII.* Umbrian school. Works by Giovanni Boccati, Antoniazzo Romano, Luca Signorelli, Marco Palmezzano, Girolamo Genga, Bartolomeo Caporali, Melozzo da Forlì. *Room XVIII.* Called the 'Tribuna', architecture and decoration by Buontalenti (1585-89). It contains the antique sculptures of the Medici collection, and a series of 16th-century portraits; the *Venus dei Medici,* discovered in the 18th century at Hadrian's Villa at Tivoli, and obtained for the Uffizi by Cosimo III. It may be attributed to Cleomenes, the son of Apollodorus the Athenian, active in the 1st century B.C. The *Apollino,* copy of a work by Praxiteles; the *Arrotino* (knife-grinder, the popular name for this unique copy of an original of the 3rd or 2nd century B.C. of the

Scythian about to flay Marsyas. Some scholars consider it to be the original). The *Wrestlers,* copy of a Pergamene sculpture; *Dancing Faun,* Greek copy of the 3rd century B.C.; *Torso of a satyr,* Pergamene sculpture of the 2nd century B.C. Among the portraits are *Cosimo il Vecchio,* by Pontormo; *Bartolomeo Panciatichi, Lucrezia Panciatichi; Don Garzia; Eleonora di Toledo with her son Giovanni. Room XIX.* Perugino and Francia. Portrait of *Baldassare,* a monk of Vallombrosa, and portrait of *Francesco delle Opere* (signed and dated 1494); both by Perugino; *Pietà* and portrait of *Evangelista Scappi,* by Francia. *Room XX.* Mantegna, Dürer and Cranach. *St Dominic* by Cosmè Tura, painted for the church of S. Luca at Ferrara; Triptych with *Adoration of the Shepherds* (painted in Florence 1466-67) and *Madonna of the Quarries* (1488-89) by Mantegna. Works by Dürer: *Madonna and Child* (signed and dated 1526); *Portrait of his father,* an early work; *Adoration of the Magi,* (initialled and dated 1504); large *Calvary,* (initialled and dated 1505). Works by Cranach: portrait of *Luther,* (signed and dated 1543); *St George;* portrait of *Luther,* (initialled and dated 1529); *Self-portrait* (signed and dated 1550); *Adam,* (initialled and dated 1528) and *Eve. Room XXI.* Venetian school. Works by V. Carpaccio and Cima da Conegliano. Works by Giovanni Bellini: *Sacred Allegory* (c. 1490); *Portrait of a gentleman; Lamentation over the dead Christ;* works by Giorgione: *The Child Moses before Pharaoh; Judgment of Solomon;* the so-called *Gattamelata,* attributed to Giorgione; works by Dürer: *Apostles* (initialled and dated 1516). *Room XXII.* Holbein, and other Flemish artists. *Adoration of the Magi* by Gerard David; *Deposition* by A. Altdorfer; *St Florian's farewell and martyrdom,* (initialled 1525-30). Portrait of *Richard Southwell* by Holbein (dated 1536); portrait of *Thomas More,* (school of Holbein). *Room XXIII.* Correggio, North Italian and Flemish painters. Works by Correggio: *Madonna in Adoration* (a work of his early maturity), *Rest on the flight into Egypt; Madonna in Glory. Room XXIV.* Miniatures of the 15th to the 18th centuries. These are Italian, English, French and German. *Room XXV.* Raphael and Michelangelo. Also works by Granacci, Mariotto Albertinelli (*Visitation* dated 1503, and predella), and Agnolo Bronzino (*Holy Family,* signed). Works by Raphael: portrait of *Perugino,* an early work; portrait of *Francesco*

Maria della Rovere; Leo X with Giulio dei Medici and Luigi de' Rossi (1518-19); *Madonna of the goldfinch* (painted in 1506 for the marriage of Lorenzo Nasi); portrait of *Julius II* (attributed). Works by Michelangelo: *Holy Family* (known as the Doni tondo, painted in 1504-5 for the marriage of Agnolo Doni). *Room XXVI.* Florentine Mannerists. Works by Cecchino Salviati, and A. Berruguete; works by Andrea del Sarto: *Banner of the Compagnia di S. Jacopo del Nibbio; Madonna of the Harpies* (signed and dated 1517); altarpiece and predella; *Portrait of a lady with a book;* works by Rosso Fiorentino: *Moses defending the daughters of Jethro* (c. 1520); *Portrait of a girl;* works by Pontormo: *Martyrdom of St Maurice; Portrait of a lady; The Expulsion from Paradise. Room XXVII.* Florentine Mannerists. Works by Pontormo: *Madonna and Child with saints. Portrait of a man;* portrait of the musician *Francesco dell'Ajolle; Charity,* (c. 1530), *Supper at Emmaus;* works by Rosso Fiorentino: *Putto playing the lute,* and *Madonna with Child and saints,* executed for the Arcispedale di S. Maria Nuova, also works by D. Beccafumi, Bachiacca, D. Puligo, Franciabigio and Jacopino del Conte. *Room XXVIII.* Titian and the Venetian masters of the 16th century. Works by Titian: *Venus of Urbino* (1538); Portrait of *Ludovico Beccadelli; Venus and Cupid;* portrait of *Francesco Maria della Rovere,* Duke of Urbino; *Knight of Malta; Flora. Room XXIX.* Parmigianino and the Emilian Mannerists. Works by Parmigianino: *Madonna with the long neck; Portrait of a man.* Other works by Garofalo, Dosso Dossi and Amico Aspertini. *Room XXX.* The Emilian school and Parmigianino. *Room XXXI. Witchcraft; Madonna in Glory with St Sebastian,* both by Dosso Dossi. *La Fornarina* (1512) by Sebastiano del Piombo, to whom *The Sick Man* (1514) is also attributed. *Portrait of a young man* (c. 1505) by Lorenzo Lotto. *Room XXXII.* Sebastiano del Piombo and other Venetian masters. *Death of Adonis* (1511-12) painted by Sebastiano del Piombo in Rome, under the influence of Raphael and Michelangelo. *Passage XXXIII.* Small paintings by various masters of the late 16th century. Works by Alessandro Allori, Ligozzi, Poppi and Bronzino. Portrait of *Francis I* by François Clouet. *Room XXXIV.* Veronese and other Venetian masters. Work by Veronese: *Martyrdom of St Justina,* an early work; *St Agatha; Esther and Ahasuerus.* Works by Moroni: portrait of *G. Antonio Pantera*: portrait of *Conte Pietro Secco Suardi* (signed and dated 1563); *Portrait of a man with a book. The Transfiguration* by Girolamo Savoldo; *Portrait of a man* (signed and dated 1546) by Tintoretto. *Room XXXV.* Tintoretto and Baroccio. Works by Tintoretto: *Leda* (a late work); portrait of *Jacopo Sansovino* (1566); *Portrait of an Admiral.* Works by Baroccio: *Noli me tangere,* (signed and dated 1590); portrait of *Francesco Maria II della Rovere; Madonna del Popolo* (1575). Room *XXXVI.* Caravaggio and works of the 17th and 18th centuries. Works by Caravaggio: *The young Bacchus,* a masterpiece of his early period; *Medusa* (after 1590); *Sacrifice of Isaac,* painted for Cardinal Maffeo Barberini (c. 1590). *Room XXXVII.* Rembrandt. Also Italian and Flemish works of the 16th and 17th centuries. Works by Rembrandt: *Self-portrait as an old man* (c. 1664); *Portrait of a Rabbi* (so-called, signed and dated 1658); *Self-portrait as a young man. Room XXXVIII.* 17th century. Works by Italian and foreign artists, including the *Erection of the statue of an emperor* by G. B. Tiepolo (c. 1726). *Room XXXIX.* Guardi and 17th-century Venetian paintings. Two views of Venice by Canaletto; *Landscape with a canal* and *Seashore with an arch* by F. Guardi. *Room XL.* Genre paintings by Giuseppe Maria Crespi. *Susanna and the Elders* by G. B. Piazzetta; *Gypsies* by Magnasco. *Room XLI.* Rubens. *Henri IV at the battle of Ivry; Henri IV's entry into Paris;* portrait of *Isabelle Brandt* (c. 1620); *Triumphal entrance of Ferdinand of Austria into Antwerp* (1635). *Room XLII,* called the 'Sala di Niobe', contains a temporary arrangement of 17th-century French painting, and the famous *Niobe* group discovered in Rome in 1583, and brought to Florence by Grand Duke Pietro Leopoldo. These statues are Roman copies of Hellenistic originals of the 3rd or 2nd century B.C. A staircase between *Room XXV* and *XXXIV* leads to the Vasari Corridor, connecting the Uffizi and the Palazzo Pitti with its famous collection of self-portraits. 36, 40, 47, 49, 52, 67, 111, 114, 116, 117, 118, *138, 140,* 145, 146, 147, 148, 149, *150,* 152, 157, 164, 166, 168, *174, 175,* 177, *196,* 198, 201, *204,* 217, 219, 235, 236.

Museo dell'Antica Casa Fiorentina
Palazzo Davanzati. Open in summer from 9.30 to 4.30, and in winter from 9.30 to 4. Sundays and public holidays from 9 to 1.

A collection of works of art and objects of use from various galleries and bequests, so arranged as to create the atmosphere of a wealthy Florentine house of bygone days.

Museo Archeologico Centrale dell'Etruria
Piazza SS. Annunziata 9 [GD]. Open in summer and winter from 9.30 to 4. Sundays and public holidays from 9.30 to 1. Closed on Mondays.
The museum is housed in the Palazzo della Crocetta, possibly built by Giulio Parigi for the Grand Duchess Maria Maddalena of Austria. The collections, which go back to the time of Cosimo il Vecchio and Lorenzo il Magnifico, were brought here in 1880. *Ground floor*: Greek, Etruscan and Roman sculpture, and *Museo Topografico della Etruria. First floor; Museo Egiziano,* Etruscan, Greek and Roman antiquities, *Gabinetto Numismatico* and *Collezione dei Preziosi. Second floor.* Prehistoric section, dealing with Etruscan contacts with Italy and the eastern Mediterranean, and containing terracottas, plaster casts and facsimiles of Etruscan painting. The vestibule gives access to the 'Sala delle Muse di Ferente', containing the collection of Greek, Etruscan and Roman sculpture. Montalvo sarcophagus with the *Death of Meleager* (from a Greek original of the 4th century B.C.); *Bonus Eventus,* marble statue of the Augustan age; *Artemis Laphria,* from a Greek original of the 5th century B.C.; sepulchral lion from the Agro di Tuscania, 4th or 3rd century B.C. *Museo Topografico dell'Etruria.* In a series of rooms are arranged objects of all kinds according to the locality where they were found. These provide some understanding of the Etruscan people, their country and their civilization. The best represented localities are Tarquinia, Tuscania, Vatulonia, Populonia and Chiusi. In the garden are tombs and monuments which have been reconstructed with the use of authentic materials. *Museo Egiziano* is on a par with that of Turin, these being the two most important Egyptian collections in Italy. The original nucleus of the museum is the Nizzoli collection. Later acquisitions came from the Tuscan expedition to Egypt under I. Rossellini in 1828, contemporary with the excavations carried out by Champollion and Schiaparelli. *First floor: Room I.* Statues and fragments: *Bust of a Pharaoh* of the 26th Dynasty (7th to 6th centuries B.C.) in red basalt. *Room II.* Reliefs. Relief of a tomb (18th Dynasty); relief with an artisan at work (663-

525 B.C.); polychrome relief of the *Goddess Hathor and Pharaoh Setis I* (19th dynasty, *c.* 1292 B.C.); relief with scribes (18th dynasty, *c.* 1400 B.C.). *Room III.* Sarcophagi, mummies, urns, papyri and inscribed tablets. *Portrait of a young woman. Rooms IV* and *V.* Sarcophagi, mummies, stelae and Coptic textiles. *Room VI.* Statuettes in limestone and wood. *Maid preparing beer,* and *Maid preparing flour* (6th dynasty). *Room VII.* Statuettes of divinities, amulets, scarabs and plants. *Room VIII.* Precious chariot of the time of Rameses II in perfect condition. Ceramics and other objects. *L'Antiquarium Etrusco-greco-roman* occupies *Rooms IX* to *XXII* on the first floor. Etruscan, Greek and Roman sculptures and bronzes. Outstanding exhibits are the *Idolino* in *Room XIII,* a rare Greek work of the Attico-Peloponnese school of the 5th century BC; *Chimaera wounded by Bellerophon,* 5th century, with an Etruscan inscription; *Orator,* funerary statue in the Etruscan style, 3rd century. *Rooms XVI-XVIII* contain the *Gabinetto Numismatico.* The collection of coins is divided into three groups: Medieval and modern Italian coins, especially those of Florence and Tuscany: Antique Italian coins: a selection of Roman coins of the Republic and the Empire arranged according to the iconography of the Emperors. The collection of precious stones occupies *Rooms XIX* and *XX* and includes gems, glass, gold and silver work, and a collection of carved precious stones including those of Lorenzo il Magnifico signed by famous Greek artists. The prehistoric section on the second floor (*Rooms I* and *II*) is devoted to finds made in various localities of Tuscany. *Rooms III-VI* contain objects found in parts of Italy outside Etruria. These are of use in the comparative study of Etruscan civilization. *Rooms VII-XV* contain vases and terracottas, arranged in chronological order. The vases come from various local and foreign places of manufacture. There are also architectural ceramics and clay figures from various Etruscan localities. *Room XI* contains the famous François vase painted by the Greek artist Klitias (6th century BC). Room *XVI* contains the collection of Etruscan plaster casts. *Room XVII* is devoted to reproductions of the most important Etruscan frescoes.

Museo Arcivescovile di Cestello
Lungarno Soderini 19 [HA]. *Open in summer from 6 to 7 and in winter from 4 to 5.*
The museum is housed in the Se-minario Maggiore, a former Cistercian monastery. The old refectory contains works of art from the whole diocese: furniture, early 14th-century wooden statues, precious manuscripts and choir books, a *Crucifixion* attributed to Lorenzo Monaco, a predella attributed to Paolo Uccello, and a *Crucifixion* by Giovanni di Francesco, formerly in S. Andrea a Brozzi.

Museo Bardini
Piazza dei Mozzi [JC]. *Open from 9 to 4. Sundays and public holidays from 9 to 12.*
Donated by the antiquarian Stefano Bardini to the Municipality of Florence in 1923. It contains sculptures, paintings, tapestries, weapons and works of decorative art of various periods. Amalgamated with the Galleria Corsi, donated to the Municipality in 1937. 236.

Museo di 'Firenze com'era'
Via S. Egidio 21 [HD]. *Open in summer and winter from 10 to 4. Sundays and holidays from 10 to 12.*
This comprises eight rooms on the first floor of the former Convento delle Oblate. It contains paintings, drawings, prints and photographs of Florence, from the 15th century to the present day. 230.

Museo della Fondazione Horne
Via dei Benci 6. Open on Mondays and Thursdays from 10 to 1 and 3 to 5. Closed in September.
The Palazzetto Horne belonged originally to the Alberti, and then to the Corsi who had it rebuilt in the 15th century. It has been attributed to Giuliano da Sangallo. The building, together with the collection of pictures and other works of art, furnishing etc., was bequeathed to the state by the Englishman Herbert Percy Horne. Among its notable works are: *First floor, Room A. Madonna and angels,* stucco tondo attributed to Luca della Robbia; *Room B. Madonna* in polychrome stucco by Rossellino; *Holy Family* by Beccafumi; *Room C.* Decorative Florentine furniture of the 15th and 16th centuries. *Room D. Allegory of music* by Dosso Dossi; part of a polyptych with *Three saints* by P. Lorenzetti; diptych by Bernardo Daddi with *Crucifixion, Madonna and saints; St Stephen* by Giotto. *Room E. Esther* by Filippino Lippi. *Room F. St Julian,* part of a predella attributed to Masaccio. *Second Floor. Room G.* Collection of drawings by Italian and foreign masters of the 15th to the 19th centuries. 152, 172, 236.

Museo Mediceo
Via Cavour 1 [GC]. *Open summer*

and winter 9 to 1 and 3 to 5.30. Sundays and public holidays 9 to 12. The museum occupies four rooms in the Palazzo Medici-Riccardi. *Room I.* Medici tapestries on cartoons by Stradano (1569-70) and a painting of the *Arrival of Charles VIII. Room II.* Medici portraits. Paintings of the Medici castles of Cafaggiolo and Trebbio by Justus Utens (1599) in the large lunettes. The present passage was once Lorenzo's writing room. It contains an important *Madonna and Child* by Filippino Lippi (*c.* 1450). *Room III.* Small portraits painted by Bronzino for Cosimo I; death mask of Lorenzo. *Room IV.* Notable portraits including: *Cosimo I as a youth* by Pontormo; *Cosimo I as a boy* by Ridolfo Ghirlandaio; small portraits of the sons of Cosimo I painted from life by Bronzino; a rare portrait of *Bianca Cappello* by A. Allori. The courtyard gives access to the chapel, a work of Michelozzo (*see* Palazzo Medici, p. 19). 114.

Museo Nazionale, or **Museo del Bargello** - *see also* **Palazzo del Podestà** *Via del Proconsolo 4* [HC]. *Open in summer from 9.30 to 4.30, and in winter from 9.30 to 4. Sundays and holidays from 9 to 1. Closed on Tuesdays.*
One of the most important museums in Italy, set up in 1859 by the provisional city government to house works of art from the Uffizi and elsewhere. It contains works by Donatello, the della Robbias, Michelangelo, the Carrand collection of minor works, the Ressman collection of weapons and the Franchetti collection of textiles. *Ground floor, Room I.* The cannon of St Paul, made for Ferdinando II by the Florentine Cosimo Cenni; the cannon known as Il Falcone, also by Cenni, made for Cosimo II in 1620. Armour and weapons of the 9th to 17th centuries, including the famous suit of 16th-century Milanese armour, said to have been that of Charles V. *Room II.* Italian and foreign fire-arms of the 18th and 19th centuries. Courtyard with arcades on three sides, an open staircase on the fourth side (1345-67) and an octagonal well in the centre. Coats of arms on the walls of successive Podestà, and Giudici di Ruota. The second storey has trilobate Gothic windows. Among the statues in the arcade are Ammannati's *Allegory of the Earth* and *Allegory of Temperance* from the Boboli Gardens; the *Oceanus* (formerly in the Boboli gardens) and *Virtue conquering Vice* (1570), both by Giambologna. *Sala del Trecento.* Florentine

sculpture of the 14th century including *Madonna and Child* by Tino da Camaino, and holy water font of the school of Nicola Pisano. *Sala di Michelangelo.* Two marble niches by Benedetto da Rovezzano. *Brutus* (*c.* 1540) by Michelangelo, carved, according to Vasari, after the death of Lorenzino de' Medici, the murderer of Duke Alessandro; *Madonna and Child with the infant St John,* tondo (1504); *David,* begun in 1531 for Baccio Valori; *Drunken Bacchus,* carved in Rome in 1497/99. *First floor.* In the Verone or Loggia, sculptures by Giambologna, including his famous *Mercury* (*c.* 1540). The Salone del Consiglio Generale, also called the Salone di Donatello; *St George* (1416), formerly in Or San Michele, by Donatello; *David* in bronze (1430), made for Cosimo il Vecchio by Donatello. Bust of a woman, bust of a boy, and *Madonna and Child,* bas-relief by Desiderio da Settignano; *St Bernardino,* wooden statue by Vecchietta; *Sacrifice of Isaac,* bronze panel by Ghiberti, submitted for the competition for the door of the Baptistry (1401); *Sacrifice of Isaac* by Brunelleschi, executed for the same purpose as Ghiberti's; panels and sculptures by Luca della Robbia, including the *Madonna del Roseto* (*c.* 1460). The *Collezione Carrand* occupies seven rooms. Sala della Torre. Tapestries and carpets. Salone del Podestà, or Salone del Duca d'Atene. Gold and enamelwork, arranged in chronological order. Cappella del Podestà, or Cappella di S. Maddalena. Rectangular, barrel-vaulted, decorated with frescoes attributed by some to Giotto. Illuminated missals; a rare portable Byzantine ikon of the 11th century; 15th-century inlaid stalls and reading desk; in the sacristy, precious materials and embroideries of the 11th to the 16th centuries, and two 15th-century paintings. Sala degli Avori. Polychrome wooden statues of the 14th and 15th centuries of the Umbrian, Marchigian and Sienese schools. The ivories are Byzantine, Mesopotamian, Sicilian-Arabic, Moorish, Roman, Carolingian, Romanesque and Gothic, Italian, German, French and Flemish. Sala delle Oreficerie. Chalices, processional crosses, monstrances, thuribles, reliquaries, including a 15th-century Tuscan reliquary bust of St Ignatius, patriarch of Constantinople. Precious copes and dalmatics. Sala delle Maioliche. Majolica ware from Florence, Siena, Faenza, Urbino and other Italian factories of the 15th and 16th centuries, including parts of a service made for Guidobaldo II della Rovere by Orazio Fontana. *Sec-*

ond floor. Sala di Giovanni della Robbia e del Cellini. Enamelled terracottas by Giovanni della Robbia, including a *Madonna and Child with the infant St John,* tondo framed in flowers and fruit; works by Cellini: *Ganymede riding the eagle* in bronze, and *Ganymede,* an antique marble statue of Apollo restored by Cellini; models for the *Perseus; Narcissus, Apollo and Hyacinth,* formerly in the Boboli gardens; colossal bust of Cosimo I, one of his best works; *Perseus rescuing Andromeda,* bronze relief for the base of the *Perseus* in the Loggia dei Lanzi. Sala di Andrea della Robbia. Glazed terracottas including the *Madonna of the Architects* (1475) and the *Madonna of the pillow*; also the *Madonna and Child with the infant St John,* polychrome stucco by Antonio Rossellino. Sala del Verrocchio. Bust of *Battista Sforza,* Duchess of Urbino, by Francesco Laurana; works by Mino da Fiesole: Portrait of *Rinaldo della Luna,* signed and dated 1461; *Madonna and Child,* bas-relief tondo (*c.* 1481); tabernacle. Works by Rossellino: bust of *Francesco Sassetti* (1464); *Madonna and Child with angels,* polychrome stucco; *Adoration of Christ,* marble tondo (*c.* 1470); bust of *Matteo Palmieri,* signed and dated 1468. *Young soldier,* possibly a portrait of Giuliano de' Medici, and *Hercules and Anteus* by Pollaiuolo. Works by Verrocchio: bust of *Piero di Lorenzo de' Medici*; the *Resurrection* (terracotta relief formerly in the Arcispedale di S. Maria Nuova (*c.* 1480); *Death of Francesca Pitti Tornabuoni,* relief for her tomb in S. Maria Novella; *David,* bronze executed for the villa at Careggi. Sala del Camino, or Sala del Sansovino. This is dominated by the great fireplace made by Benedetto da Rovezzano for the Casa Borgherini. The frieze is carved with the story of Croesus and Cyrus and contains statues of the 16th and 17th centuries. Works by Sansovino: *Madonna and Child,* relief in polychrome papier mâché; bronze tabernacle; *Bacchus,* inspired by the antique and executed before 1520. Other works of art include a portrait of *Costanza Bonarelli* by Gian Lorenzo Bernini, and 16th-century Tuscan candelabra. Sala dei Bronzi. A collection of small bronzes of different schools and periods. Sala della Torre. Italian tapestries and textiles of the 15th and 17th centuries. Alongside the Salone del Verrocchio, two small rooms contain the Medici collection of medals. This is the richest collection of ancient and modern Italian medals. *46, 70, 72, 77, 81, 118,* 120, 129, 130, *135, 145, 147, 149,* 164, *166,* 181, 184, *186,* 192, 205, *207, 233,* 236.

Museo Nazionale di Storia della Scienza
Piazza dei Giudici 1 [JC]. *Open from 9 to 1.*
A collection made in 1930 of instruments and scientific objects in the old Medici collections (formerly on view in the Tribuna di Galileo and the observatory near the Museo Zoologico), from the Arcispedale di S. Maria Nuova and various other bequests.

Museo dell'Opera del Duomo
Piazza del Duomo 9 [HC]. *Open in summer from 10 to 1 and from 3 to 6, and in winter from 10 to 4. Sundays and public holidays 10 to 1.*
A collection of works of art and church furnishings from the Duomo, the Baptistry and the Campanile. The Vestibule contains marble bas-reliefs with figures of saints and prophets by Baccio Bandinelli, originally in the choir of the Duomo. The Sala dell'antica facciata del Duomo has a collection of fragments from the façade of 1587, including the *Madonna and Child, S. Reparata, Madonna of the Nativity* and a statue of *Boniface VIII* by Arnolfo di Cambio; also designs of the old façade. In the Ottagono delle oreficerie are precious reliquaries of the 13th to the 18th centuries. The Sala delle Cantorie contains the two choir galleries by Luca della Robbia (1433-39), formerly under the dome of the Cathedral; also the sixteen statues which once stood in the niches of the Campanile, including the *Habakkuk* (known as the 'Zuccone') by Donatello. The Sala dell'Altare contains the famous Gothic-Renaissance altar from the Baptistry, of gilded and enamelled silver; also the silver cross by Betto Betti, Antonio Pollaiuolo and M. Dei; intarsia picture of *S. Zanobi* by Giuliano de Maiano; twenty-seven panels embroidered in silver and gold (1466-80) designed by Antonio Pollaiuolo; a statuette of *Christ blessing* by Andrea Pisano; a 12th-century gospel cover, possibly from Constantinople. In the Sala dei Modelli is the model for the lantern, possibly made by Brunelleschi himself; also early projects and wooden models for the Duomo. 31, *51,* 75, *82,* 87, 88, *116,* 120, *133,* 145.

Museo dell'Opera di S. Croce
Piazza S. Croce 16 [JD]. *Open in summer from 9 to 12 and 3 to 6, and in winter from 10 to 12 and 3 to 5. Sundays and public holidays from 10 to 12.*

The museum is arranged in the old refectory of the convent of S. Croce. It is decorated with fine frescoes of Taddeo Gaddi, and contains paintings and sculptures, some of which come from the church and the convent. *Room I. Crucifixion* by Cimabue, badly damaged in the floods of 1966; fragments of the fresco of the *Triumph of death* by Orcagna; *St Louis*, bronze by Donatello (1423), designed for Or San Michele; *SS. John Baptist and Francis*, fresco by Domenico Veneziano; *Coronation of the Virgin* by Maso di Banco, *Deposition* by Taddeo Gaddi. *Room III* is the old Cappella Canigiano, a Gothic building altered in the Renaissance. It contains the *Stigmata of St Francis*, and *Tobias and the angel*, glazed terracotta altarpiece by Andrea della Robbia. *Room IV* contains one of Bronzino's masterpieces, the *Christ in Limbo* (1552). 114.

Museo di S. Marco, or Museo dell'Angelico

Piazza S. Marco [GC]. *Open in summer from 9.30 to 4.30, and in winter from 9.30 to 4. Sundays and public holidays from 9 to 1. Closed on Mondays.*

The convent of S. Marco was rebuilt and enlarged by Michelozzo (1437-52) in a harmonious Renaissance style that preserves the monastic character of the building. The plain exterior is pierced with small windows, and the interior surrounds an arcaded cloister. The building houses about a hundred works of art, including frescoes and pictures by Beato Angelico. The vestibule leads into the Chiostro di S. Antonino, by Michelozzo, which is closed in between the church, the refectory, the guest-house and the chapter room. There are 17th-century frescoed lunettes beneath the arcade, including some by Poccetti. The guest house (Ospizio dei Pellegrini) is a rectangular hall and now contains pictures by Angelico which were formerly in different churches in Florence. These include the *Linaiuoli tabernacle* (1433); the *S. Marco altarpiece*, formerly in the convent church, and two episodes from the lives of *SS. Cosmas and Damian*, parts of a predella; *Deposition* (*c.* 1435) formerly in S. Trinita; a series of small paintings of the *Life of the Virgin* (*c.* 1433-35) done with the delicacy of a miniaturist; the *Last Judgment* (*c.* 1430), formerly in S. Maria Nuova. The Sala del Lavabo, with *Madonna and saints* by Fra Bartolomeo, leads to the large Refectory which contains, among other works, the *Last Judgment*, a detached fresco by Fra Bartolomeo (1499-

1501). The Chapter Room contains a fresco of the *Crucifixion* by Angelico, an impressive composition featuring a number of the saints connected with the founding of religious orders. On the first floor is the dormitory, which occupies the three sides of the Chiostro di S. Antonino. It is divided into cells opening onto a corridor, which were frescoed by Angelico and his assistants between 1439 and 1445. Among the most famous of these are: *Jesus appearing to Mary Magdalen*; the *Annunciation*; the *Transfiguration*; the *Coronation of Mary*. The Prior's quarters, where Girolamo Savonarola lived, contain a portrait of him by Fra Bartolomeo, also other frescoes. Savonarola's study has a collection of his writings, and objects that he used. Among the frescoes in the cells of the novitiate are the *Baptism of Christ* and *Madonna and child enthroned with saints*. The cells of Cosimo contain the *Epiphany*, executed in collaboration with Benozzo Gozzoli. The library is a very elegant building by Michelozzo (1444). Returning to the ground floor one comes to the small refectory which contains the *Last Supper*, a large fresco by Domenico Ghirlandaio. The adjacent Chiostro di S. Domenico is also by Michelozzo, with Ionic capitals supporting the arcade. 111, 117, 230.

Museo Stibbert

Via Stibbert 26. Open in summer and winter from 9 to 4. Sundays and public holidays from 9 to 12.

An important collection of works of art of various kinds, but especially weapons of every provenance and period. The Villa Stibbert was formerly the Villa Davanzati. 236.

Museo Zoologico

Palazzo Torrigiani.

Founded by Grand Duke Pietro Leopoldo in 1775, it is now closed to the public due to re-arrangement.

Pinacoteca dello Spedale degli Innocenti

Piazza SS. Annunziata, 12 [GD]. *Open in summer from 9 to 1 and 3 to 6, and in winter from 9 to 12 and from 2 to 5.*

Room I. Paintings by major Tuscan artists of the 16th and 17th centuries, and illuminated antiphonals. *Room II. Adoration of the Magi* (1488) by Domenico Ghirlandaio. *Room III. Madonna and saints* by Piero di Cosimo and *Madonna of the Innocents* (1450-55) relief in white terracotta by Luca della Robbia. *Room IV.* Portraits, manuscripts and autographs.

Uffizi - *see* Galleria degli

Historic Buildings and Churches

Arciconfraternita della Misericordia
Piazza del Duomo [HC].
An institution originally dedicated to free medical care. The present site was occupied in 1576, and altered soon after by Alfonso Parigi. Further alterations were made in the 18th century. It contains numerous works of art, especially in the Stanzone dei Capi di Guardia.

Arcispedale di S. Maria Nuova
Piazza S. Maria Nuova [HD].
Founded in 1287, it is the oldest hospital in Florence. The design of the façade and of the right wing is attributed to Bernardo Buontalenti. The portico decorated with busts of the Medici was added by Giulio Parigi (1611-18). 30, 111, 117, 130, 145, 168.

Badia Fiesolana
This was originally the cathedral of Fiesole. It was taken over by the Benedictines, and later by the Augustinians of the Lateran. It was enlarged under Cosimo il Vecchio by Brunelleschi. The original Romanesque façade can be traced stylistically to that of S. Miniato. The interior has the typical harmony of Brunelleschi. In the sacristy there is an elaborate marble lavabo of the 15th century. Renaissance cloister with a vestibule leading into the refectory, which has a large fresco by Giovanni da S. Giovanni (1629) of *Christ served by the angels*. 16, 109.

Badia Fiorentina
Via del Proconsolo and via Dante Alighieri [HC].
Benedictine church founded in the 10th century, altered in the Cistercian style in the 13th century and completely transformed during the Baroque period (1627). The hexagonal pointed campanile is of special note, with its four orders of coupled windows, Romanesque (1310) and Gothic (1330). The porch and vestibule with Corinthian columns are both by Benedetto da Rovezzano (1495). The interior is of the Greek cross design, and contains among other works of art the *Apparition of the Madonna to St Bernard* by Filippino Lippi (1480) and the tomb of Count Ugo by Mino da Fiesole (1469-70). In the left transept (corresponding originally to the principal chapel) there are fragments of frescoes, recently discovered, with episodes from the life of the Virgin by Giotto and his assistants. In the apse there are inlayed choir stalls by Francesco and Marco del Tasso (1501). In the Chiostro degli Aranci (15th century) there are tombstones of Florentine families from the 13th century onwards on the lower part of the walls, and frescoes of the life of St Benedict on the upper part. The Pandolfini chapel is also by Benedetto da Rovezzano. 12, 26, 30, 40, 47, 130, 152, 172, 218.

Badia di S. Salvatore a Settimo
Strada statale 67, Tosco-Romagnola (10.4 km from the centre of Florence).
First mentioned in the 10th century, it was originally surrounded by a wall with towers which also enclosed the church of SS. Salvatore e Lorenzo. It originally belonged to the Cluniac Benedictines, and later to the Cistercians who owned it until 1782. It was badly damaged during the last war. The church has been restored and the campanile entirely rebuilt. Wide Romanesque façade, three-aisle nave with open timber roof, and apse in the style of Brunelleschi. In the choir there is a marble tabernacle attributed to Giuliano da Maiano. In the Capella di S. Quintino to the left of the high altar, frescoes by Giovanni di S. Giovanni (1629) and valuable reliquaries. Interesting 11th-century sarcophagus in the Cappella di S. Jacopo. From the small courtyard behind the church one can see a small 15th-century cloister and a 14th-century building with pointed arches. In the actual monastery there is a laybrothers' hall (Sala dei Conversi) which is a fine example of Cistercian architecture, also a chapter room.

Baptistry
Piazza del Duomo and Piazza S. Giovanni [HC].
There is some controversy as to the date when this building was begun. The 5th, the 11th and the 12th centuries have all been suggested. It occupies the site of a 1st-century building, possibly the Praetorium, some of the materials of which are incorporated in the building. It is octagonal in design, with a revetment of geometrically shaped slabs

of white and green marble, a pilaster course surmounted by a pediment and rounded arcade. The attic is 13th century, covered by a pyramidal roof with pointed lantern which hides the cupola. The Baptistry is famed for its three doors of gilt bronze. The south door is by Andrea Pisano, and the north and east doors are by Lorenzo Ghiberti. The south door was modelled in 1330 and is divided into twenty-eight panels. The upper series depicts the life of John the Baptist, and the lower one the Virtues. The decoration of the door-jambs is by Vittorio Ghiberti, the son of Lorenzo. The north door was the first to be put up (1403-24) and it was done in collaboration with Donatello and Paolo Uccello. This also contains twenty-eight panels with episodes from the New Testament, evangelists and doctors of the church. The east door, which Michelangelo called the 'Door of Paradise', is Ghiberti's masterpiece. He was assisted here by his two sons, and by Michelozzo, Benozzo Gozzoli and others. It is divided into ten panels showing biblical episodes, and these are framed by twenty-four small statues of sibyls and prophets linked together by portrait heads in round frames, one of which is a self-portrait of Ghiberti. The *Baptism of Christ* on the pediment is by Andrea Sansovino. The interior walls are divided into two orders, the upper one pierced by the windows of the gallery. Alterations carried out in the 16th and 18th centuries are clearly discernible. Among the many fine works of art are a baptismal font of the school of Pisano (1371), the tomb of the anti-pope John XXIII by Donatello and Michelozzo, and a wooden statue of the *Magdalen* also by Donatello (1435-55) by the side of the tribune. The mosaics of the dome were done in the 13th and 14th centuries, possibly by Venetian artists, after cartoons by Florentine painters including Cimabue and Coppo di Mercovaldo, the latter probably being responsible for the design of the *Last Judgment*. 15, 16, *26*, *31*, 36, 49, 56, 67, 70, 72, 93, 105, 107, 129, 145, 169, 218.

Bargello - *see* Palazzo del Podestà

Biblioteca Mediceo Laurenziana
Piazza S. Lorenzo 9 [GC]. *Open in summer from 8 to 2, and in winter from 10 to 4. Closed Saturdays at 1.*
Michelangelo was commissioned for the design of the library in 1524 by Clement VII, and it was completed in 1578. It consists of a hall (known as the ricetto) with two orders. The walls are treated in a sculptural

manner, with a powerful articulation of architectural elements. The monumental staircase was designed by Michelangelo but carried out by Ammannati. It gives access to a rectangular hall, grandiose and austere in character, with a wooden ceiling and benches with reading desks, also designed by Michelangelo. Founded by Cosimo I and augmented by Lorenzo di Medici, the library houses valuable manuscripts and illuminated liturgical books. 180, 182, 219.

Boboli Gardens - *see* Giardino di Boboli

Borgo degli Albizi
From via Giuseppe Verdi to via del Proconsolo
Important buildings: Palazzo Nonfinito (q.v.); No. 28, Palazzo Vitali (formerly dei Pazzi) by Bartolomeo Ammannati; No. 26, Palazzo Matteucci Ramirez di Montalvo, also by Ammannati (1568); No. 18, Palazzo Altoviti (formerly Albizi) and later Valori and Guicciardini; No. 12, Palazzo degli Albizi (early 16th century). The Albizi were rivals of the Medici. No. 15, Palazzo degli Alessandri (14th century). No. 11, 16th-century house with a bust of Cosimo II by Fancelli and a high medieval tower. It belonged to the Donati, who also owned the house with overhanging eaves and the tall 13th-century towered house that stand near the entrance to via Palmieri. 12, 22, 136, 184.

Cappelle Medicee
Piazza Madonna degli Aldobrandini [GC]. *Open from March to October from 9 to 5, November to February from 9 to 4. Sundays and public holidays from 9.30 to 12.30.*
These are the Cappella dei Principi adjoining the presbytery of S. Lorenzo, and the Sagrestia Nuova, commissioned by Leo X as a mausoleum chapel for the Medici. The Cappella dei Principi is a sumptuous Baroque building on an octagonal plan with a dome. It is decorated with precious marbles and gilt bronze, and contains the six tombs of the Grand Dukes of Tuscany. The New Sacristy, so-called for its being the companion to Brunelleschi's Sacristy, was begun by Michelangelo in 1520 and finished by Vasari in 1557. It is square in plan, with a dome, and its architecture is designed to emphasize the tombs. Michelangelo designed the tomb of Lorenzo II, Duke of Urbino, with its statues of *Dawn* and *Dusk*, and that of Giuliano, Duke of Nemours, with the statues of *Day* and *Night*. For the third tomb, which was to receive the body of Lorenzo il Magnifico, Michelan-

gelo produced only the unfinished group of the *Madonna and Child*. *178, 180.*

Cappella de' Pazzi
Entrance alongside the church of S. Croce [JD]. *Open in summer from 9 to 12 and from 3 to 6, and in winter from 10 to 12 and from 3 to 5. Sundays and public holidays, 10 to 12.*

Designed by Brunelleschi and begun in 1430 for Andrea de' Pazzi, this is one of the finest examples of Renaissance architecture. It consists of a pronaos of Corinthian columns surmounted by an attic in the centre of which there is a large arch corresponding to the one at the entrance of the chapel. On the pediment there is a frieze with cherubims' heads by Desiderio da Settignano. The rose design in the atrium is by Luca della Robbia, also the tondo with St Andrew over the carved wooden door, which is by Giuliano da Maiano (1472). The walls of the rectangular interior are divided up by pietra serena pilasters. Flat dome with a lantern, and small square presbytery with a small dome in which there is a window attributed to Alessio Baldovinetti. The frieze with medallions of apostles is the work of Luca della Robbia. *89, 92, 96, 130.*

Cappella Rucellai
Via della Spada [HB] (*now connected to the neighbouring church of S. Pancrazia*).

This chapel contains the Edicola del Santo Sepolcro, a tempietto modelled on the Holy Sepulchre at Jerusalem. It was designed by Leon Battista Alberti, for Giovanni Rucellai, in 1467. *105, 129.*

Carmine, or S. Maria del Carmine
Piazza del Carmine [JA].

The Romanesque-Gothic church was destroyed by fire in 1771, and only the façade and the Brancacci and Corsini chapels were saved. It was rebuilt a few years later. It is built on the Latin cross plan with a single nave, and side chapels. The decoration is Baroque. The Cappella Brancacci (to the right of the crossing) is famous for its cycle of frescoes with scenes from the life of St Peter, and the *Original Sin*, begun by Masolino (1424-25), continued by Masaccio (1426-27) and finished by Filippino Lippi (1484-85). Masolino is responsible for the upper frescoes on the right: *Temptation of Adam and Eve*, *St Peter curing the cripple and bringing Tabitha back to life*. Also the *Preaching of St Peter*, lower down to the left of the altar. Masaccio painted the *Expulsion from Paradise* on the upper part of the left wall. This is Masaccio's masterpiece, and it inspired Raphael and Michelangelo. His *Payment of the Tribute Money* is a scene of lively and complex realism in which he finds some interesting solutions to problems of perspective. His *Distribution of the Goods of the Community* is on the lower part of the back wall, to the right. *St Peter healing the sick with his shadow* is on the left. *St Peter enthroned* and *St Peter restoring the son of Theophilus*, on the lower part of the left wall, were completed by Lippi. The choir vault was painted in the 18th century, and the monument in the choir is that of Pier Soderini by Benedetto da Rovezzano. The Cappella di S. Andrea Corsini (to the left of the crossing) is a sumptuous design of Pier Francesco Silvani (1675-83). In the cupola a fresco by Luca Giordano depicts the saint's apotheosis. *76, 78, 81, 81, 114, 172, 218.*

Casa di Bianca Cappello, formerly dei Corbinelli
Via Maggio, 26 [JB].

A good example of a nobleman's house, altered by Buontalenti (*c.* 1570-74) for the Grand Duke Francesco I.

Casa Buonarroti
Via Ghibellina, 70

The house was bought by Michelangelo for his nephew Leonardo, and decorated by his grand-nephew Michelangiolo il Giovane. It is now a museum. In the courtyard there is a headless statue by Arnolfo di Cambio, from the original façade of the Duomo. The Galleria Buonarroti is on the first floor (*open summer 9.30 to 4, Sundays and holidays 9 to 1, closed on Tuesdays*). In *Room 1* there are works of Michelangelo which include the marble bas-relief of the *Madonna and Child* (1490-92) and the *Battle between the Lapiths and Centaurs* (*c.* 1492), two of his important early works. In *Room 3* there is a statue of Michelangelo, and paintings, of scenes from his life, of the 17th century. *Room 4*, the study of Michelangiolo il Giovane, contains his bust. *Room 5* contains a *Holy Family* designed by Pietro da Cortona. In *Room 6* there are portraits of famous Italians. *Room 7* contains a della Robbia canephorus. In *Room 8* there is a wooden model for the façade of S. Lorenzo, and in *Room 9* portraits and paintings by artists of various periods. *Room 10* contains portraits of Michelangelo, and his own manuscripts. *162, 164, 167, 180, 181, 181, 236.*

Cascine
A large public park extending 3 km. along the right bank of the Arno to the confluence of the Mugnone. It takes its name from the old Medici farms. 232, 233.

Casino di S. Marco
Via Cavour, 63
Now Palazzo della Corte d'Appello, built by Bernardo Buontalenti in 1574 for Francesco I. The courtyard, with a fountain and statue of the school of Giambologna, was originally the 'Giardino di S. Marco' where the Medici had their sculpture collection, which was visited and studied by the principal artists of the Renaissance. 164.

Cenacolo di Foligno
Via Faenza 42 [GB]. *Open from April to September from 9 to 12 and from 3 to 6, and from October to March from 10 to 4.*
Originally the refectory of the convent of S. Onofrio, which belonged to the Franciscan nuns of Foligno. The fresco of the *Last Supper* is one of Pietro Perugino's finest works (1490).

Cenacolo del Ghirlandaio
Borgo Ognissanti, 42 [HB]. *Open in summer from 7.30 to 12.30 and from 1.30 to 8, and in winter from 8 to 12.30 and from 1.30 to 7.*
Originally the refectory of the convent of Ognissanti, with a fresco of the *Last Supper* by Domenico Ghirlandaio (1480).

Cenacolo di S. Apollonia e Museo di Andrea del Castagno
Via XVII Aprile, 1 [GC]. *Open summer and winter from 9 to 12, and from 2 to 6. Sundays and public holidays 9 to 12.*
Some of the most important works of Andrea del Castagno are to be seen in the former convent of S. Apollonia. In the refectory are his *Last Supper* (*c.* 1450), a *Crucifixion*, *Deposition* and *Resurrection*, episodes from the life of S. Eustachio (1462), a group of frescoes from the Villa Pandolfini at Legnaia showing portrait-figures, a *Crucifixion with Madonna and saints*, a large lunette from S. Maria Nuova, and a *Pietà*. 118.

Cenacolo di S. Salvi
Via Andrea del Sarto, 16. Open in summer from 9.30 to 4.30, and in winter from 9.30 to 4. Sundays and public holidays from 9 to 1.
This is the old refectory of the Abbazia. Beyond the gallery containing altarpieces of the Florentine school, there is the Sala del Lavabo, with bas-reliefs by Benedetto da Rovezzano. The *Last Supper* in the refec-

tory is a masterpiece by Andrea del Sarto (1519). 168.

Cenacolo di S. Spirito
Piazza S. Spirito, 26 [JB]. *Open summer and winter from 9 to 1. Sundays and public holidays 9 to 12.*
In the refectory of the old Augustinian convent there are some important frescoes by Andrea Orcagna, who was assisted here by his brother, Nardo di Cione (*c.* 1360). The subjects are the *Crucifixion* and the *Last Supper*. The building is occupied by the Fondazione Salvatore Romano, whose collection contains Romanesque sculptures by Tino da Camaino, Jacopo della Quercia, and others of the school of Donatello.

Certosa del Galluzzo
Strada statale 2, via Cassia, dopo il Ponte sull'Ema. Open from November to February from 9 to 12 and from 2 to 4, and in summer from 9 to 12 and 2 to 6, except May to August when it is open until 7.30.
Begun in 1342, later enlarged and restored since the war, it belongs to the Cistercians. The Palazzo degli Studi, of pietra viva with single arched Gothic windows, was founded by Niccolò Acciaiuoli as a school for teaching the liberal arts to boys. The interior is of the 14th century. In the Pinacoteca on the first floor are some fine works. Five large lunettes in fresco by Pontormo (1522-25) formerly in the main cloister. *Madonna and Child with the infant St John* by Lucas Cranach (1514), *SS. Francis and Jerome* with an *Annunciation* above them, from a polyptych attributed to Masolino or possibly by the young Angelico. The church of S. Lorenzo has a late Renaissance façade, much restored during the last century. The interior is divided into two parts, in the Carthusian style. In the front part, the lay-brothers' choir, there is a chapel of the Madonna in the form of a Greek cross. In the monks' choir, three spans with cross vaults and Gothic pilasters, carved and inlaid stalls of the late 16th century. Fine cupboards of the 18th century in the Sacristy and a chapel for the relics with frescoes by Poccetti. A staircase leads down to the underground chapels which include a chapel of St Andrew with the tomb of Cardinal Agnolo Acciaiuoli (1409) once attributed to Donatello but possibly by Francesco da Sangallo. A visit to the convent begins with the parlour with its 16th-century stained glass, then follow the 16th-century middle cloister, the chapter room with a tomb by Francesco da Sangallo (1545) and fresco by Mariotto

Albertinelli (1506). Then comes the great cloister with relief busts by Andrea and Giovanni della Robbia, the refectory with 15th-century pulpit, and the small cloister in the style of Brunelleschi. There is also a guesthouse which has given hospitality to many famous people, and a pharmacy where the monks sell their liqueurs. *12, 177.*

Chiostri di S. Maria Novella
Piazza di S. Maria Novella [HB]. *Open in summer from 9 to 6, and in winter from 9 to 4. Sundays and public holidays from 9 to 12.*
The Chiostro Verde, so called from its frescoes in terra verde, is Romanesque with large, slightly flattened arches. The walls were frescoed by Paolo Uccello, illustrating the book of Genesis. To avoid deterioration, these frescoes are now on view in the refectory and the entrance to the refectory. Particularly impressive are the *Flood* and the *Sacrifice of Noah*, with their dramatic quality and surprising perspective. A passage from the refectory leads to the Chiostro Grande, with frescoes of the late 16th century. The old library is on the ground floor, and the Cappella dei Papi, with frescoes by Pontormo (1515) is on the first floor. The north side of the Chiostro Verde leads into the Cappellone degli Spagnuoli. This is the old convent chapel, built by I Talenti after 1350, and put to the use of Eleonora da Toledo's Spanish retainers in 1540. The interior is rectangular with pointed arches, and is entirely frescoed by Andrea da Firenze and his assistants (*c.* 1355). The subject matter is taken from the 'Specchio della vera penitenza', a work by I Passavanti who was prior of the convent. It is one of the most interesting cycles of 14th-century Tuscan art. Behind the chapel is the Chiostrino dei Morti with its tombs, and to the left the Cappella funeraria degli Strozzi, with frescoes recently attributed to Andrea Orcagna. 116.

Chiostro della Scalzo
Via Cavour, 69. Open summer and winter from 9 to 12 and from 2 to 4. Sundays and public holidays 9 to 12.
Courtyard with portico of the early 16th century, and frescoes by Andrea del Sarto (1514-26) on the life of St John the Baptist.

Convento di S. Maria Maddalena
Via Faentina
Originally a hospice of the Dominicans, now a convent. 15th-century building recently restored, and famous for its frescoes by Fra Bartolomeo.

Duomo (S. Maria del Fiore)
Piazza del Duomo [HC].
The building was begun in 1296 by Arnolfo di Cambio, on the site of the cathedral of S. Reparata. Recent critics affirm that Arnolfo's original design was considerably different from the final construction. After an interruption of several decades, the work was continued under Giotto's direction, and after his death a more elaborate design was submitted by Francesco Talenti and Lapo Ghini (1357). The dome, which is a daring work by Brunelleschi, was finished in 1434. The ensemble gives an impression of unity, despite the variety of styles in its various parts. The exterior is basically Romanesque, the interior Gothic, the dome is pure Renaissance, and the façade (designed by E. de Fabris) is of the 19th century. The oldest part of the church is the portion on the left side where the door opens onto the Campanile, with statues of *Gabriel* and the *Virgin Annunciate* attributed to Niccolò Lamberti. Next to this door is the Porta dei Canonici of the late 14th century. From the back of the cathedral with its three large Gothic arched tribunes, there is a good view of the high drum and the octagonal dome covered in red tiles between marble ribs, and the lantern in the form of a tempietto. The Renaissance gallery over the drum is by Baccio d'Agnolo, and because of criticism by Michelangelo, it was left unfinished. On the left side of the Duomo, the Renaissance Porta della Mandorla is surmounted by an *Assumption* in a mandorla by Nanni di Antonio di Banco (1414-21). The pinnacles at the sides support prophets attributed to Donatello. The *Annunciation* in the lunette is by Domenico and Davide del Ghirlandaio (1491). The dimensions of the interior are impressive (length 153 m., width of the aisles 38 m. and of the transept 90 m.). It is built on the Latin cross plan, with three aisles. Work has recently been carried out in restoring the underground church of S. Reparata. The design for the polychrome pavement is attributed to Baccio d'Agnolo. The stained glass of the internal façade is by Lorenzo Ghiberti, that of the oculi in the drum by Ghiberti, Donatello, Paolo Uccello and Andrea del Castagno, and that of the nave by Agnolo Gaddi. The heads of prophets at the corners of the clock-face are by Paolo Uccello. The frescoes of the *Last Judgment* in the cupola are by Vasari, Federico Zuccari and assistants. Attached to pilasters are eight 16th-

century statues of apostles. The octagonal marble choir is by Baccio Bandinelli (1555). On the high altar stands a bronze crucifix by Benedetto da Maiano (1495-97). The three tribunes have polygonal apses. Five radial chapels lead off from these, and alongside the middle chapel are the sacristies. The Sagrestia Vecchia or Canons' Sacristy, which has a lunette of the *Ascension* by Luca della Robbia over the door, and two of his angels bearing candle-sticks within. The lunette of the Sagrestia Nuova or Mass Sacristy contains a *Resurrection* by Luca della Robbia, and the bronze door is also by him, in collaboration with Michelozzo and Maso di Bartolomeo. This is divided into ten compartments showing the Virgin, the Evangelists, and doctors of the church. The inlaid cupboards are by Antonio Manetti, and the marble lavabo is of the 15th century. In the first chapel of the left tribune stands Michelangelo's dramatic *Pietà*. The frescoed monument to Giovanni Acuto (John Hawkwood) in the left aisle is of exceptional interest. It is by Paolo Uccello and dated 1436. The other equestrian monument is of Niccolò da Tolentino, by Andrea del Castagno (1456). The campanile was begun by Giotto in 1334 and continued by Andrea Pisano and later by Francesco Talenti. It was completed in 1359 and is 81.75 m. in height. The revetment is in polychrome marble. There are coupled windows on two floors, and triple windows on the top floor which is covered by an attic. The base is covered with two zones of bas-relief which are examples of the finest Italian Gothic work. The first zone is by Andrea Pisano, possibly using designs by Giotto. It shows the life of man from the creation onwards. The second is by Orcagna and followers of Pisano, and it deals with the planets, the virtues, the liberal arts and the sacraments. *26, 30, 30, 31, 40, 49, 52, 53, 56, 65, 68, 74, 75, 76, 81, 82, 87, 88, 103, 105,* 107, 116, 117, 120, 134, 157, 164, 169, 172, 181, 183, *217, 224,* 229, 230, *235.*

Duomo di Fiesole
An 11th-century building enlarged in the 13th, and considerably restored during the 19th, especially the façade. The campanile has the form of a crenellated tower, and was built in 1213. The interior is of basilica type, with three aisles, and presbytery raised over a crypt. To the right of the presbytery, the Cappella Salutati has frescoes of evangelists and saints by Cosimo Rosselli, the tomb of Leonardo Salutati by Mino da Fiesole (1464), who also did the reredos. The *Madonna enthroned with the Child and saints* on the high altar is by Bicci di Lorenzo (*c.* 1440). In the sacristy there are some fine vestments and altar plate. In the crypt, which belongs to the earlier building, there is some fine Sienese iron work of the 14th century. 30, 130, *131.*

Fortezza
Near S. Miniato al Monte
It was built in a few months under the direction of Michelangelo, and strengthened by Francesco da Sangallo and others in 1553. The decorated part is by Tribolo.

Fortezza da Basso, or Fortezza di S. Giovanni Battista
At the termination of Via Faenza.
Built by Pier Francesco da Viterbo and Alessandro Vitelli (1534-35) and designed by Antonio da Sangallo on a pentagonal plan. The impressive walls facing the via Faenza are decorated with large ashlar diamonds, alternating with rounded forms recalling the Medici crest. It was built for the Medici, and since 1967 it has been occupied by the Gabinetto dei Restauri della Soprintendenza alle Gallerie di Firenze, which is one of the largest and most up-to-date offices of its kind in the world.

Fortezza di S. Maria del Belvedere, now the Forte di S. Giorgio
Via del Belvedere e via di San Leonardo.
Built by Buontalenti (1590-95) at the orders of Grand Duke Ferdinando I, and designed by Don Giovanni de' Medici. The three-storey Palazzetto di Belvedere is built over it. *177, 199.*

Giardino di Boboli
Entrance in the Piazzale di Palazzo Pitti [KB]. *Open in summer from 8.30 to 7.30, and in winter from 8.30 to 5.30.*
One of the finest examples of a garden in the Italian style, commissioned by Eleonora da Toledo in 1550, laid out by Tribolo, Ammannati, Buontalenti, and completed by Alfonso Parigi among others. The Grotta del Buontalenti (1583-88) is to the left of the entrance. The decoration is by Poccetti, and among the statues is Giambologna's *Venus* (1573). The main path leads to the Amphitheatre, a scenic construction of 17th- and 18th-century work. In the centre of the Vivaio di Nettuno, a fine 16th-century bronze statue of *Neptune* stands on a small island. The terraced Giardino del Cavaliere contains the *Fontana delle scimmie* (monkey fountain) of Tacca. The

'Viottolone', a straight path with no plants, leads to the Piazzale dell'isolotto, designed by A. Parigi, with Giambologna's *Fontana dell'Oceano* in the centre. *96, 102, 184, 192, 196, 229, 233.*

Loggia del Bigallo
On the corner of via dei Calzaiuoli [HC].
Attributed to Alberto Arnoldi (1352-58), it was built for the Compagnia della Misericordia, who used it for showing foundlings to the public. An outstanding example of religious and secular architecture, richly decorated with sculpture. Among its many works of art are a 13th-century *Crucifixion*, a tabernacle by Bernardo Daddi (1333), and inside the loggetta a statue of the *Madonna between two angels* by A. Arnoldi (1359-64) and a predella by Ridolfo del Ghirlandaio (1515). The building is now used by the Orphanage. *56.*

Loggia del Grano
On the corner of via dei Castellani and via de' Neri [JC].
Built as a market, the upper part was used as a grain store. It was transformed into a theatre in the 19th century. Designed by Giulio Parigi at the order of Cosimo II (1619).

Loggia dei Lanzi (also known as the **Loggia della Signoria** and the **Loggia dell'Orcagna**)
Piazza della Signoria [HC].
Built for the public ceremonies of the Signoria by Benci di Cione and Simone Talenti (1376-81), and not, as is traditionally supposed, by Orcagna. It gets its name dei Lanzi from the guard of lancers of Cosimo I. The building is a typical example of Florentine Gothic-Renaissance, with three round arches on the front, and one at the side. The sculptures of the *Virtues* were designed by Agnolo Gaddi (1384-89). The most notable sculptures in the Loggia are the bronze *Perseus* of Benvenuto Cellini (1553), the *Rape of the Sabine women* (1583) and the *Hercules slaying the centaur* (1599), both by Giambologna. *49, 54, 56, 58, 184, 186, 192, 207, 222.*

Loggia di Mercato Nuovo
Near the Palazzo di Parte Guelfa
An elegant building by G. Battista del Tasso (1547-51) on a square plan with four arches and pillars at the corners decorated with niches. It is occupied by stall-holders. In the middle of the south side, the *Fontana del Porcellino* by Pietro Tacca (*c.* 1612) is a reproduction of the antique marble boar in the Uffizi.

Monastero di S. Apollonia
ex Via S. Gallo, 25 [GC].
Probably an 11th-century foundation, rebuilt in the 14th and 15th centuries, and now occupied by the Centro Italiano delle Relazioni Universitarie con l'Estero. It contains the fine Chiostro della Badessa and the *Last Supper* of Poccetti can be seen in the old refectory.

Ognissanti
Piazza Ognissanti [HB].
An old church rebuilt in the Baroque period. The façade by M. Nigetti was much restored in the 19th century. The campanile is early 14th century, with coupled and triple windows. Single-aisled nave rebuilt in the 17th and 18th centuries. By the second altar to the right, frescoes by Domenico and Davide Ghirlandaio (*c.* 1470) of the *Madonna della Misericordia* protecting the Vespucci family, and a *Pietà*. Between the third and the fourth altars, the fresco of *St Augustine in his study* is by Botticelli (1480). The companion piece to this is Domenico Ghirlandaio's *St Jerome* (1480) to the left of the nave. The *Paradise* in the dome over the presbytery is by Giovanni di S. Giovanni (1616-17). In the sacristy, a painted crucifix of the school of Giotto, and a fresco of the *Crucifixion* by Taddeo Gaddi. To the left of the crossing is the cloister in the style of Michelozzo, with Ionic columns and 17th-century frescoes of the life of St Francis. *149.*

Or San Michele (or **S. Michele in Orto**)
Via dei Calzaiuoli [HC].
An 8th-century oratory on this site was replaced by a grain market, built in 1290 by Arnolfo. It was burned down in 1304 and rebuilt and enlarged by F. Talenti, Neri di Fioravante and Benci di Cione in 1337. The loggia was closed in and turned into a church in 1380 by Simone Talenti. A light upper storey was added with coupled windows, for the storage of grain. The lower part consists of a closed arcade with Gothic-Renaissance decoration. The pilasters are ornamented with niches to hold statues of the saints invoked for the protection of various crafts. On the east side (*in the via dei Calzaiuoli*) to the left: niche of the Arte di Calimala (importers of foreign cloth) designed by Ghiberti, with his bronze statue of *St John Baptist* (1414-16): niche of the Tribunale di Mercanzia (Merchants' Guild) by Donatello and Michelozzo (1425) with a bronze statue of *St Thomas* by Verrocchio (1464-83): niche of

the judges and notaries (1403-6) with a bronze statue of *St Luke* by Giambologna (1601). On the south side (*via dei Lamberti*): niche of the woodworkers and second-hand dealers (1411) with Donatello's marble statue of *St Mark* (1411-13): niche of the furriers (15th century) with a statue of *St James*: niche of the doctors and apothecaries, possibly by S. Talenti (1399) with a marble group of the 15th century, niche of the goldsmiths and silk-weavers (mid-14th century) with a bronze statue of *St John the Evangelist* by Baccio di Montelupo (1515). On the west side (*via dell'Arte della Lana*) niche of the exchange, designed by Ghiberti and containing his bronze *St Matthew* (1419-22): niche of the wool-workers with a bronze statue by of *St Stephen* by Ghiberti (1426): tabernacle of the farriers, with a marble statue of *St Eligio* and a bas-relief (1415) by Nanni di Banco. On the north side (*via Orsanmichele*) niche of the butchers (mid-14th century) with a marble statue of *St Peter*, an early work of Donatello (1408-13): niche of the tanners (1405-10) with a marble statue of *St Philip* by Nanni di Banco: niche of the bricklayers, carpenters and masons (*c.* 1408) with marble statues of the four *Crowned Saints*, and a bas-relief by Nanni di Banco: niche of the armourers (1416) with a bronze copy of Donatello's marble *St George* (now in the Bargello) and his bas-relief of *St George rescuing the king's daughter*. Some of the medallions over the niches are by Luca and Andrea della Robbia. The interior is divided into two aisles with round arches on pilasters. Marble tabernacle by Andrea Orcagna (1349-59) with episodes from the life of the Virgin, remarkable for its perfect fusion of architecture, sculpture and painting. On the pilasters there are paintings and frescoes of the 15th and 16th centuries. 11, 30, 49, 55, 77, 81, 96, 120, 130, 145, 169, 192, 235.

Orti Oricellari
Via degli Oricellari, in the Palazzo Venturi-Ginori [GA].
Bernardo Rucellai transferred the Platonist Academy to this site in 1489. In the centre of the garden is a colossal statue of *Polyphemus* by a pupil of Giambologna.

Palazzo degli Albizi
Borgo degli Albizi [HC].
Restored by Gherardo Silvani (1626-32), its early 16th-century façade retains the character of the previous century.

Palazzo Antinori, formerly Boni and Martelli
Piazza Antinori [HB].
Built *c.* 1465 in the style of Giuliano da Maiano with smooth ashlar facing, overhanging eaves and an elegant courtyard with porticos. Now occupied by the British Institute. 136.

Palazzo dell'Arte della Lana
Via Or San Michele [HC].
Built in 1308 for the important Wool Guild, and now occupied by the Società Dantesca. It consists of a house with a crenellated tower, and a smaller building which has kept its original wooden roof. The Tabernacle of S. Maria della Tromba (late 14th century) comes from the Piazza di Mercato Vecchio, and contains an *Enthroned Madonna with angels and saints* by Jacopo del Casentino. There are some 14th-century frescoes.

Palazzo Bartolini Salimbeni
Piazza S. Trinita [HB].
Built by Baccio d'Agnolo (1517-20) and inspired by the classical forms that he studied in Rome. 174.

Palazzo Busini, later Quaratesi
Piazza d'Ognissanti [HB].
A notable building of the first half of the 15th century with 16th-century graffiti decoration, and an overhang on small arches to support the upper floors. 107.

Palazzo dei Capitani di Parte Guelfa
Piazza di Parte Guelfa
Begun in the early 14th century with crenellated façade and loggetta staircase. Enlarged in the 15th century by Filippo Brunelleschi and Francesco della Luna, with later additions by Vasari, who is also responsible for the hanging loggetta decorated with the Medici crest in polychrome stone by Giambologna. Notable among its 14th and 15th century rooms are the Sala dell'Udienza with a late Gothic wood and stone ceiling, the small Consigliatoio and the Salone Brunelleschiano with a ceiling by Vasari, and a fine lunette of Luca della Robbia in glazed terracotta.

Palazzo Castellani
Piazza dei Giudici
Three-storey medieval building restored during the 19th century. Originally the seat of the Giudici di Ruota, and now occupied by the Museo Nazionale di Storia della Scienza and the Accademia della Crusca (2nd floor). Among its curiosities are the old seats for the Academicians, in the form of bread baskets.

Palazzo Davanzati
Via Porta Rossa, 9 [HC].
An interesting example of a 14th-

century nobleman's house. The interior has been restored and appropriately furnished. Three-storey tower structure, with a large Renaissance loggia and overhanging roof. It is occupied by the Museo dell'Antica Casa Fiorentina.

Palazzo Gondi
Piazza S. Firenze [HC].
A fine example of Florentine civil architecture, built by Giuliano da Sangallo (1490-94) with an interesting use of ashlar facing. The left side is a 19th-century addition. The courtyard is notable for its capitals, its fountains, and a Roman statue which probably came from the Roman theatre, on the site of which the Tribunale di Mercanzia now stands. 10, 138, 218.

Palazzo Guadagni
Piazza S. Spirito [JB].
Attributed to Cronaca (1503-06) and also to Baccio d'Agnolo. Typical Florentine nobleman's house, basically a fortress but with its aspect softened by the airy colonnaded loggia, projecting roof, and elegant courtyard with flattened arches and Renaissance columns. 172.

Palazzo Larderel
Via Tornabuoni [HB].
A noble building by G.A. Dosio (1580).

Palazzo Medici, later **Riccardi**
Via Cavour [GC].
A superb example of Florentine Renaissance architecture. Three storeys with graded ashlar, and a heavy cornice by Michelozzo (*c.* 1444-60). It was built for Cosimo il Vecchio, and occupied by the Medici until 1659. It is now occupied by the Prefettura. The porticos of the courtyard are decorated with graffiti, Medici emblems, bas-reliefs and fragments of Roman sculpture. The signed statue of *Orpheus* is by Baccio Bandinelli. In the second courtyard, there are the remains of a loggia by Michelozzo, and a Baroque garden in the Italian style. The interior contains the Museo Medici, and a chapel with some famous frescoes by Benozzo Gozzoli of the *Journey of the Magi* (1459-60), which incorporate a number of Medici portraits. There is also a frescoed gallery' by Luca Giordano (1682-83). 96, 99, 108, *110*, 114, 116, 120, *127*, 133, 134, 135, *145*, 166, 181, 182, 218, *229*.

Palazzo Nonfinito
Via del Proconsolo, 12 [HC].
Begun in 1593 for Alessandro Strozzi, it was left unfinished. The ground floor is by Bernardo Buontalenti, the first floor by Vincenzo Scamozzi, and the courtyard by Cigoli. 190, 229.

Palazzo Pandolfini
Via S. Gallo, 74
An elegant and sober building designed by Raphael and built by Giovanni Francesco and Aristotele da Sangallo (*c.* 1520) for Bishop Pandolfini. 166, 173.

Palazzo dei Pazzi, later **Quaratesi**
Via del Proconsolo, 10 [HC].
Designed by Giuliano da Maiano (1462-72) for Jacopo dei Pazzi. A good example of the more florid type of palace, with rusticated ashlar facing on the ground floor, and plaster on the walls of the two upper floors. Rectangular coupled windows. On the corner (the 'canto dei Pazzi') is the Pazzi coat of arms. The capitals in the courtyard are attributed to Benedetto da Maiano. It is now occupied by the Istituto Nazionale di Previdenza Sociale. *112, 136.*

Palazzo Pitti - *see also* **Giardino di Boboli**
Piazza Pitti [JB]. *Open in summer from 9.30 to 4.30, and in winter from 9.30 to 4. Sundays and public holidays, 9 to 1. Closed on Tuesdays.*
The most grandiose of the Florentine palaces, at the foot of the hill of Boboli. It now contains the Galleria d'Arte Moderna, the Galleria Palatina, and the Museo degli Argenti. Begun in the mid-15th century, designed by Brunelleschi for Luca Pitti, it was completed by Ammannati between 1558-70 after being acquired by Eleonora da Toledo. Enlarged by Giulio and Alfonso Parigi (1620-40) and G. Ruggeri in the 18th century with two projecting wings called rondò. Further enlargements on the garden side were made during the last century. An imposing atrium with Doric columns (1850) leads into Ammannati's courtyard, which is enclosed on three sides by the palace and the terrace. On the terrace is the 16th-century *Artichoke fountain;* the grotto of *Moses* (a 17th-century design), and the statue of *Hercules reclining*, a Roman copy of the *Farnese Hercules* in the museum at Naples. In the richly frescoed Cappella Palatina there is a bronze Crucifix attributed to Giambologna. A collection of fine plate and reliquaries may be seen in the sacristy. The great staircase, with Giambologna's bronze *Genius of the Medici* on the third landing, leads to the royal apartments, a series of finely appointed rooms which were occupied by the houses of Medici Lorraine, and later of Savoy, until the palace passed to the State under Vittorio Emanuele III. Of particular note is the Sala delle Nicchie, with its portraits of the Medici princes by Sustermans. The Sala dei Pappagalli

contains a portrait of the Duchess of Urbino by Titian (1547). The Sala della Stufa was frescoed by Pietro da Cortona in 1537, who painted the rooms of Venus, Jove, Mars and Apollo in 1540-42. The Appartamento degli Arazzi consists of five rooms with Florentine, Gobelins and Beauvais tapestries. The ballroom is richly decorated with 18th-century stucco. *96, 98, 102,* 135, 182, 184, 196, *196,* 198, 201, 205, *208, 213,* 217, 218, 221, 222, 227.

Palazzo del Podestà, or **Bargello**
Piazza S. Firenze [HC].
The oldest part of the building (1254-60) lies between Via del Proconsolo and Piazza S. Firenze. Built alongside the Volognana tower as a house for the Capitano del Popolo, it was then used by the Podestà, the Consiglio di Giustizia and finally by the Bargello. The large window in the Sala del Consiglio was designed by Benci di Cione (1345). The crenellations are built over a pointed arcade. It is now occupied by the Museo Nazionale q.v. *26, 34, 46, 47, 55, 70, 118,* 218, *233.*

Palazzo Rosselli del Turco, formerly **Borgherini**
Borgo SS. Apostoli
A magnificent building designed by Baccio d'Agnolo (1517). A bas-relief of Benedetto da Maiano is let into the wall. 174.

Palazzo Riccardi, see **Palazzo Medici**

Palazzo Rucellai
Via della Vigna Nuova, almost in front of the Loggia dei Rucellai [HB].
Designed by Alberti (1446-51) and built by Bernardo Rossellino. The superimposed orders of the exterior reveal the classical ideal that inspired Florentine tradition in building, and was to be widely influential. The large trilobate, coupled windows are part of the medieval heritage. 102, *102,* 103, 108, 135.

Palazzo della Signoria, or **Palazzo Vecchio**
Piazza della Signoria [HC].
The construction of the original nucleus was carried out from 1298 to 1314. It was a rectangular building faced with rusticated ashlar. It had two courses of coupled windows, and an overhanging battlemented gallery. Additions were made in 1343 under the Duke of Athens, in 1495 by Cronaca, and in 1511 on the side facing the piazza. The development of the rear part was done by Battista del Tasso (1549-55) and B. Buontalenti (1588-92). The rectangular tower is finished off with an overhanging crenellated chamber and small belfry. Originally used by the

Signoria, it was temporarily the residence of Cosimo I and his son Francesco, who then moved into the Palazzo Pitti, whence it acquired the name of Palazzo Vecchio (the old palace). It is now occupied by the Municipio. On the steps is a copy of the *Marzocco* in the Bargello, the lion holding the shield with the lily of Florence. It stands on a plinth designed by Donatello (*c.* 1438). The statue of *Judith and Holofernes* by Donatello and assistants (*c.* 1460) was originally in the Palazzo Mediceo. A copy of Michelangelo's *David* (now in the Galleria dell'Accademia) stands in front of the façade. The interior is noteworthy for its late Renaissance and Baroque decoration. There is little left of the original work. The first courtyard, designed by Michelozzo (1453) was decorated for the wedding of Francesco, the elder son of the Grand Duke (1565), with stucco on the columns and fresco in the gallery. The porphyry fountain in the centre of the courtyard has a bronze statue by Verrocchio of a *Winged putto with a fish* (1476) which comes from the Medici Villa at Careggi. In the Camera dell'Arme, to the left, is the only remaining part of the 14th-century building. The great staircase by Vasari (1560-63) leads to the Salone dei Cinquecento on the first floor (53 m. in length, 22 m. in width, and 18 m. in height). This is the work of Cronaca (1495) who used designs by Leonardo and Michelangelo among others. It was intended for the assemblies of the Consiglio Generale del Popolo. The ceiling, by Vasari and his assistants (1563-65) tells the story of Florence and of the Medici family. At the entrance are tapestries from the Medici factory inspired by Andrea del Sarto's frescoes of John the Baptist. The walls were frescoed by Vasari and his assistants. The dais is on the north side. The niches contain statues by Bandinelli, and the paintings above them are by I. Ligozzi and Cigoli. In front of the dais, in the central niche, is Michelangelo's *Victory,* designed for the tomb of Julius II in Rome (*c.* 1525) and brought to Florence in 1565. The study of Francesco I de' Medici is accessible to the right. It was richly decorated by Vasari and V. Borghini (1570-72). The stuccoes and frescoes on the ceiling are by Poppi, and there are portraits of Cosimo and Eleonora by Bronzino in the lunettes. The niches contain bronze statuettes by artists of the late 16th century. On the cupboard doors are tondi by Bronzino, Santi di Tito, Giovanni

Stradano and others. A stairway leads to the Tesoretto, which was the study of Cosimo I, with paintings of the arts and sciences. To the left of the dais is a passage to the Sala degli Otto di Pratica, with a ceiling by Benedetto da Maiano and two Gobelins tapestries; also the Sala dei Dugento by Benedetto and Giuliano da Maiano (1472-77), with a coffered ceiling by Benedetto da Maiano and his assistants, and tapestries made after cartoons of Bronzino, Francesco Salviati and Pontormo. The Salone dei Cinquecento also leads to the Quartieri Monumentali: the Quartiere di Leone X, comprising six rooms frescoed by Vasari and assistants with subjects from the lives of the Medici: the Quartiere degli Elementi (2nd floor) with five rooms and two terraces, with architecture by Battista del Tasso (c. 1550), decorations by Vasari and assistants (1555-59), and 16th-century Florentine tapestries on cartoons by Giovanni Stradano. On the Terrazza del Saturno, the bronze *Diavolino* is by Giambologna: the Quartiere di Eleonora da Toledo, the wife of Cosimo I, has five rooms and a small chapel completely decorated by Bronzino (c. 1564). One of these rooms, the Camera Verde, was painted by Ridolfo del Ghirlandaio, and the dining room has a fine 15th-century marble washbasin. A short corridor leads to the Cappella della Signoria (1511) painted by Ridolfo del Ghirlandaio (1514) and restored in the 19th century, and then on to the Sala dell'Udienza, with architecture by Benedetto da Maiano and a fine carved ceiling by Giuliano da Maiano. The frescoes depicting the story of Camillus are the work of Francesco Salviati (1550-60). The marble doorway is by Giuliano and Benedetto da Maiano (1476-78). It leads into the Sala dei Gigli, a large hall with a fresco by Domenico Ghirlandaio and assistants (1481-85). From here a landing leads into the covered gallery. The tower is accessible up to the second row of battlements. The mezzanine on this level was fitted up by Michelozzo for the use of the Priors' families. It is occupied by a part of the Loeser collection of 14th-16th-century Tuscan painting and sculpture. In the second courtyard, the Cortile della Dogana, the pilasters supporting the Salone dei Cinquecento are by Cronaca. The third courtyard, the Cortile degli Uffici, is part of the extension of the Palazzo. *9*, 10, 26, 27, 30, *49*, 55, 75, 107, 120, 136, 139, 145, *145*, 149, 161, 164, *179*, 181, 182, 183, *183*, 184, *184*, 186-190, *191*, 201, *204*, 205, 227.

Palazzo Spini, later **Ferroni**
Piazza S. Trinita [HB].
One of the most important buildings of medieval Florence (1289), with three floors and battlements. Partly altered when it was restored in 1874. *33, 152.*

Palazzo Strozzi
Via Tornabuoni [HB].
The most famous palace of the Florentine Renaissance, built for Filippo Strozzi. Begun by Benedetto da Maiano (1489) with the assistance of Jacopo Rosselli and Cronaca, who built the classically inspired cornice and the elegant courtyard. Graded ashlar facing, and fine iron lanterns of the period. It is now occupied by the Gabinetto Vieussieux and others. 108, *114*, 138, 139.

Palazzo dello Strozzino
Piazza Strozzi [HB].
Begun by Michelozzo (1458), the upper floor with coupled windows is by Giuliano da Maiano (1461-65). It is similar to the Palazzo Medici-Riccardi. 136.

Palazzo Torrigiani
Via Romana, 17
Known as La Specola on account of the observatory installed here by Grand Duke Pietro Leopoldo. The Museo Zoologico or the Tribuna di Galileo, set up by Leopoldo II in 1841, occupies a semi-circular room, richly decorated. 174.

Palazzo degli Uffizi
Piazzale degli Uffizi [JC].
Begun by Vasari in 1560 at the behest of Cosimo I for the administrative offices and tribunals of the Florentine state. Completed in 1580 by Alfonso Parigi and Bernardo Buontalenti, following Vasari's designs. It consists of two parallel parts flanking a long piazzale which stretches from the Arno to the Piazza della Signoria. The niches contain twenty-eight 19th-century marble statues of famous Tuscan personalities. The Palazzo is now occupied by the Galleria degli Uffizi and the Archivio di Stato. 16, 182, 190, 192, 198, 219.

Palazzo Vecchio - *see* **Palazzo della Signoria**

Palazzo dei Vescovi
To the right of S. Miniato al Monte [KD].
Begun in 1295, it was the summer residence of the bishops of Florence until 1594, when it was incorporated into the convent of S. Miniato. It has suffered some damage and alteration in the course of centuries. The bishops' coats of arms are to be seen in the Salone. *20.*

Piazza della SS. Annunziata [GD]
Surrounded by the three arcades of the Annunziata (17th century), the Spedale degli Innocenti (by Brunelleschi, 1419-26) and the Confraternita dei Servi di Maria (by Antonio da Sangallo and Baccio d'Agnolo, 1516-25). On the corner of the via dei Servi is the Palazzo Riccardi Mannelli, formerly Grifoni, by Ammannati (1557). Equestrian statue of *Ferdinando I*, by Giambologna, in the centre of the piazza. At the sides, two marble fountains with bronze sea beasts, by Pietro Tacca (1629). 192, *195, 198*, 201.

Piazza di Bellosguardo
Surrounded by fine villas of the 16th and 17th centuries, one of which is the 'Ombrellino' where Galileo lived.

Piazza di S. Croce [JD]
Among the palaces here are the Palazzo Seristori, formerly Cocchi, attributed to Baccio d'Agnolo (1469-1474), and the Palazzo dell'Antella, formerly dei Cerchi, by Giulio Parigi (1619). The piazza was a place for public meetings in the Middle Ages, and for tournaments during the Renaissance. 10, 21, 174.

Piazza S. Maria Novella [HB]
Pentagonal in shape, closed on the north side by the façade of S. Maria Novella and on the south side by the Loggia di S. Paolo (1489-96), which is similar to the Loggia degli Innocenti, with medallions and a lunette by Andrea della Robbia. In the centre, two obelisks are supported on two bronze tortoises by Giambologna.

Piazza della Signoria [HC]
The political centre of Florence, opened up in the 13th-14th centuries after the demolition of certain Ghibelline houses, among which was that of the Uberti. Besides the Palazzo Vecchio and the Loggia dei Lanzi, the piazza is famous for its fountain decorated with statues of seagods, the work of Ammannati and assistants. To the left of the fountain is the equestrian statue of *Cosimo I de' Medici* by Giambologna (1594). 10, 149, 184, 192, *192*.

Piazzale Michelangelo
At the end of the Viale dei Colli [KD]
Designed by the architect Giuseppe Poggi and laid out in 1865-70, it affords a fine view of the city. 229.

Ponte alla Carraia [HB]
Destroyed during the last war, it has been rebuilt to the original design of Ammannati (1559). It was commissioned by Grand Duke Cosimo I. 232.

Ponte alle Grazie [JC]
This was a very solid construction, built in 1237. It derived its name from a nearby chapel dedicated to the Madonna. Destroyed during the last world war, it has been rebuilt in a modern design. 232.

Ponte S. Trinita [JB]
Destroyed during the last war, it has been rebuilt as Ammannati designed it. Originally built in 1557 to replace an older bridge, it has three arches on stout pylons. The statues are of the 16th century, and represent the seasons. *172*, 181, 182, 184, *188*, 232, 234.

Ponte Vecchio [JC]
The oldest bridge in Florence, in existence from the end of the 10th century. Rebuilt in 1345, probably by Neri di Fioravante or, according to Vasari, by Taddeo Gaddi, it is built on three very solid arches. It has shops on both sides, reserved for the goldsmiths by Ferdinando I. 12, *72*, 182, *226*, 232, 234.

Porta Romana
Piazza della Calza [KA].
This imposing 14th-century tower with barrel vault is a remnant of the medieval fortifications. Inside the arch is a fresco of Franciabigio. 234.

Porta S. Frediano [HA]
Early 14th-century barrel-vaulted building, also known as the Porta Pisana. The remains of the battlements connecting it with the medieval walls can still be seen. *23*, 234.

Porta S. Giorgio
At the end of costa S. Giorgio [KC].
Built in 1324. Inside the arch are 14th-century capitals and a fresco by Bicci di Lorenzo. 25, 43.

Porta S. Niccolò
At the end of Via S. Niccolò [KD].
14th-century towered building with no opening apart from the doors communicating with the embankment and the three arcaded terraces. In the hall there is a 14th-century fresco. 43.

Rotonda di S. Maria degli Angeli
Via degli Alfani
Begun by Brunelleschi after his visit to Rome in 1433 and never completed. Its plan is octagonal, with eight two-apsed chapels. It has been much restored. 92.

S. Ambrogio
Piazza S. Ambrogio [HD].
One of the first churches to be built in Florence, it was altered at the end of the 13th century. The interior has undergone several alterations including that of Foggini in

1716. The Gothic façade is of the 19th century. Single-aisle nave. Noteworthy are the marble tabernacle by Mino da Fiesole (1481-83) angels by the della Robbias (1513), and a painting of angels and saints by Alessio Baldovinetti, all in the Cappella del Miracolo. There are also frescoes by Nardo di Cione and the 'Maestro di Figline', recently detached and restored, and a *Visitation* by Andrea Boscoli (1547). 67, 114.

S. Andrea a Brozzi
Strada statale 66, Pistoiese.
An 11th-century church rebuilt in the 15th century. The portico is of the 17th century. Single-aisle nave. *Annunciation* and *SS. Eustachio and Antonio Abate* attributed to Giovanni da Ponte, but possibly by the Portuguese Alvaro Pirez. *Madonna enthroned with saints* and *Baptism of Christ*, frescoes by Domenico Ghirlandaio and assistants.

SS. Annunziata
Piazza SS. Annunziata [GD].
Erected in 1250 as an oratory for the Servites, and completely rebuilt by Michelozzo and assistants (1444-81). The long nave terminates in a wide circular tribunal inspired by the Rotonda di S. Maria degli Angeli of Brunelleschi, slightly modified at the suggestion of Alberti. There is an arcaded portico with Corinthian columns in front of the façade. The middle door leads to the atrium or Chiostrino dei Voti, designed by Michelozzo with early Cinquecento Florentine frescoes: *The Assumption* by Rosso Fiorentino (1517), *The Visitation* by Pontormo (1516), *The Birth of Mary* by Andrea del Sarto (1514), *The Nativity* by Alessio Baldovinetti (1460-62). Baroque interior with a fine carved ceiling (1664-69) designed by Volterrano. The marble Tempietto on the left was designed by Michelozzo (1448-61) to house a venerated fresco of the *Annunciation* (Florentine school, 14th century). The adjacent chapel is inlaid with precious marble, and there are marble decorations in the third and sixth chapels on the right. In the third chapel in the right transept, is a marble *Pietà* by Baccio Bandinelli who is buried there. The dome of the presbytery contains a fresco by Volterrano, the *Coronation of the Virgin*. The presbytery is surrounded by nine chapels, the central one of which was transformed by Giambologna (1594-98). It contains works by him, and paintings of the early 16th century. The chapel to the left of this contains a *Resurrection* by Bronzino (*c.* 1550).

The sacristy was designed by Michelozzo. The Cappellino delle Reliquie at the entrance of it was decorated by Passignano. Andrea del Castagno's fresco of the *Trinity* (1454-55) is to be seen over the altar of the second chapel on the left, and there are remains of other of his frescoes in the adjoining chapel, decorated in the Baroque style by Foggini (1692). In the Chiostro dei Morti, designed by Michelozzo, there is a fresco of the *Madonna del Sacco* by Andrea del Sarto (1525). The cloister opens on to the Cappella della Confraternita di S. Luca, which contains the tombs of some famous Tuscan artists, and numerous works of the 16th and 17th centuries. The Cappella del Capitolo, also accessible from the cloister, is in the Baroque style. A fragment of fresco attributed to Botticelli may be seen over the door of the Sagrestia della Madonna, in the passage leading to the piazza. 88, 112, 117, *129*, 130, 146, 168, 177, 217, 218.

SS. Apostoli
Piazza del Limbo
Late 11th century, and altered in successive centuries. Romanesque façade, with a porch attributed to Benedetto da Rovezzano. The interior has kept its basilical character, apart from the chapels added in the 16th century. Three-aisled nave and semi-circular apse. In the right aisle, the third chapel contains Vasari's *Immaculate Conception* (1541). In the left aisle are the terracotta tabernacle by Giovanni della Robbia, and the tomb of Oddo Altoviti by Benedetto da Rovezzano (1507). 16, 172.

S. Carlo dei Lombardi
Via dei Calzaiuoli, opposite Or San Michele [HC]
A small church begun by Neri di Fioravante and Benci di Cione, and completed by Simone Talenti in *c.* 1384. A *Deposition* by Niccolò di Pietro Gerini, originally in Or San Michele, stands over the high altar. 55.

S. Croce
Piazza S. Croce [JD].
One of the most important Gothic basilicas in Italy from the point of view of its architecture and for the number of works of art it contains. Begun in the second half of the 13th century on the site of a small Franciscan convent. It was completed in the second half of the 14th century, and consecrated in 1443 in the presence of Eugene IV. The façade and campanile are both of the 19th century. The long 14th-century portico

on the left is of considerable architectural interest. The length of the interior is 115 m., the width 38 m. in the aisles, and 73 m. in the crossing. Egyptian cross plan with three aisles, and pointed arches on octagonal truss-bearing pilasters. Vasari carried out alterations in 1560. Many tombstones of the 14th to the 19th century are let into the floor. A marble pulpit by B. da Maiano (1472-76) stands in the central aisle. On the first pilaster in the right aisle there is a delicate bas-relief by A. Rossellino (1478), the *Madonna del Latte*. Opposite this is the tomb of Michelangelo by Vasari. Canova's monument to Vittorio Alfieri stands near the third altar. Remains of Andrea Orcagna's fresco, the *Triumph of Death; St John the Baptist and St Francis* by Domenico Veneziano; *The Annunciation* by Donatello, in collaboration with Michelozzo (1435) in polychrome stone; the tomb of Leonardo Bruni (past the entrance to the first cloister) by Bernardo Rossellino (1369-1444). In the right transept is the Cappella Castellani or Cappella del Sacramento, frescoed by Agnolo Gaddi and assistants (after 1383) with stories of the saints. Next comes the Cappella Baroncelli, frescoed by Taddeo Gaddi (1332-38), a pupil of Giotto, with the *Life of Mary*, his masterpiece. The sacristy corridor is by Michelozzo, and the sacristy itself is 14th century. This is a square room with panels and frescoes of the 14th and 15th centuries. In the 14th-century Cappella Rinuccini there is a polyptych by Giovanni del Biondo (1379) and frescoes by Giovanni da Milano and assistants (*c.* 1366) with episodes from the lives of Magdalen and Mary. The Cappella del Noviziato, or Cappella dei Medici is the work of Michelozzo (1434). The altar piece in enamelled terracotta is by Andrea della Robbia (*c.* 1480). On the two sides of the Cappella Maggiore is a series of five chapels. From right to left: the Cappella Velluti, with remains of frescoes by the school of Giotto; the Cappella Calderini, later Riccardi, rebuilt by Gherardo Silvani (*c.* 1620), of which the ceiling was decorated by Giovanni da S. Giovanni; Cappella Giugni, later Bonaparte, with an early stained glass window and the tomb of Giulia Bonaparte Clary; Cappella Peruzzi, one of the most noteworthy on account of its frescoes by Giotto (after 1320) depicting the history of St John the Evangelist and St John the Baptist. The Cappella Bardi, also frescoed by Giotto (after 1317) with the history of St Francis,

and a late 13th-century altarpiece; Cappella Maggiore with frescoes by Agnolo Gaddi (*c.* 1380) of the legend of the *Finding of the Cross*. The polyptych on the altar is by Nicolò Gerini; Cappella Tosinghi e Spinelli, now the Cappella Sloane, with frescoes of the *Assumption* by the workshop of Giotto, and a polyptych by Giovanni del Biondo (1372) and predella by Neri di Bicci; Cappella Capponi, restored during the 19th century; Cappella Pulci e Beraldi, with frescoes by Bernardo Daddi and assistants (*c.* 1330), and an enamelled terracotta altarpiece by Giovanni della Robbia; Cappella Bardi di Vernio with the history of *S. Silvestro,* fresco by Maso di Banco (pre-1350). In the left transept are the Cappella Niccolini (17th century) with a dome frescoed by Volterrano and two paintings of the *Virgin* by Bronzino; Cappella Bardi with a wooden crucifix attributed to Donatello, and the 14th-century Bardi tomb; Cappella Salviati, re-designed by Gherardo Silvani. In the right aisle, the tomb of Carlo Marsuppini by Desiderio da Settignano, *Pietà* by Bronzino, and frescoes by Mariotto di Nardo (*c.* 1400). Alongside the church is the entrance to the cloisters, the Cappella dei Pazzi, and the Museo dell'Opera di S. Croce. The first cloister is of the 13th century. The Cappella Pazzi occupies one side of it, then there is an arcade with a loggia, and above it a portico with wide arches and 14th-century frescoes. The second cloister is approached through a door by Benedetto da Maiano (*c.* 1450). It was designed by Brunelleschi, finished in 1453 and decorated by Rossellino. 30, 36, *39,* 40, 46, 47, 49, 50, *50,* 58, 60, 81, 88, 89, *92, 96,* 114, 120, 130, *131,* 136, 198, 218, 221, 230, 235.

S. Domenico di Fiesole

15th-century church with 17th-century campanile and portico. Single aisled nave with side chapels of the 15th and 16th centuries. The *Madonna and Child with angels and saints* is by Fra Angelico (1430) who lived in this convent. In the old chapter room there are frescoes by him of the *Crucifixion* and the *Madonna and Child*. 111, 148, 157.

S. Egidio

Adjoining the Arcispedale di S. Maria Nuova [HD].
Rebuilt in 1418-20 and designed by Lorenzo di Bicci. Single-aisled nave altered in the 17th century. It contains a number of 16th- and 17th-century works, also the 14th-century tomb of Folco Portinari, *Madonna and Child* by Andrea della

Robbia, *Deposition* by Alessandro Allori (1579) and a painting by Volterrano. The portico leads into the Chiostro delle Medicherie, built by Bicci di Lorenzo in 1422, with octagonal pillars. *Pietà* by Giovanni della Robbia and a stucco lunette of the *Madonna* attributed to Michelozzo. At the end of the portico, in what was once part of the Chiostro della Ossa, is the stairway leading to the Sala della Presidenza, which contains a fresco of the *Crucifixion* by Andrea del Castagno. 114, 148.

S. Felice
Piazza S. Felice
An ancient church rebuilt in the 14th and 15th centuries, and partially restored in 1926. Façade by Michelozzo (1457) of a single order, with richly carved doorway. Single-aisled nave with a high enclosed choir at the back, with a 16th-century grill, for the Dominican nuns of the adjoining convent. Frescoes and paintings of the 14th- and 15th-century Florentine school, and a painted cross recently attributed to Giotto. Next to the church (*entrance in via Romana 8-10*), is the Oratorio dei Bini, with a Renaissance porch and medieval walled structure. The oratory contains some interesting works of the 15th- and 16th-century Florentine school. 25.

S. Felicita
Piazzetta S. Felicita
Built on the site of an early Christian cemetery and considerably altered, especially during the 18th century, it has kept its portico by Vasari, with the corridor over it connecting the Uffizi with Palazzo Pitti. Neoclassical interior, Egyptian cross design with single nave and side chapels. The Cappella Capponi (designed by Brunelleschi but completely altered) contains a *Deposition* and frescoes by Pontormo. In the sacristy there is a polyptych by Taddeo Gaddi and a painting of *S. Felicita* by Neri di Bicci. In the chapter room, or Stanza delle Reliquie, 14th-century frescoes. The choir is by Cigoli, with 17th-century paintings. 15, 177, 218, 222.

S. Firenze
Piazza S. Firenze [HC].
17th-century complex consisting of the old convent of the Filippini, the church to the right now occupied by the Tribunale, and the church dedicated to S. Filippo Neri on the left (originally the Oratorio di S. Firenze) with a Baroque interior and Florentine paintings and sculptures of the 18th century. The façades are 18th century. 229.

S. Francesco
Fiesole
14th-century Franciscan church, later altered. The façade, the side, the vestibule and the fresco in the lunette are of the early 15th century. Gothic interior with a single aisle. *Annunciation* over the high altar attributed to Raffaellino del Garbo. The Chiostro grande leads to the remains of the Etruscan Acropolis.

S. Frediano, formerly S. Maria degli Angeli
Piazza di Cestello [HA].
An old church rebuilt at the end of the 17th century, with a curious Baroque campanile. Latin cross plan with side chapels. Paintings and frescoes of the 18th-century Florentine school, and *Madonna of the Smile,* a fine statue of the Pisan-Florentine school (third chapel on the left). 12, 25, 217, 218.

S. Gaetano
Piazza Antinori [HB].
11th-century church, rebuilt in the Baroque style by Matteo Nigetti (1604), with later alterations. Façade by Gherardo and Pier Francesco Silvani (1633-48). *Martyrdom of St Laurence* by Pietro da Cortona (1653) and *Crucifixion with saints* by Filippo Lippi. 11, 217.

S. Giovanni Battista dell'Autostrada del Sole
Campi Bisenzio
An important contemporary work by Giovanni Michelucci (1961). Sculptures by Pericle Fazzini, Emilio Greco, Venanzo Crocetti, mosaics by B. Saetti, windows by C. Avenali, decorations by A. Biancini, A. Biggi, G. D'Aloisio, Dilvo Lotti, L. Montanarini, L. Venturini and J. Vivarelli. 234.

S. Giovannino dei Cavalieri
Via S. Gallo
Originally the Oratorio di S. Maria Maddalena (1326) and in 1553 altered and dedicated to S. Niccolò, it is known by the name of the patron of the Knights of Malta. A vestibule leads into the three-aisled nave with open timber roof. Of interest are the two altars with stone cornices in the Gothic-Renaissance transition style, and the *Crucifix* by Lorenzo Monaco in the apse.

S. Giovannino degli Scolopi
Via dei Martelli [HC].
Begun by Ammannati (1579), together with the adjoining convent, and finished by Alfonso Parigi il Giovane in 1661. The façade shows the influence of Michelangelo. Late Renaissance interior, with statues and altarpieces by artists of the 16th century. Ammannati is buried in the chapel that bears his name.

S. Giuseppe
Via dei Malcontenti [JD].
Built by Baccio d'Agnolo in 1519, the façade is 18th century. Single aisle with side chapels. A large painted cross by Lorenzo Monaco near the entrance, *S. Francesco di Paola* by Cigoli (second altar on the right), *Nativity* by Santi di Tito (third altar on the right).

S. Jacopo sopr'Arno
Borgo S. Jacopo [JB].
12th-century Romanesque church, with later alterations. The columns of the three-arched portico are part antique, part 12th and 13th century. These once belonged to the church of S. Donato a Scopeto. The cornice is supported on corbels in the shape of heads. The 17th-century campanile is by Gherardo Silvani. Three-aisled nave altered in the 18th century, with frescoes and altarpieces by Florentine artists of the same period.

S. Leonardo in Arcetri
Via S. Leonardo [KC].
11th-century church, very much restored. Basilical interior with a single aisle. Among its treasures are works of the 16th-century Tuscan school, and a 13th-century pulpit originally in S. Pietro a Scheraggio.

S. Lorenzo
Piazza S. Lorenzo [GC].
The basilica, consecrated by S. Ambrogio, was renovated in the 11th century, and rebuilt at the expense of the Medici in 1442. It was designed by Brunelleschi, and finished after his death by A. Manetti (1447-60). The dome of the Cappella dei Principi is by Nigetti, that of the Sagrestia Nuova by Michelangelo, and the campanile by F. Ruggieri (1740). Latin cross plan, with three-aisled nave and round arches on Corinthian columns. One of the most important examples of Florentine Renaissance architecture. In the central aisle there are two bronze pulpits by Donatello (*c.* 1460) with bas-reliefs of the *Resurrection* and the *Deposition*. In the second chapel of the right aisle, *Marriage of the Virgin* by Rosso Fiorentino (1523). At the end of this aisle is a marble tabernacle by Desiderio da Settignano. To the left is the Cappella dei Martelli, with the *Annunciation* by Filippo Lippi (*c.* 1440), and the Sagrestia Vecchia di S. Lorenzo, designed by Brunelleschi (1420-29) and decorated by Donatello (1435-43) with four medallions with episodes from the life of St John the Evangelist, four tondi with Evangelists and a frieze of cherubs' heads. It is square in plan with white walls ribbed with

pietra serena, and a hemispherical dome with lantern. Also by Donatello are the bronze doors of the Porta dei Martiri and the Porta degli Apostoli, and the polychrome terracotta bas-reliefs. To the left of the entrance is the bronze and porphyry tomb of Giovanni and Piero dei Medici by Andrea del Verrocchio (1472). Terracotta bust of S. Lorenzo attributed to Donatello. The cloister of S. Lorenzo to the left of the church is in the style of Brunelleschi (15th century). (*See also* Cappelle Medicee, and Biblioteca Mediceo Laurenziana). 11, 15, 88, 89, *89,* 92, 93, *93,* 96, *96,* 108, 114, 129, 130, 134, 139, 145, 166, 177, *178,* 179, 180, *181,* 198, *208, 218,* 235.

S. Lucia dei Magnoli
Via de' Bardi [JC].
An old church known as 'fra le rovinate' (among the ruins), notable for a painting of *S. Lucia* on a gold ground, by P. Lorenzetti.

S. Marco
Piazza S. Marco [GC].
The church and adjoining convent were built on a site occupied by the oratory of the Silvestrine monks in 1299. When the Silvestrine order was suppressed in the 15th century, they passed to the Dominicans and were enlarged by Michelozzo (1437-52) at the orders of Cosimo il Vecchio. Single-aisle nave on Latin cross plan, altered in the 16th and 17th centuries, and Baroque façade. Noteworthy are the *Madonna and child enthroned* by Fra Bartolomeo (1509), a large mosaic from the oratory of Pope John VII at Rome (705-707), the *Vision of St Thomas Aquinas* by Santi di Tito (1593). In Michelozzo's sacristy (1437-43) may be seen a precious Greek pallium of the 15th century. To the left of the presbytery is the Cappella del Sacramento, with late Cinquecento paintings and sculptures. In the left aisle, Cappella di S. Antonio by Giambologna, richly decorated with frescoes, paintings and statues of the 16th and 17th centuries. 30, 108, 112, *126,* 148, 167, 168, 218, 219.

S. Margherita a Montici
Via Pian dei Giullari
Situated on top of a hill. Medieval fragments are still visible in this old church, which contains a marble shrine attributed to Sansovino, and two paintings by the Maestro di S. Cecilia, *Madonna and Child enthroned,* and *S. Margherita.*

S. Maria dell'Impruneta
Via Cassia-Tavernuzze-Impruneta.
11th-century basilica, rebuilt in the 15th century, surrounded by walls

and towers, and altered since the 16th century. The high bell tower with crenellations and Romanesque windows, some single and some coupled, are of the 13th century. The portico on the façade is by Gherardo Silvani. Single-aisle nave restored after the war, timbered roof and polygonal apse. Two niches in the style of Michelozzo by the presbytery, with statues by Luca della Robbia. In the sacristy, a painting and a polyptych of the 15th century, also vestments and plate. The first and second cloisters are respectively of the late 16th and the 14th centuries. The second cloister leads into the crypt (11th century) with cushion capitals.

S. Maria del Fiore - *see* Duomo

S. Maria Maddalena dei Pazzi
Via della Colonna. (Closed on Sundays and public holidays).
Founded in the 13th century, together with the adjoining Benedictine convent, and altered by Giuliano da Sangallo (1480-92) who designed the magnificent cloister. The nave is single-aisled and contains works by artists of the 15th-17th centuries, including Carlo Portelli and Luca Giordano. In the chapter room of the convent, there is a famous fresco of the *Crucifixion* by Perugino (1493-96). 136, 148, *154*, 158, 218, *235*.

S. Maria Maggiore
Piazza S. Maria Maggiore
Pre-11th century, rebuilt in the Gothic style in the second half of the 13th century, possibly by Arnolfo, but according to Vasari by Maestro Buono. Interior in the Cistercian style with three aisles. Façade by Buontalenti (1595). The *Madonna and Child enthroned,* a painted woodcarving attributed to Coppo di Marcovaldo, is to be seen in the chapel on the left.

S. Maria Novella
Piazza S. Maria Novella [HB].
Dominican church built on the site of a 10th-century oratory, and later enlarged. It was completed in 1360. The façade was begun in 1350. The lower part is Romanesque-Gothic, and the upper part, designed by Alberti, is Renaissance. Alberti also designed the classical middle portal. The campanile and most of the building are the work of Fra Iacopo Talenti. To the right of the façade, the old cemetery wall turns into via degli Avelli, where the tombs of Florentine families may be seen. The interior of the church is built on an Egyptian cross plan, with grouped pilasters. On the entrance wall, fresco attributed to Botticelli, and others of the 14th-century Florentine

school. The glass in the windows is thought to have been designed by Andrea di Buonaiuto. In the second span of the right aisle, tomb of Beata Villana by B. Rossellino (1451). In the Cappella della Pura (sixth span) a wooden crucifix by Baccio di Montelupo. In the right transept, Cappella Rucellai (14th century) with Nino Pisano's *Madonna and Child,* and the tomb of Fra Lionardo Dati by Ghiberti (1425). Next come the Cappella dei Bardi and the Cappella di Filippo Strozzi, frescoed by Filippino Lippi. The tomb of Filippo Strozzi is by Benedetto da Maiano (1491-93). The Cappella Maggiore contains a cycle of frescoes by Domenico Ghirlandaio (1485-90), assisted by his brother Davide and the young Michelangelo. Also remains of the original ceiling decoration with busts of prophets by Andrea Orcagna (1340-48). The Cappella Gondi by Giuliano da Sangallo (1503) contains a wooden crucifix by Brunelleschi (*c.* 1410-15), and the Cappella Gaddi is late 16th century. In the left transept, the 14th-century Cappella Strozzi has important frescoes by Nardo di Cione, brother of Andrea Orcagna, who painted the *Redeemer enthroned with saints* over the altar (1357). Beyond the Cappella del Campanile is the Sacristy (1350) with a polychrome lavabo by Giovanni della Robbia (1498) and an early *Crucifixion* by Giotto. In the left aisle is a marble pulpit designed by Brunelleschi and executed by Buggiano (1448). Also a fresco by Masaccio of the *Trinity, the Madonna and St John* (*c.* 1427). 28, 30, 40, 49, 51, 72, *74*, 75, 81, 88, *103*, 105, *105*, *111*, 112, 116, 138, *142*, 146, 149, 152, *152*, *161*, 177, 229, 232.

S. Martino a Gangalandi
Strada statale 67, Lastra a Signa, via Livornese.
Romanesque church altered in the 15th and 16th centuries. Octagonal font with reliefs by the school of Ghiberti. Of great interest is the circular apse with stone pilasters and cornices, possibly designed by Alberti who was prior of the church (1432-72).

S. Michele a S. Salvi
Piazza di S. Salvi
Vallombrosan abbey church begun in the 11th century. The portico is a 16th-century addition, as is also the alteration of the interior. Latin cross plan with rectangular apse. In the nave there is a painting by Passignano. In the sacristy a bust of S. Giovanni Gualberto (16th century). Romanesque cloister with bas-reliefs by Benedetto da Rovezzano and re-

mains of 14th-century frescoes. In the Cappella del Sacramento, tabernacle attributed to Benedetto da Rovezzano, and paintings of the Florentine school.

S. Michele Visdomini (San Michelino)
Via dei Servi
14th-century building, rebuilt in the 17th century by Michelangelo Pacini. It contains an important painting by Pontormo, the *Holy Family with saints* (1518) over the second altar on the right. Other altar paintings by Empoli, Poppi and Passignano. 177.

S. Miniato al Monte
On Monte alle Croci [KD].
A perfect example of Florentine Romanesque, altered during the 11th century, and completed at the beginning of the 13th century. The façade is in two orders, the lower having five arches on Corinthian columns, with a marble revetment in geometrical designs. The false window in the tympanum is surmounted by a 13th-century mosaic. Elegant campanile begun in 1500, and completed by Baccio d'Agnolo. The interior has a revetment of white and green marble. It is divided into three aisles with grouped pilasters, and has 14th- and 15th-century frescoes. There is a wide variety of capitals. The timbers of the central nave roof are painted, and part of the pavement is 13th-century marble inlay with signs of the zodiac and other symbols. The Cappella del Crocifisso by Michelozzo (1448) takes the form of a shrine, with coffered ceiling in glazed terracotta by Luca della Robbia. Raised presbytery enclosed by a marble screen, with a pulpit of *c.* 1207. The choir has 15th-century carving and inlay. 13th-century apse mosaic restored by Baldovinetti in 1491. Over the left altar, a painting of *S. Miniato* by Jacopo del Casentino. In the left aisle, the Cappella del Cardinale di Portogallo by Antonio Manetti (1461-66), is a perfect piece of Renaissance design. The decoration of the roof is by Luca della Robbia. In a niche on the right, Antonio Rossellino's monument to the Cardinal of Portugal. In the left niche, a painting of the *Annunciation* by Baldovinetti, and in the central one, two angels by Antonio Pollaiuolo. In the sacristy, frescoes by Spinello Aretino and assistants (14th century) with the history of St Benedict, and a 15th-century reliquary bust in gilded wood. The crypt is of the 11th century, with seven small aisles. In the cloister are remains of a fresco by Paolo Uccello of the

Lives of the Fathers. 14, *14*, 15, 16, 20, 28, 105, 116, 117, 130, 229.

S. Niccolò sopr'Arno
At the end of via S. Miniato
12th-century church rebuilt in the 16th century. Single-aisle nave with open timber roof, and paintings of the 15th and 16th centuries. In the sacristy, Renaissance shrine with lunette frescoed by Piero del Pollaiuolo of the *Madonna della cintola.* 25.

S. Pietro Scheraggio
Between piazzale degli Uffizi and via della Ninna [JC].
Outstanding Romanesque church, consecrated in 1068, later altered. In 1561 incorporated into the Uffizi buildings. Excavations have uncovered a columned portico and a 'confessio' of the early 9th century. Frescoed brick columns of the old building can be seen in via della Ninna. 16.

S. Remigio
Piazzetta S. Remigio
Founded in the 11th century, rebuilt in the 14th century, the nave has three aisles with pointed arches on octagonal pillars. *Madonna with Child* attributed to Cimabue or one of his followers. 51.

S. Salvatore al Monte, also known as S. Francesco al Monte
Near Piazzale Michelangelo [KD].
Old oratory donated to the Franciscans of Fiesole and rebuilt in its present form by Cronaca (1499) by order of the Calimala merchants. Basilical interior with two orders. 15th- and 16th-century works in the second chapel on the left. 16th-century *Deposition* in polychrome terracotta and 16th-century choir stalls. 139, 229.

S. Simone
Piazzetta S. Simone
13th-century church restored by Gherardo Silvani (1630). Single-aisled nave. Painting attributed to the Maestro di S. Cecilia (1307) over the first altar on the right, of *St Peter enthroned.* Two 15th-century tabernacles. Small Gothic tabernacle (1363) with a 15th-century bust of a woman on the left of the nave.

S. Spirito
Piazza S. Spirito [JB].
Augustinian church, one of Brunelleschi's masterpieces. Begun in 1444 on the site of a small church. Completed by others with some variation on the original design. Campanile by Baccio d'Agnolo. The dome was designed by Brunelleschi and executed by Salvi d'Andrea (1479-81) who is responsible for the internal façade with large rose window and stained

glass of the *Descent of the Holy Spirit* after a design by Perugino. Latin cross plan, three aisles with Corinthian columns which continue into the transept and the apse, grafting a central plan on to a basilical one in the space surmounted by the dome. The small semi-circular chapels contain a large number of works of art. In the right aisle, 16th-century polychrome wooden statue of *S. Nicola da Tolentino,* and two angels by Franciabigio (third chapel): *Expulsion of the Money Changers from the Temple* by Giovanni Stradano (fourth chapel); *Martyrdom of St Stephen* by Passignano (sixth chapel); the high altar is a monumental work of Giovanni Caccini and assistants (1599-1608). The wooden crucifix is attributed to the young Michelangelo. In the right transept, a painting by Filippino Lippi (*c.* 1490) and marble tomb of Neri di Gino Capponi attributed to Bernardo Rossellino (1458) behind a bronze grill. In the apse, from right to left, polyptych by Maso di Banco (second chapel); Allori's *Adulteress* (1577) (fifth chapel); *The Annunciation,* 15th-century Florentine school (seventh chapel). Left transept, *Madonna enthroned with Child and saints* by Cosimo Rosselli (1482); Cappella Corbinelli, architecture and sculpture by Andrea Sansovino (1492) with 17th-century balustrade; *Adoration of the Trinity* attributed to F. Granacci; *Madonna enthroned with Child and saints* by Raffaele dei Carli (1505). Left aisle, *Madonna enthroned with saints* of the school of Fra Bartolomeo; *Madonna with St Anne and saints* by Ridolfo and Michele Ghirlandaio. The door beneath the organ leads to a vestibule built by Cronaca (1492-94), designed by Giuliano da Sangallo, and then on to the Sacristy, also designed by him. This is a large octagonal room ribbed with pietra serena, with a dome designed by Antonio del Pollaiuolo. *Miracle of St Fiacre* over the altar, painted by Alessandro Allori. The first cloister is by Giulio and Alfonso Parigi, the second by Ammannati (1564-69). This leads to the Cappella Corsini, with the Gothic tomb of Neri Corsini. 49, 92, *106, 109,* 114, 136, 139, 152, 166, 177, 236.

S. Stefano al Ponte
Piazza S. Stefano al Ponte
12th-century church with Romanesque façade the lower part of which is of the first half of the 13th century. The rectangular interior is by Ferdinando Tacca, who also executed the altarpiece on the third altar to the left, the *Stoning of St Stephen.* The surrounding altars are of the 16th century, and the marble steps to the presbytery were designed by Buontalenti. 217.

S. Trinita
Piazza S. Trinita [HB].
Built in the second half of the 13th century on the site of a Vallombrosa church of the 11th century. Façade by Buontalenti (1593-94). Gothic interior with three aisles, transept, and pointed arches. In the right aisle: 14th-century wooden crucifix in the first chapel. Frescoes (*c.* 1420-25) and *Annunciation* by Lorenzo Monaco in the fourth chapel. In the sacristy, Renaissance tomb of Onofrio Strozzi by Piero di Niccolò Lamberti (1421). To the right of the presbytery is the 15th-century Cappella Sassetti, containing a famous cycle of frescoes by Domenico Ghirlandaio (1483-86) who also painted the *Adoration of the shepherds* over the altar. The tombs of Francesco Sassetti and his wife Nera Corsi are attributed to Giuliano da Sangallo (1485-91). In the second chapel to the left, in the left transept, is the tomb of Bishop Benozzo Federighi by Luca della Robbia (1455-56). The left aisle contains a wooden statue of the *Magdalen* by Desiderio da Settignano and Benedetto da Maiano (1464-65). Access to the cloister of the convent of S. Trinita is in Via Parione. The convent is now occupied by the Facoltà di Magistero. It was rebuilt by A. Parigi (1584) after designs by Buontalenti. 29, 36, 66, 111, 117, 130, 138, 149, 152, 172, 174, 190.

Spedale degli Innocenti
Piazza SS. Annunziata [GD]
Begun by Filippo Brunelleschi (1421-24) and completed by Francesco della Luna in 1445. The nine wide arches are supported on Corinthian columns, and the spandrels contain ten enamelled terracotta tondi by Andrea della Robbia (*c.* 1463). Under the portico are frescoes by Poccetti. Over the left door, *The Eternal Father surrounded by Martyred Innocents* by Giovanni di Francesco (1459). This leads into the Cappella di S. Maria degli Innocenti, which contains *The Blessed Virgin in Glory* by Matteo Rosselli, and an *Annunciation* by Mariotto Albertinelli. In the first cloister, in the style of Brunelleschi, an enamelled terracotta *Annunciation* by Andrea della Robbia. The so-called Chiostro delle Donne is also in the same style, with elegant columns. It has recently been restored. 82, *87,* 88, 93, 108, 130, 152, 235.

Spirito Santo e S. Giorgio sulla Costa
Costa S. Giorgio
The church belongs to the adjoining convent, founded in the 14th century and modernized at the beginning of the 18th century. Noteworthy 18th-century interior with high tribune. Ceiling fresco by A. Gherardini, *St George in glory;* on the right of the altar, *Madonna with Child and angels* mentioned by Ghiberti and others as a work of Giotto and accepted as such by many modern scholars.

Stadio Communale
Viale Manfredo Fanti.
Built of reinforced concrete in 1932 by Pier Luigi Nervi. One of the finest stadiums in Italy, it can hold 55,000 spectators. 231.

Stazione Centrale di S. Maria Novella [GB]
Built in 1935, it was designed by the 'Gruppo Toscano', directed by the architect Giovanni Michelucci. It is one of the first achievements in Italy in the field of functional architecture, and has been carefully designed to fit into the historical background of the city. 231.

Teatro Romano, Excavations and Museum
Fiesole. (The excavations may be visited from 9 to 5. The museum is closed from 12 to 2). The Roman theatre is of the 1st century B.C. but received improvements during the 1st and 2nd centuries A.D. It is built on the Greek pattern and could hold 300 spectators, being carved out of the hillside (34 m. in diameter). It is divided into four sections, with an orchestra on three steps, and a stage 26.4 m. wide and 6.4 m. in depth. The ruins of the baths against the Etruscan walls beyond the theatre date from the 1st century B.C. with enlargments carried out under Hadrian. It is still possible to identify the swimming baths, the heating system, calidarium, sudatorium, and frigidarium. A straight road leads from the baths to the Etruscan-Roman temple, which was rebuilt in the last days of the Republic without alteration to the Etruscan decoration of the tympanum. The sanctuary was divided into three, with a tetrastyle pronaos 'in antis'. The remains of the Etruscan temple are at a lower level, and to the right there are remains of an Etruscan doorway. The museum consists of three rooms containing material that has been excavated or donated. 9, 16.

Tribunale di Mercanzia
Piazza della Signoria [HC].
Built in 1359 on the site of a Roman theatre. It contains a medieval room used by the merchants.

Via dei Ginori
From piazza S. Lorenzo to Via S. Gallo [GC].
This street takes its name from the palace of the Ginori family, No. 13, attributed to Baccio d'Agnolo. On the same side of the street are other important 15th- and 16th-century palaces. No. 7, Palazzo Donati (formerly Neroni), No. 9, Palazzo Barbolani di Montauto (formerly Gerini), No. 15, Casa Ginori (formerly Masi, once occupied by Baccio Bandinelli), No. 19, Palazzo Taddei (by Baccio d'Agnolo, 1503-04), occupied by Raphael in 1505, No. 23, Palazzo Tolomei, later Garzoni.

Via dei Pucci [HC]
This takes its name from the great Palazzo Pucci, the outside of which was rebuilt in the 17th century by P. Falconieri, who preserved the elegant windows on the ground floor, and Ammannati's loggia . There are two courtyards within, and the rooms contain frescoes by Giovanni da S. Giovanni, and various works of art. At the corner of the street is the *Tabernacolo delle cinque lampade* (tabernacle with five lamps) on the right side of which is a niche frescoed by Cosimo Rosselli.

Via dei Servi
From Piazza del Duomo to Piazza della SS. Annunziata.
Church of S. Michele Visdomini, (q.v.); No. 12, Palazzo Fiaschi Cuccoli (formerly Almeni, attributed to Ammannati), No. 15, Palazzo Niccolini (formerly Montauto, by Domenico di Baccio d'Agnolo). 88.

Via S. Niccolò [KD]
A street of old houses and palaces. Palazzo del Rosso is 16th century (No. 54), Palazzo Demidoff (No. 56), Palazzo Nasi, later Strozzi-Ridolfi, with 16th-century façade and an interesting courtyard, Casa Nasi, formerly Quaratesi (No. 107) is late 15th century. At the end of the street are the three historic 13th-century Palazzi de' Mozzi.

Via Tornabuoni [HB]
Among the most interesting and elegant streets in Florence, it contains palaces dating from the 15th to the 19th centuries. 12.

Villa medicea di Careggi
A medieval manor transformed and enlarged after 1457 by Michelozzo for Cosimo il Vecchio. It was the meeting place of the Florentine Platonist Academy. 110, *120*, 130, 145.

Villa medicea di Castello
16th-century building of great simplicity, the favourite residence of the Medici. Of particular interest is the terraced garden by Tribolo (*c.* 1540) with the fountain of *Hercules and Cacus.* In the centre of the park is a fishpond with a statue by Ammannati. *122,* 146.

Villa medicea della Petraia
Via della Petraia (Castello di Sotto).
Built by Buontalenti (1576-89), it comprises two storeys and a square tower. The garden, by Tribolo, is in the Italian style. Tribolo also designed the fountain. The villa stands on a terrace, with a fishpond alongside. Under the arches in the courtyard are frescoes by Volterrano (1636-48) dealing with the Medici family. To the right there is a roof garden with a fountain by Tribolo and at the summit a statue by Giambologna. There is a large park with fishponds. *117, 122.*

Villa medicea del Poggio a Caiano
Strada statale 66, Pistoiese.
Commissioned by Lorenzo il Magnifico and built by Giuliano da Sangallo, later partially altered by the Grand Dukes. It is decorated with smooth courses of pietra serena, and stands on a wide terrace over an arcade. A double staircase leads to the central terrace and entrance loggia with a frieze in terracotta bas-relief attributed to Andrea Sansovi-

no. The Salone is barrel-vaulted with gilt coffering, and contains allegorical paintings by Franciabigio, Alessandro Allori and Andrea del Sarto. Pontormo's masterpiece, *Vertumnus and Pomona* (1521) is on the right wall at the entrance. The villa is noted also for its park and garden with lemon trees. 134, 136, *136,* 168, 177, 205.

Villa di Poggio Imperiale
Viale di Poggio Imperiale.
A magnificent building standing on the site of an old castle which came into the possession of Maria Maddalena, the widow of Cosimo II, who was of the imperial house of Austria. It was she who had the place enlarged by Giulio Parigi in 1620. The rear façade is 18th century, and the neo-Classical front is early 19th century, with two orders, a central loggia and two low wings. The interior is richly decorated with paintings and stuccoes by Tuscan artists. It is now the seat of the Educandato Statale della SS. Annunziata. 201, 218, 221.

Villa I Tatti
Settignano. The villa may be visited on Wednesdays in summer, by previous appointment.
A low building with large garden in the Italian style, restored by Bernard Berenson who formed an important library and made a rich collection of works of art. 236.

Painters, Sculptors and Architects

Alberti, Leon Battista
(Genoa 1404-Rome 1472). Architect and man of letters, who made a decisive contribution to Renaissance architecture. Worked for Giovanni Rucellai in Florence from 1442-60. He designed the Palazzo Rucellai and the loggia. He built the Cappella del S. Sepolcro near the church of S. Pancrazio and the façade of the church of S. Maria Novella. He also made designs for the choir of SS. Annunziata, and the apse of the church of S. Martino a Gangalandi near Lastra a Signa is attributed to him. 65, 67, 75, 88, 102, *102,* 105, 106, 108, 114, 116, 129.

Albertinelli, Mariotto
(Florence 1474-1515). Painter. Pupil of Cosimo Rosselli and Piero di Cosimo. He often collaborated with Bartolomeo della Porta. Fresco of the *Crucifixion* in the Certosa del

Galluzzo (1505). *Visitation* (1503) in the Uffizi. Two paintings of the *Annunciation,* one in the Galleria dell'Accademia (1510), the other in the Spedale degli Innocenti. *Madonna enthroned* (signed and dated 1514) in the church of S. Michele at Volognano, on the outskirts of Florence. 168.

Allori, Alessandro
(Florence 1535-1607). Painter. Pupil and assistant of Bronzino. Influenced by Michelangelo, whose work he studied in Rome (1554-59). Very active in Florence: S. Maria Novella (Cappella Gaddi, 1575); *Gathering of the manna* in the refectory. Works in the churches of SS. Annunziata (Cappella Montanto, 1550), S. Spirito, S. Maria del Carmine, S. Marco, S. Niccolò sopr'Arno. Paintings in the museums: Galleria dell'Accademia, Uffizi, Museo dell'Opera del

Duomo, Museo dell'Opera di S. Croce, Museo Mediceo, Museo dell'Ospedale degli Innocenti (frescoes taken from S. Maria Nuova). Frescoes at the Villa di Poggio a Caiano and the Carmine and in the Cappella di S. Luca near SS. Annunziata. 168, 190, 192, 201, 205.

Allori, Cristofano
(Florence 1577-1621). Painter. Son of Alessandro Allori. *Judith* in the Galleria Pitti, and other works in the Uffizi, Casa Buonarroti, SS. Annunziata, S. Trinita. 208.

Ambrogio di Baldese
(Florence 1352-1429). Painter. Frescoes in the Loggia del Bigallo, in collaboration with Nicolò Gerini.

Ammannati, Bartolomeo
(Settignano 1511-Florence 1592). Architect and sculptor. Collaborated with Sansovino in Venice. In Rome in 1555. Called to Florence by Duke Cosimo I. Exponent of Florentine Mannerism. Worked on the Boboli gardens. Built the Palazzi Riccardi-Mannelli, formerly Grifoni (1557), Pitti (1558-70), Vitali, formerly Pazzi, Ramirez di Montalvo, formerly Almeni, Mondragone (*c.* 1568-70), della Commenda di Castiglione. He also built the Ponte S. Trinita (1566-69), the fountain in Piazza della Signoria (1563-75), the second cloister in the church of S. Spirito (1564-69). Sculptures by him are in the Villa di Castello (the fountain of *Hercules and Cacus*) and the Museo del Bargello. 181, 184, *188*, 190, 192, *192, 195, 223*, 229, *233*.

Andrea da Firenze (Andrea di Bonaiuto)
Painter, active in the 14th century. His chief work is the grand cycle of frescoes (*c.* 1355) in the chapter room of S. Maria Novella, which in the 17th century became the Cappellone degli Spagnuoli. 51.

Andrea Del Sarto
(Andrea d'Agnolo; Florence 1486-1531). Painter, pupil of Piero di Cosimo, he worked in France at the invitation of Francis I. Frescoes in the Chiostrino dei Voti and the Chiostri dei Morti in SS. Annunziata, the Chiostro dello Scalzo and the Cenacolo di S. Salvi (the famous *Last Supper*, 1519-27). Paintings in the Uffizi and the Galleria Palatina. 168, 205.

Andrea Pisano
(known as Andrea da Pontedera; Pontedera *c.* 1295-Orvieto 1349). Sculptor, architect and goldsmith. He worked in the Duomo at Orvieto in 1310 and the following years. In Florence he executed the south door of the Baptistery (1330-36) and di-

rected work on the Campanile of the Duomo after the death of Giotto (1337). 49, 56. 58, *65, 66,* 72.

Angelico, Fra
(Fra Giovanni da Fiesole, called l'Angelico; Vicchio di Mugello 1387-Rome 1455). Painter and friar of the convent of S. Domenico at Fiesole. Active in the development of Florentine painting with the other great artists of the early 15th century. He frescoed the cloister and the cells of the convent of S. Marco in Florence (now the Museo dell'Angelico where there are many other of his celebrated works) between 1436-43. His *Madonna and Child* (*c.* 1445) is in the Uffizi; other works in S. Domenico at Fiesole. 111, 112, 114, 119.

Antico
(Alari Bonacolsi Pier Iacopo, called l'Antico; Mantua *c.* 1460-Gazzuolo, Mantua, 1528). Sculptor, goldsmith and medal-maker. Medals in the Museo del Bargello (Sala dei Bronzi).

Arnoldi, Alberto
(Active Florence in the second half of the 14th century). Has sculptures in the Campanile of the Duomo (the *Sacraments*), in the Loggia del Bigallo (*Madonna*, 1361), in the Bargello (bas-relief in the lunette above the door of the Cappella del Podestà). 49, 56.

Arnolfo di Cambio
(Colle di Valdelsa 1245-Florence 1308?). Architect and sculptor. Trained in the school of Nicola Pisano, he spent some time in Perugia and Rome, returning to Florence in 1296 where he began the Duomo and the Palazzo della Signoria and probably S. Croce. The Museo del Duomo has sculptures by him from the original façade of the Duomo. One of his statues is in the Casa Buonarroti. *9,* 30, 31, 36, *39,* 46, *51,* 53, 55, 58, *65,* 75, 82.

Baccio D'Agnolo
(Baglioni; Florence 1462-1543). Architect and sculptor in wood. His principal works in Florence are the Palazzi Serristori, formerly Cocchi (attributed, 1469-74), Bartolini Salimbeni (1517-20), Taddei and Borgherini. 173, 174, 180.

Baccio da Montelupo
(Baccio Sinibaldi; Montelupo 1469-Lucca 1535). Architect and sculptor. Works in Florence: wooden crucifix in S. Maria Novella (1501), bronze statue of *St John the Evangelist* in Or San Michele, and a wooden crucifix in the Museo di S. Marco. 169.

Baldovinetti, Alessio
(Florence 1425-99). Painter. Works in the churches of SS. Annunziata

(*Nativity* 1460-62), S. Miniato al Monte (*Annunciation* 1466-67). In the Uffizi, *Annunciation* and *Madonna and child with saints*. In the Galleria dell'Accademia, *Trinity and saints*. In the Museo di S. Marco, the *Life of Christ* and *St Anthony adoring the Cross*. 117, 130, 134, 146.

Bandinelli, Baccio
(Florence 1488-1560). Sculptor, much patronized by the Medici. Among his important works are the octagonal choir of the Duomo (1555), the self-portrait medal in the Museo dell'Opera del Duomo (1556), and *Hercules and Cacus* on the steps of the Palazzo della Signoria (1533). Other works in the Museo del Bargello, the Uffizi, the first cloister of S. Croce (*Eternal Father*, 1548), the Boboli Gardens, and a *Pietà* in SS. Annunziata. 89, 139, 182, *184*, 186.

Bartolini, Lorenzo
(Savignano 1777 - Florence 1850). Sculptor. As a young man in Paris, he trained with David and Ingres. Then in Tuscany he became director of the Academy of Fine Arts at Carrara and visiting lecturer in the Academy at Florence. Principal works: monuments to Leon Battista Alberti, Charlotte Bonaparte, Princess Zamoyska in the S. Croce; monuments to Nespoli in the SS. Annunziata and to Demidoff in the square of the same name. Statue of Niccolò Macchiavelli in the portico of the Uffizi, as well as many portraits and gesso-works. 221, 222.

Bartolomeo, Fra
(Della Porta Baccio, Florence 1472-Pian di Mugnone 1517). Painter. Entered the Dominican order in 1505. Influenced by Raphael. Works in the Museo di S. Marco taken from S. Maria Nuova (fresco of the *Last Judgment*, 1499-1501); in the Galleria Palatina (*Deposition, c.* 1516) and in the Uffizi. Frescoes in the convent of S. Maria Maddalena (*Annunciation*, 1515 and *Noli me tangere*, 1517). 167, 168.

Beccafumi, Domenico
(Domenico di Iacopo di Pace; Montaperti, Siena, 1486-1551). Painter, influenced by Perugino, Sodoma, and Raphael. Works in the Uffizi, Museo Horne, and Galleria Palatina.

Benci di Cione
(Died Florence 1388). Architect. Gave his name to two examples of Florentine Gothic architecture: the church of S. Carlo dei Lombardi (1349-50), which he built with the help of Neri di Fioravante, and the Loggia dei Lanzi (1376) which he built with the help of Simone Talenti. *55*, 56.

Benedetto da Maiano
(Maiano 1442-Florence 1497). Sculptor and architect, an original artist who remained independent of the influence of Donatello. Famous for his marble pulpit in S. Croce (1472-76) and the marble doorway of the Sala dell'Udienza (1481) in the Palazzo della Signoria. Other works in S. Maria Novella (tomb of Filippo Strozzi, 1491-93) and in the Duomo (bronze crucifix, 1495-97). He designed the Palazzo Strozzi and worked on the Sala dei Dugento with Giuliano (1472-77). *114, 129, 135, 136, 145.*

Benedetto da Rovezzano
(Canapale, Pistoia 1474-Vallombrosa after 1552). Sculptor and architect, follower of Benedetto da Maiano and Giuliano da Sangallo. In Florence from 1505 to 1515, he designed the doorway (1495) and vestibule for the Badia Fiorentina and the Cappella Pandolfini. Sculptures in the Museo del Bargello (two niches from the Palazzo Cepparello, formerly Salviati), and in the churches of S. Michele a S. Salvi and S. Maria del Carmine (tomb of Pier Soderini). 169.

Bertoldo di Giovanni
(Florence, *c.* 1420-91). Sculptor and medallist. Follower of Donatello. He was principal of the Medicean school at the convent of S. Marco. Notable among his sculptures in the Bargello are the bronze reliefs of an *Equestrian Battle*, the *Crucifixion*, the *Pietà* and various small statues.

Botticelli, Sandro
(Filipepi, Sandro; Florence 1444-1510). Painter. Pupil of Filippo Lippi, influenced by Pollaiuolo, Andrea del Castagno and Verrocchio. He was an innovator who greatly influenced Florentine painting. Principal works in the Uffizi (Room V); *Primavera* (*c.* 1476-78) painted for the villa of Lorenzo di Pierfrancesco de' Medici at Castello, *Madonna of the Magnificat*, *Birth of Venus*. Other works in the Galleria dell'Accademia, the Galleria Corsini and the Galleria Palatina. Fresco of *St Augustine* in the refectory of Ognissanti (1480). In the Uffizi *Annunciation*, fresco taken from S. Martino della Scala. Attributed *Madonna and Child enthroned* in the Oratorio del Vannella at Settignano. 134, 136, *140*, 146, 147, 148, 152.

Bronzino
(Agnolo Tori, called Il Bronzino; Monticelli, Florence 1503-1572). Painter and poet. Pupil of Raffaellino del Garbo and Pontormo. An original portrait painter who con-

tributed to the development of Florentine Mannerism. Portrait of Laura Battiferri in the Palazzo della Signoria, Medici portraits in the Uffizi, and a series of small Medici portraits in the Museo Mediceo. Other works in S. Croce, SS. Annunziata, the Galleria dell'Accademia, and S. Maria Novella. His first work, *Martyrdom of San Lorenzo*, in the Certosa del Galluzzo. *174, 177, 182, 186, 188.*

Brunelleschi, Filippo
(Florence 1377-1446). Architect and sculptor. Initiator of the Italian Renaissance. His theory of perspective and his new conception of reality are of fundamental importance. He had made a close observation of Roman architecture while in Rome and embraced the humanistic ideals of classical literature. His training as a goldsmith is apparent in his panel *The Sacrifice of Isaac* for the second door of the Baptistry, now in the Bargello. His first works after his definitive return to Florence are the Casa Lapi, and the wooden crucifix in S. Maria Novella. In 1417 he was called in as consultant and built the dome of the Cathedral after 1420. This is a bold construction of eight segments connected with pointed arch ribs. At this period he also designed the portico of the Ospedale degli Innocenti, the Sagrestia Vecchia in S. Lorenzo, and he also worked on the Palazzo dei Capitani di Parte Guelfa (1428). The Cappella dei Pazzi (1430) and the rotunda of S. Maria degli Angeli remained incomplete and S. Spirito begun in 1444. The central portion of the Palazzo Pitti is attributed to him. *16, 31, 56, 59, 65, 65, 67, 70, 72, 75, 82, 87, 88, 92, 92, 93, 96, 96, 98, 98, 103, 106, 106, 108, 109, 112, 114, 130, 134, 136, 139, 180, 196, 235.*

Buonsignori, Stefano
(Died in Florence 1589). Artist and cartographer. Author of the most famous perspective plan of Florence (1575) and of some of the 53 maps painted on the doors of the wall-cupboards in the Guardaroba at the Palazzo Vecchio (1575-84). *189, 219.*

Buontalenti, Bernardo
(Florence 1536-1608). Architect. Follower of Michelangelo, and influenced by Ammannati, he is one of the major exponents of late Florentine Mannerism. A versatile artist, he worked for the most part in the service of Cosimo I and his sons Francesco and Ferdinando. His first work was the Villa del Pratolino (1569) for Bianca Cappello (this was rebuilt in the early 19th century). Then came the Casino di S. Marco (1574), now Palazzo della Corte d'Appello, the designs for the portico of the Arcispedale di S. Maria Nuova and for the Villa della Petraia (1576-89) and di Artiminio (1594). In the Uffizi he built the room called 'La Tribuna' (1585-89) and the so-called Porta delle Suppliche. In 1576 he was working on the Boboli gardens. He built the famous grotto which houses the *Slaves* of Michelangelo. In 1593 he designed the façade of S. Trinita and a little later began the Palazzo Nonfinito. The Palazzi Corsini and Gerini (Via Ricasoli) have also been attributed to him. *177, 184, 190, 192, 198, 199, 201, 201, 207, 230.*

Canova, Antonio
(Possagno 1757-Venice 1822). Sculptor. Leader of the neoclassical school in Italy who achieved European fame early in his life. A prolific artist, he had a great influence on the sculpture of the beginning of the 19th century. In Florence, the monument to *Vittorio Alfieri* in S. Croce, the large bust of *Napoleon* in the Galleria d'Arte Moderna and the statue *Italic Venus* in the Palazzo Pitti. *221.*

Cellini, Benvenuto
(Florence 1500-1571). Sculptor, writer and goldsmith. An exponent of the Mannerist style. He came to Florence after spending some time in France at the court of Francis I and here produced the bronze *Perseus* (1553) on the Loggia dei Lanzi. The bust of *Cosimo I* and other works are in the Bargello. *54, 164, 183, 186, 192.*

Cimabue
(Cenni di Pepo, Florence *c.* 1240-Pisa 1302). Painter. Predecessor of Giotto, working along the same lines as Giunta Pisano and Coppo di Marcovaldo, but surpassing them in his handling of masses. Two of his most important works are in Florence: the *Madonna in Majesty* in the Uffizi (formerly in S. Trinita) and a *Crucifixion* in the Museo dell'Opera di S. Croce, damaged in the 1966 floods. *36, 40.*

Ciseri, Antonio
(Ronco 1821-Florence 1891). Painter. Pupil of Bezzuoli in Florence. Executed paintings with historical and religious subjects as well as excellent portraits. Principal works in the church of S. Felicita and the Galleria d'Arte Moderna in the Palazzo Pitti.

Cronaca
(Simone del Pollaiuolo, called Cronaca, Florence 1457-1508). Architect and sculptor. Togheter with Giuliano da Sangallo he developed Brunelles-

chi's architectural style with a tendency to classical grandeur. Among his principal works are the courtyard and cornice of the Strozzi palace (1496), the Salone del Cinquecento in the Palazzo Vecchio (1495) and the church of S. Salvatore al Monte (*c.* 1500). 136, 139, 164, 172.

Daddi, Bernardo
(Florence, active during the first half of the 14th century). Painter. Follower of the late style of Giotto, as is shown by his frescoes in the Cappella Pulci e Beraldi in S. Croce (*c.* 1330). His lively and original use of colour and his more massive forms may be observed in the Tabernacle of the Museo del Bigallo (1333). *Madonna of grace* (1347) in Or San Michele, and a diptych in the Museo Horne. Other works in the Uffizi, one signed and dated 1328. 49.

Danti, Vincenzo
(Perugia 1530-76). Architect, sculptor and art historian. While in Florence he came under the Mannerist influence of Michelangelo. He has works in the Bargello, in S. Croce and on one of the Baptistry doors (the *Beheading of St John the Baptist*). In 1567 he published a thesis on proportion. 169, 184, 190.

De Fabris, Emilio
(Florence 1808-83). Architect. Professor of architecture and perspective at the Academy of Fine Arts, Florence. Author of the scheme for the façade of the Duomo (S. Maria del Fiore). 230.

Del Castagno, Andrea
(Mugello 1423-Florence 1457). Painter. Influenced by Paolo Uccello, his works are noted for their plastic vigour and lively colour. *Deposition* (cartoon 1444), for a window in the Duomo. *Last Supper* (*c.* 1450), *Crucifixion, Deposition and Resurrection* in the refectory of Andrea del Castagno (the former Monastero di S. Apollonia). Equestrian monument to Nicola da Tolentino, fresco in chiaroscuro mounted on canvas (1456) in the Duomo; frescoes of illustrious people in the villa Carducci Pandolfini a Legnaia. 117, 118, *129*, 235.

Del Tasso, Giovanni Battista
(Florence, 1500-55). Architect. The most original member of a well-known family of sculptors and engravers. Works in Florence include the Loggia del Mercato Nuovo, the addition to the back part of the Palazzo Vecchio, and, within this building, various ceilings in the wing of Eleonora da Toledo. He completed the carving of a ceiling designed by Michelangelo in the main room of the Biblioteca Mediceo-Laurenziana. 186, 188.

Della Francesca, Piero
(Borgo San Sepolcro, Arezzo, 1410/ 20-92). Painter, theoretician of perspective and mathematics. One of the greatest artists of the Renaissance, he exercised an important influence on northern Italian art, especially that of Venice and Ferrara. Frescoes are to be found at Rimini, Borgo San Sepolcro and at Arezzo, where his famous cycle, the *History of the Cross* is to be found in the church of San Francisco. As a young man in Florence he is mentioned as having assisted Domenico Veneziano on the lost frescoes of Sant'Egidio (Arcispedale di S. Maria Nuova). One of his masterpieces is in the Uffizi: a diptych with the portraits of Federico da Montefeltro and Battista Sforza (*c.* 1465), which came from Urbino in the 17th century. 114, 116, 117, 201.

Della Robbia, Andrea
(Florence 1435-1525). Sculptor, one of the famous family of ceramic artists. His best works are those of his youth: the tondi of the portico of the Spedale degli Innocenti (*c.* 1463) and the *Meeting of St Domenic and St Francis* in the Loggia di S. Paolo. The terracotta altarpiece in the Cappella del Noviziato in S. Croce (*c.* 1480), some medallions of the large cloister in the Certosa del Galluzzo, and his works in the Bargello are of his later period. 130.

Della Robbia, Giovanni
(Florence 1469-1529). The most important artist among the sons of Andrea, he showed a certain eclecticism. His principal works in Florence are terracottas in the Bargello, an enamelled terracotta lavabo in the sacristy of S. Maria Novella (1498), and the tabernacle in the right aisle of SS. Apostoli.

Della Robbia, Luca
(Florence *c.* 1400-82). Sculptor, and the most outstanding of the Della Robbia family. His glazed terracotta madonnas reach the highest degree of perfection. Notable examples of his work are in the Bargello and the Pinacoteca degli Innocenti. These are later than his *Cantoria* in the Museo del Duomo (1431-38). The bas-reliefs of the Campanile are of 1437-39. Lunette of *S. Pierino* in the Palazzo dei Capitani di Parte Guelfa. Tomb of Bishop Benozzo Federighi in S. Trinita (1455-56) and painted tile decoration on the ceiling of the chapel of the Cardinal of Portugal in S. Miniato al Monte. 112, 120, 130, *133*, *135*.

Desiderio da Settignano
(Settignano *c.* 1430-Florence 1464). Sculptor. Among his early works are

the medallions of the outer frieze of the Cappella dei Pazzi. The dating and attribution of his work is not always certain, but the monument to Carlo Marsuppini (c. 1453) in S. Croce is certainly by him, also the wooden statue of the *Magdalen* in S. Trinita completed by Benedetto da Maiano. Other works generally agreed to be his are in the Bargello. 129, 130, *131*.

Donatello
(Donato di Niccolò di Betto de' Bardi; Florence c. 1386-1466). Sculptor. He is the true initiator of Tuscan Renaissance sculpture. His first works are the marble *David* (1408-09) in the Bargello, the *St John Evangelist* (1407-11) in the Museo dell'Opera del Duomo, the *St Mark* (1411-13) and *St George* (1417) for Or San Michele now in the Bargello. All these clearly reveal his awareness of classical sculpture, and suggest that he must have spent some time in Rome. His major works in the succeeding years are the statues of prophets for the niches of the Campanile of the Duomo, now in the Museo dell'Opera. Notable among these is the *Habakkuk* (1423-24). The *Marzocco*, now in the Bargello, dates from 1418-20. During the following decade he produced the bronze tomb of Anti-pope John XXIII, in collaboration with Michelozzo, in the Baptistry of Florence, which also contains his later wooden statue of the *Magdalen*. For the Medici he produced a series of elegant works. These include the bronze *David* (1430-32) now in the Bargello, the *Annunciation* in S. Croce (1428-39), and the *Cantoria* of the Duomo (1433-39) in the Museo dell'Opera. He was in Padua from 1444-53, and the works he produced in Florence after that period are more expressionistic, such as the *Judith and Holofernes*, in the Piazza della Signoria (c. 1460), and the bronze pulpits in S. Lorenzo (1460-70). He also decorated the Sagrestia Vecchia (1435-43). 67, 72, 76, 81, *82*, 89, 93, *93*, 112, *116*, *118*, 120, 129, 133, 134, 142, 145, 164.

Dosio, Giovanni Antonio
(Florence 1533-Rome or Naples after 1609). Architect and Mannerist sculptor. He decorated the Cappella Gaddi in S. Maria Novella (1575-77), the Cappella Niccolini in S. Croce, and the Palazzo Arcivescovile (1573-84). The Palazzo Larderel (formerly Giacomini 1580), is also attributed to him. 192, 230.

Fancelli, Luca
(Settignano 1430-95). Sculptor and architect. Most of his work was done in Mantua for the Gonzaga family, then in Milan and Naples. In Florence he began the construction of the Palazzo Pitti from Brunelleschi's designs. 134, 157.

Fiorentino, Pier Francesco
(Active in Florence 1470-1500). Painter. Follower of Benozzo Gozzoli and of Baldovinetti, he painted mainly madonnas with a craftsman's skill. Certain works are attributed to a very similar painter, usually called the 'Pseudo Pier Francesco Fiorentino', and are more sensitive and are composed after the manner of Filippo Lippi.

Foggini, Giovanni Battista
(Florence 1652-1725). Sculptor and architect, a representative of late Florentine Baroque. He made the Cappella Feroni and tomb of Senator Donato dell'Antella (1702) in SS. Annunziata, and the marble reliefs in the Cappella di S. Andrea Corsini in the Carmine. 218.

Francesco del Tadda
(Francesco Ferrucci; Florence 1497-1585). Sculptor, noted for the re-introduction of porphyry sculpture. Medallions of Cosimo I and Eleonora di Toledo in the Museo Mediceo; basin of the fountain in the first courtyard of the Palazzo Vecchio (1555).

Gaddi, Agnolo di Taddeo
(died in 1396). Florentine painter with a flowing narrative style. Frescoes in the Cappella Castellani (c. 1385) with pupils, among them perhaps Lo Starnina, and the Cappella Maggiore of S. Croce (c. 1380). 50.

Gaddi, Gaddo
(active between 1312-13). Painter and mosaicist. Friend of Cimabue and Giotto. Vasari attributes to him in part the mosaics of *St John the Baptist* in the dome of the Baptistry.

Gaddi, Taddeo
(Died 1366). Florentine painter, perhaps the greatest pupil of Giotto. Frescoes in the Cappella Baroncelli in S. Croce, *Madonna and Child with angels* in the Uffizi (signed and dated 1355), and paintings of the *Life of Christ* and the *Life of St Francis* in the Galleria dell'Accademia. 47, 50, *60*.

Gentile da Fabriano
(Gentile di Nicolò di Giovanni Massi; Fabriano c. 1370 - Rome 1427). Painter. Lived in Florence 1422-25. One of the foremost Italian exponents of the International Gothic style. *Adoration of the Magi* in the Uffizi, painted in 1423 for Palla Strozzi, and *Four saints* in the Quaratesi polyptych (1425). 66, 114, 118.

Gerini, Niccolò di Pietro
(active between 1368-1416). Painter.
Follower of the traditions of Gaddi
and Orcagna, he was head of a prolific workshop of devotional painters.
Among many works *Almsgiving*,
detached fresco in the Loggia del
Bigallo (1386), *Crucifixion* and frescoes in the chapter room of S.
Felicita, *Deposition* in S. Carlo, a
large *Crucifixion* in the Cappella
Castellani, and a large polyptych in
the Cappella Maggiore of S. Croce.
53, 66.

Ghiberti, Lorenzo
(Florence 1378-1455). Sculptor, goldsmith, architect, painter and man of
letters. Pupil of the goldsmith Bartolo di Michele. He devoted himself
to painting after going to Rome.
Returning to Florence, he won the
prize for the second door of the
Baptistry, which was executed 1403-
24 on the same pattern as the first
door by Andrea Pisano. In 1425 he
was commissioned to design the door
known as the 'porta del Paradiso'.
By now he knew Donatello, and he
achieved a more interesting perspective, while his rich gilding heightened the decorative effect. Also important are his bronze statues of *St
Matthew* (1419-22) and *St Stephen*
(1426) at Or San Michele. He also
executed cartoons for the windows
of the internal façade of the dome,
the tribunes in the Cathedral, and
the reliquary of St Zenobius (1432-
42). His 'Commentari' offer one of
the most important sources for the
history of Florentine art. 40, 49, 67,
70, *72*, 81, 111, 134.

Ghirlandaio, Davide
(Bigordi, Davide; Florence 1452-
1525). Painter and mosaicist. Worked with his brother Domenico.
Among their attributed works are the
St Lucy and donor in S. Maria Novella, and an *Annunciation* on the
portal of SS. Annunziata. In collaboration with Domenico, the mosaic *Annunciation* in the Duomo. 152.

Ghirlandaio, Domenico
(Bigordi, Domenico; Florence 1449-
94). Painter and mosaicist. Follower of Baldovinetti and Verrocchio. He often used portraits of his
contemporaries in his frescoes and
the figures are characterized by his
acute observation. His most noted
works are in the refectory of Ognissanti (1480, the *Last Supper*), the
small refectory of S. Marco, now
a museum, the Cappella Sassetti in
S. Trinita (1483-86), the 'Sala dei
Gigli' in the Palazzo della Signoria
(1481-85), and the choir of S. Maria
Novella (1485-90). *Adoration of the
Magi* (1488) in the Pinacoteca degli

Innocenti, and a mosaic in the lunette
of the 'Porta della Mandorla' in the
Duomo (1491) in collaboration with
Davide. 134, 136, *142*, 148, 152,
152, 164.

Ghirlandaio, Michele
(Tosini, Michele, called Ghirlandaio
because he was a pupil of Ridolfo;
Florence 1503-77). Painter, follower
of Andrea del Sarto. Works in S.
Spirito and the Galleria dell'Accademia. Also a large fresco in the Porta
alla Croce.

Ghirlandaio, Ridolfo
(Bigordi Ridolfo, called Ridolfo del
Ghirlandaio; Florence 1483-1561).
Painter. Son of Domenico. He decorated the Camera Verde in the
Palazzo della Signoria, and the Cappella della Signoria. *Portrait of a
woman* (1509) in the Galleria Palatina. *Portrait of a man* in the Galleria Corsini. *Portrait of Cosimo I
at the age of twelve* in the Museo
Mediceo. Other works in S. Maria
Novella and S. Spirito.

Giambologna
(known as Bologne, Jean Boulogne,
and Giovanni da Bologna; Douai
1524-Florence 1608). Sculptor and
architect. Apprenticed at Antwerp,
he came to Rome where he was in
touch with Michelangelo. In Florence from 1562. His colossal statue
of *Oceanus* in the Bargello shows
the influence of Tribolo, and his
Mercury in the Bargello that of Cellini. His taste was distinctly Mannerist, as is seen in the *Venus rising
from the bath* in the Boboli gardens,
and the *Rape of the Sabine women*
(1583) in the Loggia della Signoria.
Elegance in movement is striking in
his equestrian statues of *Cosimo I*
in Piazza della Signoria (1594) and
Ferdinando I in Piazza della SS. Annunziata. His works, especially small
bronzes, are also in the Palazzo della Signoria, the Palazzo Pitti, the
Museo del Bargello, and the Villa
Demidoff (formerly Pratolino). His
architectural work is to be seen in
the alteration to the altars of the
church of S. Marco, the Palazzo della
Commenda di Castiglione, the fifth
chapel of the choir in SS. Annunziata (1594-98), and the façade of Palazzo Vecchietti. He also placed the
two obelisks in the Piazza S. Maria
Novella (1608). *54*, 77, *122*, *126*,
184, 190, 192, *195*, 201, 207, *221*.

Giordano, Luca
(Naples *c*. 1632-1705). Painter. Called to Florence by Marchese Francesco Riccardi, for whom he painted
the *Apotheosis of the Medici* on the
ceiling of the Galleria del Palazzo
Mediceo, and the *Apotheosis of S.*

Andrea Corsini in the saint's chapel in the Carmine (1682). Other works in the Galleria Palatina and the Uffizi. 218.

Giorgione
(Barbarelli, Giorgio, called Giorgione; Castelfranco Veneto *c.* 1478-Venice 1510). Painter, and the first of the great Venetian colourists. His *Child Moses before Pharaoh* and the *Judgment of Solomon* are in the Uffizi.

Giottino
Florentine painter, mentioned by Vasari and other authors, and now generally identified as the Giotto di Maestro Stefano who was a member of the Compagnia dei Pittori in 1368. In 1369 he accompanied Giovanni da Milano to Rome to work in the Vatican. His style is derived from Maso di Banco, 'Stefano', and others of the Lombard school (who in turn derive from Giovanni da Milano). To him are attributed the *Deposition* (formerly in S. Remigio and now in the Uffizi) and the tabernacle with *Madonna and Child enthroned with angels and saints* formerly in via del Leone and now provisionally in the Cassa di Risparmio in Florence. 51, 52.

Giotto di Bondone
(Vespignano in Mugello, or Florence *c.* 1266-Florence 1337). Painter and architect. Pupil of Cimabue, in contact with the Roman school, especially Cavallini. From Cimabue he inherited the essential qualities of Byzantine painting and classical realism. His first works in Florence were the *Crucifixion* in S. Maria Novella, the *Madonna di S. Giorgio alla Costa, The Polittico* in Bardia, and remains of frescoes of the life of the Madonna, also in Bardia. The *Madonna and Child* in the Uffizi (1310) is later than his Roman period. The frescoes of the Cappella dei Bardi and of the Cappella Peruzzi in S. Croce were executed after 1320. The frescoes largely in fragments, of the Cappella del Podestà in the Bargello are also attributed to him and to his workshop. In 1334 he was put in charge of the Opera del Duomo. He superintended work on the Campanile, which he completed up to the first floor, and probably designed the lower reliefs. Other works by him are in the Museo Horne and the Berenson collection at I Tatti. 36, 39, 40, 46, 47, 49, 51, 56, *56*, *58*, *65*, 76.

Giovanni da Milano
(also called Giovanni da Como; active 1349-69). Painter. He executed the frescoes in the Cappella Rinuccini in S. Croce (*c.* 1366), the *Pietà* (signed and dated 1365) in the Gal-

leria dell'Accademia, and part of a polyptych in the Uffizi. 50, 52.

Giovanni di S. Giovanni
(Giovanni Mannozzi; S. Giovanni Valdarno 1590-Florence 1636). Painter. Worked in Florence as a pupil of Matteo Rosselli, and in Rome where he studied the works of the Carracci. His intense activity in Florence is attested by numerous frescoes in the town and villas on the outskirts. Tabernacle with *Visiting the prisoners* (*c.* 1615) in Via dell'Isola delle Stinche, ceiling in Casa Buonarroti, *Charity* in the Arcispedale di S. Maria Nova, *Flight into Egypt* in the Cappellina dello Ospedale di S. Matteo (1626), *Paradise* in the dome of Ognissanti (1616-17), the ceiling of the Villa La Quiete near Florence (*c.* 1620), the Sala degli Argenti in the Palazzo Pitti. 205, 208.

Giovanni del Biondo
(born in Casentino, active 1377-92). Painter in the style of Orcagna. Paintings in S. Croce, Cappella Rinuccini, Cappella Maggiore, and Cappella Bardi di Vernio. Triptych in the Galleria dell'Accademia (dated 1364). *Annunciation* in the Pinacoteca degli Innocenti (1383). Other works in the Museo dell'Opera del Duomo and the Uffizi.

Giovanni dell'Opera
(Giovanni Bandini, called Giovanni dell'Opera; Castello, Florence, *c.* 1540-Florence 1599). Sculptor, pupil of Bandinelli. Active also in Urbino. Works in Florence: tomb of Michelangelo in S. Croce (1574), bas-reliefs in the Cappella Gaddi in S. Maria Novella (1575-77), *St Philip* in the Duomo. Numerous portraits, including the bust of Francesco I dei Medici on the façade of the Palazzo Riccardi-Mannelli (1577) and that of Cosimo I in the Museo dell'Opera del Duomo.

Giovanni di Francesco
(active in Florence in mid-15th century). Painter of the Carrand Triptych in the Bargello. On the strength of this work, other paintings have been attributed to him: *St Nicholas of Bari* in Casa Buonarroti (possibly the predella of the triptych), fresco of the portico of the Spedale degli Innocenti, and the *Crucifixion of S. Andrea a Brozzi* now temporarily in the seminary of the Castello.

Giuliano da Maiano
(Maiano 1432-Naples 1490). Architect and sculptor. His fine wood carving may be seen on the door of the Cappella dei Pazzi (1472) and the ceiling of the Sala dell'Udienza in the Palazzo Vecchio. He desi-

gned the upper floor of the Palazzo dello Strozzino (1461-65) and the Palazzo Pazzi (later Quaratesi 1462-72). *112, 134, 136, 139, 145, 189, 230.*

Giuliano di Baccio d'Agnolo
(Giuliano Baglioni, called Giuliano di Baccio d'Agnolo; Florence 1491-1555). Architect and sculptor. Executed diverse palaces, the octagonal choir of the Duomo, and the Canonica di S. Martino a Montughi (1539). *139, 188.*

Gozzoli, Benozzo
(Benozzo di Lese di Sandro; Florence 1420-Pistoia 1497). Painter, studied under Angelico and Ghiberti. His principal work in Florence, possibly superior to his fresco of the Camposanto at Pisa, is the *Journey of the Magi* (1459-60) in the Cappella di Palazzo Medici, an interesting mixture of the sacred and profane. Other works in the Uffizi and the Museo Horne. *119, 127, 148.*

Granacci, Francesco
(Villamagna, Florence, 1469-Florence 1543). Painter, pupil of Ghirlandaio, influenced by Leonardo and Perugino. Altar paintings in the Galleria dell'Accademia and the Uffizi. Also *The Arrival of Charles VIII* in the Museo Mediceo, and the *Trinity* in the left transept of S. Spirito. *152.*

Iacopo del Sellaio
(Florence 1442-1493). Painter. Follower of Filippo Lippi, influenced by Botticelli and Ghirlandaio. Works in the Uffizi, the Galleria dell'Accademia, the Galleria Palatina, altarpiece with *St Laurence* in S. Spirito and *St James* in Or San Michele.

Lamberti, Niccolò di Piero
(Florence, *c.* 1370-1451). Sculptor and architect. He worked in Florence with Giovanni d'Ambrogio and others on the 'Mandorla' door of the Duomo. He carved *St Luke* (*c.* 1405) for one of the niches of Or San Michele (now in the Bargello) and *St Mark* (1415) for the façade of the Duomo (now in the Museo dell'Opera del Duomo). *77, 81, 130.*

Landini, Iacopo
(called di Casentino, Florence 1297-1349 or 1358). Painter. His paintings show the influence of B. Daddi, such as the tabernacle of S. Maria della Tromba now at the corner of the Palazzo della Lana. Works in the Uffizi include a signed triptych and there is the *Life of S. Miniato* in S. Miniato al Monte.

Leonardo da Vinci
(Vinci 1452-Cloux, Amboise, 1519). Painter, architect, sculptor and scien-tist. His work was fundamental to the development of Italian Renaissance art and science. His works in Florence, where he spent his youth and occasional later periods, are the early *Annunciation*, painted in Verrocchio's workshop (1470) and an angel in the *Baptism* by Verrocchio, and the *Adoration of the Magi* in the Uffizi. *75, 134, 136, 146, 148, 152, 155, 157, 158, 164, 166, 168, 173, 204.*

Ligozzi, Iacopo
(Verona *c.* 1547-Florence 1626). Painter, invited to Florence by Bianca Cappello, where he adopted the late Mannerist style with its debt to Michelangelo and Raphael. Frescoes in the cloister of Ognissanti (1602), *Martyrdom of St Laurence* in the Cappella Salviati in S. Croce (1611). Other works in the sacristy and the right aisle of S. Maria Novella, Palazzo della Signoria (Sala dell'Udienza, *Boniface VIII receiving Ambassadors*), Galleria Palatina and the Uffizi.

Lippi, Filippino
(Prato *c.* 1457-Florence 1504). Painter. Son of Fra Filippo, and pupil of Botticelli. He completed the frescoes of Masaccio in the Cappella Brancacci. Other works of this period *Madonna and Child with saints* (1485) in the Uffizi, *Apparition of the Madonna to St Bernard* in the Badia Florentina (1480), and *Madonna with Child and the infant St John* in S. Spirito. Frescoes in the Cappella di Filippo Strozzi in S. Maria Novella (1485-1502), and *Adoration of the Magi* in the Uffizi. *75, 136, 152, 154, 161.*

Lippi, Fra Filippo
(Florence 1406/09-Spoleto 1469). Painter. The fresco of the Chiostro del Carmine now in the Uffizi belongs to his youth, when he was under the influence of Masaccio. Later he acquired a greater sense of movement and an impetuous rhythm in his design which appear in his mature works in the Uffizi: predella of the Barbadori altarpiece (1437-42), the large altarpiece with *Madonna enthroned* (1445), *Coronation of the Virgin* (1447), *Adoration of the infant Jesus* (1455) and *Madonna with angels* (*c.* 1465). *112, 114, 116, 146, 148, 158, 159.*

Lippi, Lorenzo
(Florence 1606-1664). Painter and poet. Pupil of Matteo Rosselli and friend of Salvator Rosa, with whom he founded a literary academy in Florence. His most famous paintings are *Jacob at the well* in the Galleria Palatina, and *Lot and his daughters* in the Galleria Ferroni. *208.*

Lorenzo di Bicci
(Florence c. 1350-1427). A prolific painter. His works are: the *Evangelists* in the Sagrestia Vecchia of the Duomo, the *Madonna enthroned with saints* (fresco in the 'Canto della Cuculia', 1427), *St James and St Nicholas of Bari* in the Museo Bandini at Fiesole. 53.

Lorenzo di Credi
(Lorenzo Sciarpellone, called Lorenzo di Credi; Florence c. 1459-1537) Painter, pupil of Verrocchio and follower of Leonardo and Perugino. Of his secular works, only the *Venus* in the Uffizi remains. His many religious paintings include the *Adoration of the Shepherds*, the *Annunciation* and the tondo with the *Madonna* in the Uffizi, the *Archangel Michael* in the Sagrestia Vecchia of the Duomo (1523), and the *St Bartholomew* in Or San Michele. 148.

Lorenzo di Nicolò
(Active between 1377-1444). Florentine painter. Beginning in the style of Agnolo Gaddi, he later followed the style of Orcagna. Works in the Galleria dell'Accademia and S. Croce, and a triptych on the high altar of S. Leonardo in Arcetri.

Mainardi, Sebastiano
(S. Gimignano c. 1460-Florence 1513). Painter, follower of Ghirlandaio with whom he collaborated in the Cappella Maggiore of S. Maria Novella. His best paintings are in collections outside Italy. In Florence, fresco in the Cappella del Podestà in the Bargello, the large fresco in the Cappella Baroncelli in S. Croce, and works in the Galleria dell'Accademia. 152.

Manetti, Antonio
(15th century). Architect and man of letters, follower of Brunelleschi. He designed the Cappella del Cardinale di Portogallo in S. Miniato al Monte (1461-66). Brought in after the death of Brunelleschi to complete the churches of S. Spirito and S. Lorenzo. 92, 130.

Manetti, Rutilio
(Siena 1570/71-1639). Painter in the style of Caravaggio, pupil of F. Vanni and V. Salimbeni. He has some interesting large pictures of Carthusian *beati* in the Certosa del Galluzzo.

Mariotto di Nardo
(active 1394-1424). Florentine painter, imitator of Jacopo di Cione, influenced by Nicolò di Pietro Gerini and later by Lorenzo Monaco. Almost all his work is in Florence: Galleria dell'Accademia, Museo Stibbert, S. Miniato al Monte (detached frescoes). 49, 50.

Masaccio
(Maso di Ser Giovanni di Mone Cassai called Masaccio; S. Giovanni Valdarno 1401-Rome 1428/29). The first Renaissance painter to react against the Gothic tradition. His major works are the frescoes in the Cappella Brancacci in the Carmine (1426-27) in collaboration with his master, Masolino. Also in Florence are his *Trinity* fresco in S. Maria Novella, fragments of the predella with the *Life of S. Giuliano* in Museo Horne, and *Madonna with Child, St Anne and angels* youthful work in collaboration with Masolino in the Uffizi. 67, 72, *76*, 78, 81, *81*, 110, 111, 112, 114, 152.

Maso di Banco
(Florentine painter, active in the first half of the 14th century). Pupil of Giotto. In his later phase he was influenced by Ambrogio and Pietro Lorenzetti. Frescoes of the *Life of St Silvestro* in Cappella Bardi di Vernio, in S. Croce (c. 1340). Fresco lunette of the *Coronation of the Virgin* in Museo dell'Opera di S. Croce, and *Madonna with Child and four saints* in the apse of S. Spirito. 49, 52.

Maso di Bartolomeo
(called Masaccio; Val d'Ambra 1406-died c. 1456). Sculptor, collaborator with Donatello and Michelozzo, in the late Gothic style. Bronze gate of the Cappella della SS. Annunziata (1447).

Masolino da Panicale
(Tommaso di Cristoforo Fini, called Masolino; Panicale 1383-died 1447 ?). Painter, possibly a pupil of Starnina, and exponent of the International Gothic style. He worked alongside Masaccio in the Cappella Brancacci in the Carmine (1424-45). *Madonna of Humility* in the Palazzo Vecchio. Forte Belvedere contains his fresco sketches and frescoes formerly in the Cappella della Croce in S. Agostino di Empoli (1424), and the Certosa del Galluzzo has parts of a polyptych by him (Cappella di S. Maria). 67, 72, 110.

Matteo di Giovanni
(Matteo da Siena; Borgo S. Sepolcro, Arezzo 1435-Siena 1495). Painter, Sienese, influenced by Florentine, Marche and Umbrian schools. Works in the Uffizi and the Bargello (Cappella del Podestà).

Michelangelo Buonarroti
(Caprese, Arezzo, 1475-Rome 1564). Painter, sculptor, architect and man of letters, outstanding among early 16th-century artists for his total reinterpretation of the art of the preceding century. Apprenticed to Do-

menico and Davide Ghirlandaio, he was noticed by Lorenzo de' Medici while working at the Casino Mediceo. This is the period of his *Madonna of the steps* and the *Battle of the Centaurs* in the Museo di Casa Buonarroti. He spent some time in Venice, Bologna and Rome, returning to Florence in the years 1501-05, which were very important in his development. He carved the *David* (1504), and *St Matthew* (1506) in the Galleria dell'Accademia, and the marble tondo of the *Madonna and Child with the infant St John* (1505) in the Bargello. He painted the *Holy Family* (*c.* 1503) a tondo for the marriage of Agnolo Doni, in the Uffizi, and prepared the cartoon for the fresco of the *Battle of Cascina* (1504) which was to have decorated the hall of the Cinquecento in the Palazzo Vecchio. In 1519, after another stay in Rome during which he frescoed the ceiling of the Sistine Chapel, he designed the Sagrestia Nuova in S. Lorenzo. This was finished in 1534 (tombs of Giuliano and Lorenzo de Medici). Of the same period also the celebrated sculptures of the *Slaves*, uncompleted, in the Accademia. He also designed the Biblioteca Mediceo-Laurenziana. Other works and drawings in the Galleria Buonarroti, and the Bargello. 72, 89, 133, 136, 139, 152, 157, 158, 161, *162*, 164, *164*, 166, *166*, 167, *167*, 168, 173, 177, 178, *178*, 179, *179*, 180, 181, *181*, 182, 184, 192, 198, 208.

Michelozzo
(Michelozzo Michelozzi; Florence 1396-1472). Architect, sculptor and goldsmith. Friend of Cosimo de' Medici for whom he worked. Collaborated with the greatest artists of his time. With Donatello he executed the Tabernacle of the Tribunale di Mercanzia at the east side of Or San Michele (1425) and the tomb of Anti-pope John XXIII (1422-27) in the Baptistry. His activity as an architect, under the influence of Brunelleschi, increased after a period of exile in Venice (1434). His first work was the rebuilding of the convent, church and library of S. Marco (1436-43), followed by the building of the atrium, cloister and sacristy of SS. Annunziata (1444-55). From 1444 to 1460 his works include the palazzo Medici-Riccardi, the Cappella del Noviziato in S. Croce, the Cappella del Crocifisso in S. Miniato al Monte, and the Tempietto in SS. Annunziata. About 1458 he began the building of the Medici villas at Careggi and Fiesole, and the Palazzo dello Strozzino, and also worked on the Palazzo

Vecchio. The beautiful tabernacle, which frames Donatello's *Annunciation* in S. Croce is by him. 93, 96, 99, 106, 108, 109, 110, *110*, 112, 119, 120, *120, 126*, 136, *183*, 190.

Michelucci, Giovanni
(Pistoia 1891). Architect. In collaboration with others, he built the Stazione di S. Maria Novella, an example of 'functional' architecture (1935). Also by him the church of S. Giovanni Battista on the Autostrade. 231, 233, 234.

Mino da Fiesole
(Poppi, Arezzo, 1430/31-Florence 1484). Sculptor, influenced by Desiderio da Settignano and Antonio Rossellino. One of his best works, the tomb of Bishop Salutati (1464) is in the cathedral at Fiesole. Also of this period is the tomb of Count Ugo in the Badia Fiorentina (*c.* 1469) and the marble bust of Rinaldo della Luna (1461) in the Museo del Bargello. At Badia also the tomb of Bernardo Giugni (1469-81). Among his later works is the marble tabernacle in the Cappella del Miracolo in S. Ambrogio. 129, 130, *131*.

Monaco, Lorenzo
(Piero di Giovanni, called Fra Lorenzo degli Angioli, and known as Lorenzo Monaco; Siena *c.* 1370 - died *c.* 1425). Painter and miniaturist. Trained in the Sienese school, he came to Florence where he became a Camaldulensian monk and came under the influence of Florentine painting. One of his first works is the *Pietà* dated 1404 in the Galleria dell'Accademia. His style becomes more personal with the choir books (*c.* 1409) in the Biblioteca Laurenziana, the polyptych of *The Mount of Olives* (1406-1410) and the *Coronation of the Virgin* dated 1413 in the Uffizi. There are also some crucifixes by him, including the one in S. Giovanni de' Cavalieri di Malta. Between 1420 and 1422 he painted the *Annunciation* in S. Trinita and frescoes in a chapel. Other works in the Galleria dell'Accademia. 66.

Montorsoli, Giovannangelo, Fra
(Montorsoli, Florence, (*c.* 1507-Florence 1563). Sculptor. As a youth he collaborated with Michelangelo in the Sagrestia Nuova of S. Lorenzo, where he later executed the statue of *St Cosmas* for the tomb of Lorenzo il Magnifico. He became a Servite, and decorated the Cappella della Confraternita di S. Luca in SS. Annunziata with statues in stucco.

Naldini, Battista
(Fiesole *c.* 1537-Florence *c.* 1600). Painter. Pupil of Pontormo and ex-

ponent of Mannerism. Works in S. Maria Novella, S. Croce, Museo dell'Opera di S. Croce, S. Marco and elsewhere. 190.

Nanni di Banco
(Also called Nanni di Antonio di Banco; Florence *c.* 1383 - died 1421). Sculptor. Together with Donatello he initiated a renewal of sculpture on the principles of the Renaissance but his work was interrupted by a premature death. He carved the *Assumption* for the Porta della Mandorla in the Duomo (1407-08), *Isaiah* (1408), also in the Duomo, *St Luke* (1413) in the Museo dell'Opera, and marble statues of *St Eligio, St Philip,* and the *Four Crowned Saints* (1413) in Or San Michele. 76, 77, 87.

Nanni di Bartolo
(Called il Rosso; Florence, first half of the 15th century). Sculptor, influenced by Ghiberti and Donatello. His works are in the Duomo and the Museo dell'Opera.

Neri di Bicci
(Florence 1419 - died 1491). Painter. Son and faithful follower of Bicci di Lorenzo, he had a very prosperous workshop in Florence. Florentine works include the *Annunciation* in the Galleria dell'Accademia (1464), *Coronation with saints* in the Pinacoteca degli Innocenti, *Madonna della cintola with four saints* in S. Leonardo in Arcetri (*c.* 1469). *St Felicity and her seven sons,* a painting on a gold ground, in S. Felicita, *Coronation of Mary with saints* in S. Giovannino dei Cavalieri, two paintings on a gold ground in S. Trinita, and a triptych in S. Felice.

Nervi, Pier Luigi
(Sondrio 1891). Architect of international repute. He built the Stadio Comunale, viale Manfredo Fanti (1932). 231.

Orcagna, Andrea
(Andrea di Cione, called l'Orcagna; active between 1343 and 1368). Florentine architect, painter and sculptor. Pupil of Andrea Pisano, and possibly of Daddi. His best known works is the marble tabernacle in Or San Michele (1349-59). The *Triumph of Death* in S. Croce is a carefully planned and schematic treatment. Attributed to him are frescoes in the refectory of the Cenacolo di S. Spirito (*c.* 1360). 49, 50, 58, 66.

Parigi, Giulio
(Florence *c.* 1580-1635). Architect, painter and engraver, employed at the court of the Grand Dukes. He enlarged the façade of Palazzo Pitti (1620); Palazzo dell'Antella, form-

erly dei Cerchi (1619); Loggia del Grano (1619); Palazzo della Crocetta (1620) for the Grand Duchess Maria Maddalena of Austria; he rebuilt the Villa del Poggio Imperiale (1620) and designed decorations for festivities at the Medici court. 201.

Passignano
(Domenico Cresti, called Passignano; Florence *c.* 1560-1636). Painter. Studied under F. Zuccari, whom he assisted with the frescoes of the dome in the cathedral. His paintings in Florence are in the churches of SS. Annunziata, S. Croce (*St Laurence distributing alms*), S. Marco, S. Maria Maddalena dei Pazzi (*Martyrdom of Titular Saints*), S. Spirito (*Martyrdom of St Stephen*), Spirito Santo e S. Giorgio sulla Costa (*The Pardon of S. Giovanni Gualberto*). 208.

Perugino
(Pietro Vannucci, called il Perugino; Città della Pieve 1445-Fontignano, Perugia, 1523). Painter. According to Vasari he was a pupil of Piero della Francesca at Arezzo, later studying in the workshop of Verrocchio at Florence. Until 1500 he worked mainly in Florence, Rome and Perugia. In the last decade of the 15th century he painted his frescoes in the Cenacolo di Foligno (1490) and *Crucifixion* in the chapter room of S. Maria Maddalena dei Pazzi (1493-96), *Madonna and Child with saints* (dated 1493), followed by the portrait of Francesco delle Opere (dated 1494) and other fine portraits, also *Christ in the garden* and *The Assumption* (1500). All these works are in the Uffizi. 152, *154*, 157, 158.

Pierino da Vinci
(Vinci, Valdarno, *c.* 1520-Pisa *c.* 1553). Sculptor. Nephew of Leonardo. Influenced by Tribolo in his bronze putti for the basin of the fountain at the Villa di Castello (1546). He added his own delicacy of touch to an otherwise Michelangelesque approach in his *Samson and the Philistine,* marble group in the Palazzo della Signoria, and the *Death of Count Ugolino* in the Bargello (1550).

Piero di Cosimo
(Florence 1462 - died 1521). Painter, pupil of Cosimo Rosselli. One of the most original of Florentine masters. Influenced by Signorelli, Raphael, and Leonardo, as is evidenced by his *Perseus and Andromeda* in the Uffizi. He has a poetic quality in landscape and detail in his altarpieces, such as the *Conception of the Virgin* in the Uffizi, and the *Marriage of St Catherine* in the Pinacoteca degli Innocenti. 154.

Pietro da Cortona
(Pietro Barrettini, called Pietro da Cortona; Cortona 1596-Rome 1669). Painter and architect. In Rome he was much influenced by the Carracci frescoes in Palazzo Farnese, and the works of Polidoro da Caravaggio and Rubens. Called to Florence by the Medici, who commissioned decorations in the Pitti Palace: the Sala della Stufa (1640), and five rooms of the Appartamento di Rappresentanza (1640-47). Friend and host to Michelangelo Buonarroti the Younger, works also in the Casa Buonarroti. He was also a fine architect, although his only designs for Florence were those he did for S. Firenze. 208.

Pisano, Andrea - *see* **Andrea**

Poccetti, Bernardino
(Also known as Bernardo delle Grottesche; Florence 1542/48-1612). Painter. Pupil of Michele del Ghirlandaio, active in Florence, especially in fresco. His early works re-interpret Andrea del Sarto; *St Dominic* in the Chiostro grande of S. Maria Novella. Other works are *St Catherine* (1569-82) and grotesques in S. Maria Novella, *Miracle of S. Andrea Corsini* in the Carmine (1590), *St Bruno and Carthusian saints* in the Certosa del Galluzzo (1591-97) frescoes of *Servite saints* in the Chiostro dei Morti in SS. Annunziata (*c.* 1604), frescoes in the dome of the Cappella di S. Antonino in S. Marco (1605), *Slaughter of the Innocents,* large fresco in the Pinacoteca dello Spedale degli Innocenti (1610). Numerous other works in Florence. 192.

Poggi, Giuseppe
(Florence 1811-1901). Architect. Worked in Florence following the traditional forms of Renaissance architecture. When the city became the capital of united Italy he conceived and in part carried out a vast urban plan, of which the best example is the Viale dei Colli and the Piazzale Michelangelo. 229.

Pollaiuolo, Antonio
(Antonio Benci, called del Pollaiuolo; Florence 1433-Rome 1498). Painter, sculptor and goldsmith. Worked in collaboration with his brother Piero. Like other Tuscan artists of the 15th century, his painting is full of movement obtained by his drawing of contours. His first work of note is the silver cross in the Museo dell'Opera del Duomo (1457-59). Then follow, among his paintings, the *Two angels* in fresco (1466) in the Cappella del Cardinale di Portogallo in S. Miniato al Monte, for which he also painted in collabo-

ration with Piero the *Three saints* now in the Uffizi (1467). There are also two precious little pictures including the masterpiece *Labours of Hercules.* The Museo dell'Opera del Duomo contains his designs for twenty-seven embroideries (1466-80) of subjects from the life of *St John the Baptist,* and the relief of the *Nativity of St John the Baptist,* which is part of the silver altar designed for the Baptistry (1478-80). His famous group, *Hercules and Anteus,* is in the Museo del Bargello. 129, 130, 134, 142, 143, 146, *147,* 164, 230.

Pollaiuolo, Piero del
(Florence 1441-Rome 1496). Painter and sculptor, pupil of his elder brother Antonio with whom he collaborated on the altarpiece of SS. *Vincenzo, Jacopo and Eustachio* (1466-67) now in the Uffizi, *St Michael the Archangel* (*c.* 1465) in the Museo Bardini, and on the series of *Virtues* (1469) for the Arte della Mercatanzia, now in the Uffizi, which was completed by Botticelli. 134, 146.

Pontormo
(Jacopo Carrucci, called Jacopo da Pontormo, Pontormo 1494 - died 1556). Painter. Studied with Albertinelli and Piero di Cosimo, but was principally a follower of Andrea del Sarto. His first work was the fresco of *Virtues* on the façade of SS. Annunziata now removed and that of the Cappella dei Papi in the cloisters of S. Maria Novella. His *Visitation* was painted two years later, followed by the altarpiece of S. Michele Visdomini (1518), and these are landmarks in his evolution towards an original style. In 1521 he painted a large lunette of *Vertumnus and Pomona* in the Villa di Poggio a Caiano, which is a masterpiece of composition. He painted his scenes of the *Passion* and *Supper at Emmaus* for the Certosa del Galluzzo, under the influence of Dürer's engravings (1525). These are now in the Uffizi, along with his *Venus and Cupid,* after a cartoon of Michelangelo. There is also a *Deposition* by him in the Cappella Capponi and a masterpiece, the *Annunciation,* in S. Felicita, and a *Visitation* in the parish church at Carmignano. Other works at Prato. 175, *175,* 177, 182, 188, 222.

Poppi
(Francesco Morandini, called Il Poppi; Poppi, Florence, 1544-97). Pupil and assistant of Vasari, much sought after in the court of the Medici. His best work dates from 1570 to 1584. Frescoes in the study of Francesco I in the Palazzo Vecchio, and *Crucifixion* in S. Michele a S.

Salvi. Other minor works in the Duomo, S. Marco, and S. Felicita. 190.

Portigiani, Pagno di Lapo
(Fiesole 1408-Florence ? 1470). Sculptor. Collaborated with Donatello and Michelozzo on the tomb of the Antipope John XXIII in the Baptistry. Executed the Tempietto of SS. Annunziata, designed by Michelozzo. Bas-relief of the *Madonna and Child* in the Museo dell'Opera del Duomo. Later he worked in Siena and Bologna.

Pseudo Pier Francesco Fiorentino
(active between 1477-97). Florentine painter, follower of Benozzo Gozzoli, influenced by Neri di Bicci, Andrea del Castagno and Baldovinetti. An artist of great ability, he painted mostly madonnas. His principal works are in the Galleria dell'Accademia, the Sacristy of S. Giovannino dei Cavalieri, and the Villa della Petraia.

Puligo Domenico
(Domenico Ubaldini, called Puligo; Florence 1492-1527). Painter, trained in the school of Ghirlandaio, and a follower of Andrea del Sarto, who was his friend. Works in the Galleria Corsini, the Galleria Palatina, S. Maria Maddalena dei Pazzi and in other Florentine churches.

Raffaellino del Garbo
(Florence *c.* 1470-*c.* 1525). Painter, influenced by Filippino Lippi in his *Resurrection* in the Uffizi, and also by Ghirlandaio and Perugino. Fresco of the *Multiplication of the loaves* in S. Maria Maddalena dei Pazzi (1503), *Annunciation* in S. Francesco at Fiesole.

Raffaello da Montelupo
(*c.* 1503-Orvieto *c.* 1570). Sculptor, influenced by Michelangelo and Sansovino. In the Sagrestia Nuova in S. Lorenzo, he carved *St Damian*, designed by Michelangelo. In S. Felicita he executed the tomb of Cardinal Luigi de' Rossi, and a large polychrome *Crucifixion* for the Refectory of S. Apollonia.

Raphael
(Raffaello Sanzio, or Santi; Urbino 1483-Rome 1520). Painter and architect. One of the major artists of the Renaissance. Probably a pupil of Timoteo Viti of Urbino, but a follower of Perugino. In Florence in 1504-8 he came under the influence of Fra Bartolomeo and Leonardo; later in Rome, where he spent the rest of his life, it was Michelangelo who most influenced him. The galleries of Florence contain a good number of his early and late works. Galleria Palatina: the

Pregnant woman (1506), *Madonna del Granduca* (1504-5), *Madonna del Baldacchino* (*c.* 1506), *Angelo Doni* (1506), *Maddalena Doni, Tommaso Inghirami* (early copy of the original in Boston, 1514), *Madonna della Seggiola* (*c.* 1515), the *Veiled Lady* (*c.* 1516), *Portrait of Leo X* (*c.* 1518). *Cardinal Dovizi da Bibbiena* (*c.* 1516). In the Uffizi: portrait of *Francesco Maria della Rovere,* Duke of Urbino, (*c.* 1504), *Madonna with the goldfinch* (1506), portrait of *Guidobaldo da Montefeltro and Elisabetta Gonzaga,* Duke and Duchess of Urbino, and a copy of the original portrait of Pope Julius II (1512). 75, 134, 157, 158, 164, 166, 168, *169,* 201.

Romano, Giulio
(Giulio Giannuzzi di Pietro di Pippo, called Giulio Romano; Rome 1492/99-Mantua 1546). Painter. Assistant and close disciple of Raphael, active mainly in Rome and Mantua. His works in Florence are the *Dance of Apollo and the Muses,* and the *Vision of Ezekiel* (designed by Raphael) in the Galleria Palatina, and the *Madonna and Child* in the Uffizi.

Rosa, Salvatore
(Naples 1615-Rome 1673). Painter and man of letters. After his early training in Naples and Rome he came to live in Florence from 1640 to 1649, where he had great success at the court of Ferdinando II de' Medici. In this period he matured and developed his original gifts for picturesque and romantic landscape, two examples of which are in the Palazzo Pitti: *The broken bridge* and *Seashore with towers.* He also produced many emblematic and moral paintings, such as the *Forest of philosophers,* also in the Pitti. He founded the Accademia dei Percossi in his house at the Croce al Trebbio, which became a meeting place for the intellectuals of his day, from Lorenzo Lippi to Evangelista Torricelli. He then began to write plays and satirical verses. 217.

Rosai, Ottone
(Florence 1895-Ivrea 1957). Painter, follower of the Futurist movement until 1920, when he devoted himself to scenes of everyday life in the Tuscan countryside and the streets of Florence. His works are in the Galleria d'Arte Moderna in the Palazzo Pitti, and the restaurant in the railway station of S. Maria Novella. 224.

Rosselli, Matteo
(Florence 1578-1650). Painter. Pupil of Passignano, his fame is due to the school he directed in Florence which produced certain famous painters like

Lorenzo Lippi, Giovanni di San Giovanni and il Volterrano. Among his works are those in S. Carlo, S. Croce, the Spedale degli Innocenti, SS. Annunziata, S. Marco, S. Maria Maggiore, S. Stefano al Ponte and the *Triumph of David* in the Galleria Palatina.

Rossellino, Antonio
(Antonio Gamberelli, called Rossellino; Settignano 1427-Florence 1479). Sculptor, trained in the workshop of his brother Bernardo, with affinities to Ghiberti in the refinement of his design, and to Donatello in the luminous quality of his surfaces. There is a remarkable freshness in his monument to the Cardinal of Portugal in S. Miniato al Monte (1459-61) and the busts and bas-reliefs in the Bargello. Outstanding among these is the strongly emotional portrait of Matteo Palmieri. One of his last works, the *Madonna del latte,* is in S. Croce (1478). 129, 130.

Rossellino, Bernardo
(Bernardo Gamberelli, called Rossellino; Settignano 1409-Florence 1464). Architect and sculptor. An interpreter of Alberti, as is shown by his Palazzo Rucellai (1446-51), and an important figure in the early Renaissance. Active in Florence and Rome. Pius II commissioned him to plan the new town of Pienza and to design its principal buildings. In Florence he created a new type of funerary monument that was to have considerable influence, with his tombs of Leonardo Bruni in S. Croce (1444-51), of Beata Villana in S. Maria Novella (1451), Orlando dei Medici in SS. Annunziata (1456), and Neri Capponi in S. Spirito (1458). *102, 103, 130.*

Rosso Fiorentino
(Giovanni Battista di Jacopo, called Rosso Fiorentino; Florence 1494-Paris 1540). Painter. A disciple of Andrea del Sarto, he studied the works of Raphael and Parmigianino in Rome, and acquired the classical culture that later enabled him to decorate the gallery of Francis I at Fontainebleau. An example of his classical manner is the *Moses defending the daughters of Jethro* in the Uffizi. At the age of seventeen he painted his fresco of the *Assumption* in the Chiostrino dei Voti in SS. Annunziata. His early style is developed in the *Madonna and Child with saints* in the Galleria Palatina, and the *Marriage of the Virgin* in S. Lorenzo. 175, 177.

Ruggieri, Ferdinando
(Florence, *c.* 1691-1741). Architect. In 1715 he designed a façade, in a somewhat restrained Baroque manner, for the church of San Firenze. He built the Palazzo Bastogi in Via Cavour, the campanile of San Lorenzo, the Palazzo Capponi-Farinoli (after the design by Carlo Fontana), and he enlarged the Palazzo Rinuccini, designed by Cigoli, in via S. Spirito. 218.

Rustici, Giovanni Francesco
(Florence 1474-Tours 1554). Sculptor and painter. Influenced by Verrocchio and Andrea del Sarto, but especially by Leonardo, as is shown in his terracotta groups of soldiers in the Loeser collection in the Palazzo della Signoria, and the bronze group, the *Preaching of St John Baptist,* on the north door of the Baptistry (1506-11). Among other works in the Bargello is the glazed terracotta *Noli me tangere* done in the style of the della Robbias, and a *Madonna* reminiscent of Michelangelo. 169.

Sabatelli, Luigi
(Florence 1772-Milan 1850). Painter specializing in fresco, and teacher of painting at the Accademia di Brera. His frescoes in Florence are on the ceiling and lunette of the Sala dell'Iliade of the Galleria Palatina (1819), and the *Triumph of the Religious Orders* in the Cappella del Sacramento in S. Firenze (*c.* 1830). There are paintings by him in the Cappella Ricasoli in S. Croce. 222.

Salviati, Cecchino
(Francesco de' Rossi, called Salviati; Florence 1510-Rome 1563). A painter rich in invention, pupil of Andrea del Sarto, active mainly in Rome. His paintings in Florence are in the Uffizi, the Galleria Corsini, the Museo dell'Opera di S. Croce, and his frescoes are in the Palazzo della Signoria (Sala dell'Udienza) and the Museo del Bargello. 188, 189.

Sangallo, Antonio da, il Vecchio
(Antonio Giamberti, called Sangallo; Florence *c.* 1455-1534). Architect. Brother of Giuliano, with whom he had a long collaboration. After Giuliano's death he achieved a more individual expression, as is shown in his work at Montepulciano, Arezzo and Rome. In Florence he executed the Portico della Confraternita dei Servi di Maria in the Piazza dell'Annunziata (1516-25) and designed the Fortezza da Basso (1534). 108.

Sangallo, Antonio il Giovane
(Antonio di Bartolomeo Cordini; Florence 1483-Terni 1546). Architect. Nephew of Giuliano and Antonio il Vecchio. In Rome he directed the work on St Peter's, built the church of S. Spirito in Sassia and various palaces, among them the Palazzo Farnese, and planned the Fortezza da Basso.

Sangallo, Bastiano da
(Called Aristotile da Sangallo; Florence 1481-1551). Architect and painter. Friend of Vasari, who gave him a chapter in his *Lives of the Artists*. Together with Giovan Francesco, he directed the building of the Palazzo Pandolfini in via S. Gallo, following a design by Raphael. 166.

Sangallo, Francesco da
(Francesco Giamberti, called Sangallo; Florence 1494-1576). Sculptor and architect. As a military architect he strengthened the fortress improvised by Michelangelo. His sculptures in Florence are *St Anne, the Madonna and Child* (*c.* 1526) in Or San Michele, the statue of *Paolo Giovio* in the cloister of S. Lorenzo (1560), the tomb of Bishop Angelo Marzi Medici (1546) and the tomb of Bishop Lionardo Buonafé in Certosa (1545).

Sangallo, Giuliano da
(Giuliano Giamberti, called Sangallo; Florence *c.*-1516). Architect, brother of Antonio il Vecchio, and the main heir to the Brunelleschi tradition which he refined and made more personal, and fusing it into the new ideal of Renaissance classicism. Chief works in Florence are the rebuilding of S. Maria Maddalena dei Pazzi (1480-92) and its cloister, Villa di Poggio a Caiano (1480-85), Palazzo Gondi (1490-94), Sacristy of S. Spirito (1489-92), Cappella Gondi in S. Maria Novella (*c.* 1503). 134, 135, 136, *136*, 138, 230, 235.

Sansovino, Andrea
(Andrea Contucci, called Sansovino; Monte S. Savino, Arezzo, 1460-1529). Sculptor and architect. Possibly a pupil of A. Pollaiuolo, influenced by Giuliano da Sangallo and Leonardo. Among his early works is the Cappella Corbinelli, or Cappella del Sacramento, in S. Spirito. His *Baptism of Christ* on the east door of the Baptistry was executed after a ten-year stay in Portugal. He also worked in Rome, and executed reliefs for the S. Casa at Loreto. 169, 218.

Sansovino, Jacopo
(Jacopo Tatti, called Sansovino; Florence 1486-Venice 1570). Architect and sculptor. Pupil of Andrea Sansovino whose name he adopted and whom he followed to Rome. His works in Florence reveal the influence of Michelangelo, such as the statue of *Bacchus* and the papier-mâché bas-relief of the *Madonna and Child* in the Bargello, and *St James the Elder* in the Duomo. His architectural masterpiece is the Library in Venice (1537).

Santi di Tito
(S. Sepolcro 1536/38-Florence 1603). Painter and architect. Studied in Florence under Bronzino and Baccio Bandinelli. In the years between 1569-79 he painted the *Resurrection,* the *Supper at Emmaus,* the *Crucifixion* in S. Croce, and the *Nativity* in S. Giuseppe. In 1571 he decorated the study of Francesco I in the Palazzo Vecchio. His later works such as the *Baptism of Christ* in the Cappella Corsini, and the *Raising of Lazarus* (1576) in S. Maria Novella, which also contains his *Annunciation*. His famous portrait of *Machiavelli* is in the Palazzo Vecchio. 190, 192.

Sebastiano del Piombo
(Sebastiano Luciani, called del Piombo; Venice 1485-1547). Painter, trained in the circle of Giorgione and Bellini, invited to Rome by Agostino Chigi, where he was influenced by the work of Raphael and Michelangelo. His works in Florence are the *Death of Adonis,* and a *Sick Man* (1514) in the Uffizi, and the *Martyrdom of St Agatha* (1520) in the Galleria Palatina.

Signorelli, Luca
(Cortona *c.* 1445-1523). Painter, disciple of Piero della Francesca. His *Crucifixion* in the Uffizi is related to his major work, the cycle of frescoes in the Duomo of Orvieto. Other paintings in the Uffizi, the Museo Horne, the Galleria Corsini and the Galleria Palatina. 134, 157.

Silvani, Gherardo
(Florence 1579-1675). Architect and sculptor, faithful to the Mannerism of Buontalenti during the height of the Baroque period. His works in Florence are the Palazzo Panciatichi-Ximenes (1603), a chapel in SS. Annunziata, Cappella Calderini-Riccardi and Cappella Salviati in S. Croce (*c.* 1620), Palazzo Covoni in via Cavour (1623), Palazzo Marucelli, later Fenci, in via S. Gallo (*c.* 1625), Palazzo degli Albizi, borgo degli Albizi (1626-32), restoration of the church of S. Simone (1630), S. Margherita e Maria dei Ricci, via del Corso (1640), Palazzo Giaconi, formerly Medici, via Tornabuoni, Palazzo Gianfigliazzi, now Masetti, Lungarno Corsini, Palazzo Corsini in via del Prato, the campanile of S. Jacopo sopr'Arno, and Palazzo Corsini, via Maggio 42. 217.

Silvani, Pier Francesco
(Florence 1620-Badiuzza delle Cipolle, Pisa, 1685). Sculptor, and one of the foremost Florentine architects of the 17th century. His works in Florence are S. Firenze (the side on the via dell'Anguillara, 1645 or 48),

Palazzo Corsini on lungarno Corsini (1648-56), Cappella di S. Andrea Corsini in the Carmine (1675-85) apse of S. Marco (1678), Cappella Maggiore in S. Maria Maddalena dei Pazzi (1685). 217.

Starnina
(Gherardo di Jacopo, called Lo Starnina; active between 1337-1409). Florentine painter, master of Masolino and Paolo Uccello. Frescoes in the Cappella Castellani in S. Croce, and the *Thebaid* in the Uffizi are attributed. They were executed before his departure for Spain. On his return he decorated the Cappella di S. Andrea Corsini in the Carmine.

'Stefano'
(Florentine painter active in the first half of the 14th century). No work by him can be identified with certainty in Florence, but there is no doubt that his influence was considerable in Florentine painting after the death of Giotto. His style is related to that of the late works of Giotto, and those of Maso di Banco, as can be seen in his paintings in Assisi (the lower basilica of S. Francesco e S. Chiara) and Rome (*Madonna and Child* in the Vatican Pinacoteca).

Stradano, Giovanni
(Jan van der Straet; Bruges 1523-Florence 1605). Painter, trained in Antwerp under Aersten. Friend of Vasari in Florence, where he executed many cartoons for tapestries woven in the ducal workshops, now in the Palazzo Vecchio, the Uffizi, the Museo Mediceo, and the Museo degli Argenti. Among his rare paintings are the *Crucifixion* in SS. Annunziata (1570), and the *Mercury, Ulysses and Circe* (1570) in the study of Francesco I in the Palazzo Vecchio. 190.

Strozzi, Zanobi
(Florence 1412 - died after 1471). Painter and miniaturist in the Gothic style, influenced by Beato Angelico. His most important works are the large illuminated choir books commissioned by Cosimo dei Medici for the convent of S. Marco (1446-53), now in the Biblioteca del Museo dell'Angelico.

Sustermans (or **Suttermans**), **Justus**
(Antwerp 1597-Florence 1681). Painter at the court of Cosimo II. He came to Italy from Paris, and specialized in portraits of Italian and foreign princes. His most famous portraits are those of Galileo Galilei (*c.* 1636) in the Uffizi, of Mattia dei Medici, Conte Valdemaro Cristiano, son of the king of Denmark, and Vittoria della Rovere as the Vestal

Virgin Tuccia, in the Galleria Palatina. Other portraits in the Galleria Corsini, the Museo Mediceo, and a whole series of Medici ones in the Palazzo Pitti. 217.

Tacca, Ferdinando
(Florence 1619-86). Sculptor. Son of Pietro Tacca, he collaborated with his father on the colossal statue in gilt bronze in the Cappella dei Principi (Medici chapels), and executed the altarpiece with the *Martyrdom of St Stephen* in S. Stefano al Ponte (1649). 217.

Tacca, Pietro
(Carrara 1577-Florence 1640). Sculptor. Pupil and follower of Giambologna. In Florence he executed the bronze boar in the Loggia del Mercato Nuovo (*c.* 1612) popularly known as the 'Porcellino', completed the equestrian statue of *Ferdinando I* (*c.* 1608) by Giambologna, executed the fountains with bronze sea-beasts (1629) in Piazza della SS. Annunziata, and the monkey fountain in the Boboli gardens. 192, *195, 198,* 199.

Talenti, Francesco
(Florence, died after 1369). Architect and sculptor. From 1337 he helped in the rebuilding of the structure of Or San Michele. From 1357 he supervised the building of the Duomo, helping to modify Arnolfo di Cambio's designs in order to enlarge the church; he also directed the completion of the campanile (1350-59). 53, 55, 56.

Talenti, Simone
(Florence *c.* 1340/45-died after 1381). Architect and sculptor. Son of Francesco Talenti, he worked on the construction of the Loggia dei Lanzi with Benci di Cione, and on the completion of Or San Michele and the nearby church of S. Carlo dei Lombardi (formerly S. Michele). 55.

Tintoretto
(Jacopo Robusti, called Tintoretto; Venice 1518-1594). Painter, disciple of Titian, and one of the major artists of the Venetian school. Works by him in Florence, not of his best, are to be seen in the Uffizi, the Galleria Corsini and the Galleria Palatina. Influenced by Michelangelo and the Mannerist painters.

Titian
(Tiziano Vecellio; Pieve di Cadore *c.* 1480-Venice 1576). Painter. Pupil of Giovanni Bellini, and influenced by Giorgione. He lived mostly in Venice, but was in Rome between 1543-45 and at the court of Charles V. Florence contains a large number of his early and later works. In the Uffizi: *Madonna and Child* (known as the *Madonna of the roses, c.* 1510),

Flora (1520-25), *Venus and Cupid,* the *Venus of Urbino* (1538) painted for Francesco Maria della Rovere, *Caterina Cornaro* (1542), *Eleonora Gonzaga and Francesco Maria della Rovere, Duke of Urbino* (1536-38), *Bishop Ludovico Beccadelli* (signed and dated 1552). In the Pitti: *The concert* (formerly attributed to Giorgione, but now considered to be a work of Titian (1510-13), *The Saviour* (a portrait of Tommaso Mosti, 1526), *Diego Mendoza, Philip II, Cardinal Ippolito dei Medici* in Hungarian costume (1533), *Portrait of a gentleman* (erroneously supposed to be the Duke of Norfolk, *c.* 1540), *St Mary Magdalen* (1530-40), *Julius II* (copy of the portrait by Raphael), *Portrait of Pietro Aretino* (*c.* 1545), *La Bella* (1536). In the Palazzo Pitti: *Portrait of Duchess Giulia Varano* in the Appartamento della Regina Margherita. 201. 205.

Uccello, Paolo
(Paolo di Dono, called Paolo Uccello; Prato Vecchio, Arezzo, 1397-Florence 1475). Painter. Trained in the workshop of Ghiberti, he was brought up on the late Gothic style, but concentrated on perspective and plastic values, as is evident in his Florentine works. These are the equestrian monument of Giovanni Acuto, fresco (1436), heads of prophets (1443) for the corners of the clock, and cartoons for the windows of the drum in the Duomo, *Battle of S. Romano,* one of three famous panels (*c.* 1456) in the Uffizi; frescoes in the Chiostro Verde of S. Maria Novella (*History of Noah, c.* 1455) now in the entrance to the Refectory. 116, 117.

Vasari, Giorgio
(Arezzo 1511-Florence 1574). Painter, architect, and man of letters. Author of the *Lives of the Artists,* the fullest historical work of the Renaissance that we possess. Court artist of the Medici circle, he had considerable influence on the development of late Mannerism. In 1561 he founded the Accademia del Disegno, a group of artists who decorated the Studiolo di Cosimo in the Palazzo della Signoria (1570-72). Vasari designed the great staircase (1560-63), the Salone del Cinquecento, with episodes from the history of Florence and of the Medici (1563-65), the Quartiere di Leone X, and the Quartiere degli Elementi. Vasari's architectural masterpiece is the Piazzale and the Palazzo degli Uffizi, begun in 1560 and completed by A. Parigi and B. Buontalenti. He helped to create a special type of architectural restoration, remodelling the interior

of S. Croce, S. Maria Novella (with the addition of side altars, removed in the 19th century). His numerous paintings are to be seen in the Uffizi, in S. Croce, SS. Annunziata, the Museo Mediceo, S. Maria Novella, and the Galleria Palatina. 16, 40, 52, 72, 75, 96, 109, 129, 133, 134, 145, 146, 168, 169, 186, 188, 189, 190, *191,* 196, *196,* 198, 201, *204,* 205, 229, 230, 235.

Veneziano, Domenico
(Died in Florence 1461). Painter. Exercised an important influence on the development of perspective and of light values. As a young man Piero della Francesca worked with him on the frescoes (now lost) in the church of Sant'Egidio of the Arcispedale di S. Maria Nuova. Works of his can be found in the Uffizi, in S. Croce (Museo dell'Opera) and in the Berenson Collection in the Villa 'I Tatti'. 114, 117.

Verrocchio
(Andrea di Cione, called Verrocchio; Florence 1435-Venice 1488). Painter, sculptor and goldsmith. He studied first under the goldsmith Giuliano Verrocchi, but his only remaining work from this period is the silver relief of the *Beheading of St John Baptist* for the altarpiece of the Baptistry, now in the Museo dell'Opera del Duomo. Although influenced by Donatello and Pollaiuolo, his sculpture is full of originality. His tomb for Giovanni and Piero dei Medici in porphyry and bronze (1472) is a masterpiece of decoration. His bronze *David* is of the same period, also the famous *Lady with a nosegay* in the Bargello, which also contains his fine *Resurrection.* His *Incredulity of St Thomas* in Or San Michele (1464-83) is a monumental work in bronze. His *Winged Putto with a fish* (1476) stands in the courtyard of the Palazzo Vecchio. The Uffizi contains his painting of the *Baptism of Christ and two angels.* 81, 129, 142, 145, 146, 148, *149, 150,* 157, *173.*

Volterrano
(Baldassarre Franceschini, called Il Volterrano; Volterra 1611-Florence 1689). Pupil of M. Rosselli, with whom he decorated the interior of the Villa di Poggio Imperiale. Influenced also by Pietro da Cortona. His frescoes are to be seen in the Quartiere delle Allegorie in the Palazzo Pitti, the arcades of the Villa della Petraia (1636), the dome of the Cappella Niccolini in S. Croce (1652-60), the dome of the presbytery in SS. Annunziata, and the side chapel in S. Maria Maggiore. 205, 208, 217.

FIOR

21

20

Arno Fiume